Scenic
Driving

PENNSYLVANIA

Rhonda and George Ostertag

FALCON®

HELENA, MONTANA

A FALCON GUIDE®

Falcon® Publishing is continually expanding its list of recreational guidebooks. All books include detailed descriptions, accurate maps, and all the information necessary for enjoyable trips. You can order extra copies of this book and get information and prices for other Falcon guidebooks by writing Falcon, P.O. Box 1718, Helena, MT 59624 or calling toll-free 1-800-582-2665. Also, please ask for a free copy of our current catalog. Visit our website at www.FalconOutdoors.com or contact us by e-mail at falcon@falconguide.com.

Cover photo by Eric Wunrow.
Back cover photo by Londie Padelsky.
All inside color and black-and-white photos by George Ostertag.

Library of Congress Cataloging-in-Publication Data
Ostertag, Rhonda, 1957-
     Scenic Driving Pennsylvania / Rhonda and George Ostertag
       p.   cm. — (A FalconGuide)
     Includes bibliographical references (p.   ).
     ISBN 1-56044-732-X (pbk. : alk. paper)
     1. Pennsylvania--Tours. 2. Automobile travel—Pennsylvania—Guidebooks.
 I. Ostertag, George, 1957-   . II. Title. III. Series: Falconguide.
 F147.3.O88   1999
 917.404'43--dc21   98-44269
                                                   CIP

CAUTION

All participants in the recreational activities suggested by this book must assume the responsibility for their own actions and safety. The information contained in this guidebook cannot replace sound judgment and good decision-making skills, which help reduce risk exposure; nor does the scope of this book allow for disclosure of all the potential hazards and risks involved in such activities.

    Learn as much as possible about the recreational activities in which you participate, prepare for the unexpected, and be cautious. The reward will be a safer and more enjoyable experience.

 Text pages printed on recycled paper.

Contents

Acknowledgments

We would like to thank the staffs at the Chambers of Commerce, the national parks, Pennsylvania's public agencies, and the many private organizations for their help to us in compiling the information for this book. They have been there every step of the way from research to review. We also would like to thank the people we met along the way who volunteered their ideas or faces to the book, and we would like to thank our east and west coast base camps for freeing us to do our work.

Rhonda and *George Ostertag*

Locator Map

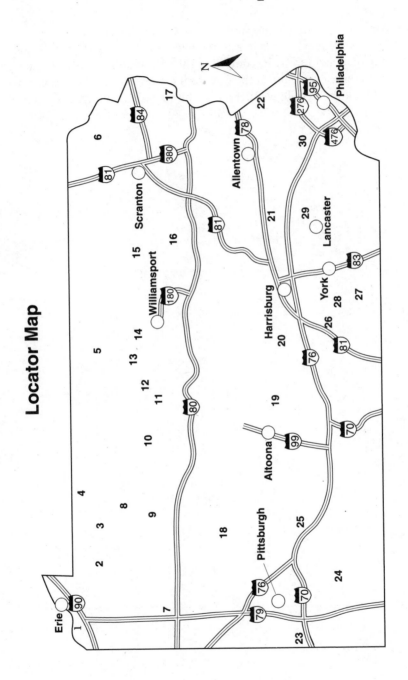

Map Legend

Scenic Drive - paved

Scenic Drive - gravel

Scenic Side Trip - paved

Scenic Side Trip - gravel

Interstate

Other Roads (paved)

Other Roads (gravel)

Railroad

Urban Area

City or Town

Picnic Area

Building

Point of Interest

Campground

Cliff

Hiking Trail

River/Creek

Lake

Interstate

U. S. Highway

State Highway

State Route

Forest or Township Road

Cemetery

Lighthouse

Lookout Tower

State Park

State or National Forest

State Boundary

P A

Map Orientation

N

Scale of Miles

0   5   10

Miles

Scenic Drive
Location

Introduction

The Commonwealth of Pennsylvania is an intriguing canvas, rolled out to cover more than 45,000 square miles, with thousands of miles of road probing its corners and unveiling its mysteries. The scenic drives that present this wealth range from short point-to-point excursions through time and place to long-distance travels across one or more of the state's many exciting regions. So strap on your seat belt, Penn's woods awaits with rich geologic, cultural, and natural tales.

A quick glance at any Pennsylvania state road map will quickly show that countless numbers of drives can be fashioned across the state. What we tried to do with this book is to compile the drives that best herald the diversity of the state's topography and history, exalt in Pennsylvania's natural beauty, and, wherever possible, invite unhurried travel. We also chose drives that allowed for frequent opportunities to stop and explore.

What we tried to avoid were routes that suffered from confusing, unmarked junctions, endless road name changes, and needless congestion. For the most part, we think we succeeded. Visitors may encounter a few more turns on some of the county- and state-forest-endorsed road tours.

The selected drives explore many of the state's premier parks, forests, mountains, rivers, private preserves and sanctuaries, and historic villages and towns. By parking and venturing away from the vehicle, Pennsylvania state travelers can stand humbled by the old-growth white pine and eastern hemlock, climb to dizzying heights atop lookout towers, get wet in the spray of waterfalls, lose themselves in an outcrop maze, or take a somber walk in the footsteps of fallen soldiers. Kettles of broadwinged hawks, a shad run, colorful flurries of falling leaves, a blueberry harvest, and pink explosions of rhododendron can put memorable, seasonal stamps on outings.

Besides enjoying great natural discovery, road travelers can share the right-of-way with Amish buggies and work wagons, purchase hand-stitched quilts, smell newly mowed hay, or bite into a just-picked apple or peach. If your tastes are more city-oriented, there are specialty shops, antique outlets, folk art displays, festivals, museums, and galleries. Taverns that once served stagecoach passengers, Conestoga wagoners, and canal boatmen now extend wayside comfort and a looking glass to the past to contemporary motorists.

Old mills, nineteenth-century covered bridges, fieldstone houses, bank barns, and stone walls dress travel along the meandering country lanes, while historic trains, trolleys, buggies, and canal barges invite drivers to shun the steering wheel for a gentler way to go. Fish hatcheries or roadside-browsing deer may welcome a second look. In Elk and Cameron counties,

Pennsylvania's lone wild elk herd—one of only two east of the Mississippi—roams protected and free, drawing camera buff and naturalist to their vast realm.

In order to keep our readers on the described tours, this collection of drives mainly stays on the marked and easy-to-follow state routes, but the collection offers only a peek in the door at the possibilities, because backroads lacing across the Keystone State promise a lifetime of discovery. For individuals with good map and directional skills or for those who enjoy the adventure of a wrong turn, the little-traveled forest and township roads are a passport to the state's hidden and unpredictable treasures. Typically, the narrowness of these roads brings nature to your side window; the road surfaces invite slower travel (and often a car wash); and the rearview mirror holds a new perspective rather than a call to speed up.

While at this writing, Pennsylvania has only a few formally designated scenic drives, we believe that this selection of 30 topnotch auto tour routes aptly showcases the state's character and unique features, and pens the signature "Pennsylvania" with pride and flair.

Weather

All of the tours in the book lend themselves to three-season travel: spring through fall. For most of the state, winter travel is also possible once the snow has been plowed or melted off the road following a snowstorm. Spring and fall offer a preferred mix of mild temperatures and low humidity. Summers can bring extremes in both categories, as well as dramatic afternoon thunder-and-lightning storms. The changes in season can dramatically transform some drives, suggesting repeat tours.

While much of your time will be passed inside the vehicle, come prepared for changeable weather, regardless of season. This will allow you to take advantage of the many opportunities to stop and explore. If you plan any hikes, carry insect repellent in spring and summer. For winter travel, it is advisable to stow these items in your trunk: traction devices (chains), and a plastic ground cover to ease installation on wet or snowy ground; extra blankets; warm, dry clothes; and additional food and water for emergencies.

Off-season travelers may find reduced hours at some parks and attractions along the described route, and even closures. A quick pre-visit phone call can prevent disappointment. Off-season and midweek touring often clear the way to greater leisure, both on and off the road.

Terrain and Geography

From the canyon walls and floodplain of the Delaware River to the lowlands of Lake Erie, and from the rugged Alleghenies to the fertile Great Valley, Pennsylvania presents a varied tapestry. But mostly, it is a mountainous state, with long ridges and rolling even-height plateaus covering fully two-thirds of its face. Hardwood forests dress the mountain flanks, with rivers, creeks, and runs carving deep, broadened chasms.

Outcrops of flagstone, sandstone, shale, quartz, and schist invite exploration and shape natural vantages. In places, fossil-bearing rocks eroded from road cuts tell the tale of an ancient sea that once covered what is now Pennsylvania. A migrating peninsula; a wildflower prairie; swamps, field, and thicket; and village and town complement travel.

For the most part, motorists will discover the state's landscape breaks roughly into four geographic regions: the Northern Tier, the Southeast–Piedmont Region, the Valley and Ridge Province, and the Western Frontier. The Northern Tier encompasses most of the northern third of Pennsylvania. It spans the state north of Interstate 80 and east from Allegheny National Forest to the Delaware River and features the drainage-cut, rolling plateaus of the Alleghenies, the Endless Mountains, and the Poconos. A national forest, state forests, state parks, and a national recreation area number among the

Stone wall, Shuman Point Natural Area.

Hay-scented ferns, Quebec Run Wild Area.

public lands that provide great access to the area. The Northern Tier holds some of Pennsylvania's wildest and least populated reaches.

The Southeast–Piedmont Region swings an arc across the southeast corner of the state, up from the Maryland border, east past Gettysburg, and north of Philadelphia to reach the Delaware River. Found in this region are lowland farms, riverine woods, a freshwater tidal marsh, and rolling hills. Much of the land is private and populated, with state, county, and city parks and a federal wildlife area among the public offerings. Private reserves and sanctuaries extend the protection of natural areas and welcome guests.

The Valley and Ridge Province then swings an arc across the central portion of the state from the Allegheny Front to the Pocono Plateau, cupping the Southeast–Piedmont Region. A quick glimpse at any road map will quickly reveal how the long arced ridges and dividing broad valleys have shaped this region, its roadways, and how the area was settled. Picturesque historic towns and family farms with bank barns, white outbuildings, and windmills grace the valleys; largely untamed forests claim the ridges. Much of the valley is privately held, while the higher lands show sizeable public holdings.

The Western Frontier then completes the Pennsylvania picture. This region can best be defined as the exception, as it lacks a single unifying character. At its northernmost reaches are lowlands and rolling hills influenced by the Great Lakes. At its midsection, you will encounter rolling hills and farmlands that are a signature of the Ohio Valley. A landscape of sharper defined hills and ridges makes up the southwest corner of the state, as the Appalachian Mountains fan into neighboring West Virginia. Despite housing two of the state's largest cities, Pittsburgh and Erie, the region is mostly quiet with pockets of settlement.

An alternative means for viewing the lay of the state is the one used by the Pennsylvania Tourism Department—it divides the state into eight regions, with breaks along county lines. The regions are Lake Erie, Allegheny National Forest, the Pocono Mountains, Valleys of the Susquehanna, Pittsburgh, Laurel Highlands, Hershey Dutch, and Philadelphia.

Lake Erie, Allegheny National Forest, and the Pocono Mountains piece together the northern tier of the state from west to east. Pittsburgh, Laurel Highlands, Hershey Dutch, and Philadelphia fill out the southern tier. Laying the final puzzle piece in place is the Valleys of the Susquehanna, at the core of the state.

Either structuring of the state can help give travelers a general sense of the area they plan to explore and help with the trip planning.

Pennsylvania History
One of the original 13 colonies that became the earliest United States, Pennsylvania holds a wealth of sites and structures of historical significance.

Keepers of the past include federal, state, county, and city agencies; private individuals and associations; and the many local historical societies. At the helm is the Pennsylvania Historical and Museum Commission.

But for many structures, history is still being written as new generations grow up in homes that date to the 1700s and businesses continue to serve patrons. Even a freshwater spring where George Washington took refreshment rests in the protection of private hands.

Motorists will discover that Pennsylvania is a tablet to our nation's past, one that traces the struggle of a burgeoning country and reaffirms the ideals of democracy. Freedom of religion is a shining thread that travels from past to present. It stretches from William Penn, the Quaker who founded this colony on principles of religious tolerance and freedom under law, to modern-day Amish and Mennonites, who choose to live aside from mainstream society to practice a simple seventeenth-century faith.

The cracked bell of freedom and Independence Hall, the encampment at Valley Forge that to this day makes visitors shiver on even the warmest days, and the hallowed ground of Gettysburg, all carry the nation's legacy, with Pennsylvania the proud keeper. Played out on Pennsylvania soils were battles of the French and Indian War, the Revolutionary War, the War of 1812, and the Civil War.

Place names and events of both war and settlement recall a proud Native American people. Even the names of French royalty brush a small chapter in Pennsylvania history—during the ousting of King Louis XVI, refugee Frenchmen sought sanctuary and a new society here. Rolling ahead in time, many Pennsylvania Quakers and freedmen participated in the Underground Railroad that helped escaping southern slaves in their quest for freedom.

Pennsylvania not only helped shape the early face of the nation, but its present face. The state's rich deposits of ore, oil, and coal sparked the start of the industrial age. Pro and con, it changed the landscape of Pennsylvania and the country. Industries and factories spewed forth product and waste, cities evolved, and transportation systems grew and improved.

Blue-and-gold Pennsylvania history markers placed by the Pennsylvania Historical and Museum Commission help sort out and unravel the intricate tale of Pennsylvania's past.

Road Systems

According to its Department of Transportation, Pennsylvania has more state-maintained roads than neighboring New York State and the six New England states combined. Interstates, U.S. highways, township and forest roads, and city streets expand the travel options.

The state's earliest roads traced Native American trade paths, while others followed rough wagon roads blazed by the military. The rolling, mountainous terrain challenged cross-state travel, with the sharp grades of the Alleghenies posing a barrier to opening the West. To this day, the steep grades still cause engines to whine in protest.

In 1818, the first state highway, Pennsylvania Road, was completed; present-day U.S. Highway 30 follows its approximate line. Another nineteenth-century benchmark was the completion of the first federally built road, the National Road, which crosses the southwest corner of the state. With the advent of the motor vehicle, the road transportation system burgeoned, and today, Pennsylvania boasts well over 100,000 miles of active roadway.

The various types of roads that crisscross the state have different merits and drawbacks. Interstates generally welcome steady, fast travel unhindered by city slowing, but they extend only limited viewing opportunity. U.S. and Pennsylvania highways can range from divided thruways to primary two-lane highways. They are direct and well maintained and can be either hurried or quiet, depending on area.

State routes, the smaller, state-maintained SR-numbered highways, generally welcome quieter, slower travel on good roads. However, these routes can be narrow and winding and may require frequent turns at junctions and stop-and-go travel through towns. As the state routes may also have little or

River Road, Delaware Gap National Recreation Area.

no road shoulder, motorists are limited as to where they can safely pull off.

All of these major routes have paved or concrete surfaces and receive regular maintenance.

The backroads of the state consist primarily of township and forest roads. Either surfaced or dirt, these routes often suffer from unmarked or confusing junctions and are sometimes rough. Yet they tend to offer the most relaxed travel and best chances for wildlife discovery and lead to the state's hidden corners. You just need to stay alert, keep your vehicle in good working order, and carry a good map or two that covers the area of travel.

In this well-settled and historic state, city and village streets may, and frequently do contribute to the driving tours. Because many communities existed during the days of horse and wagon and early homes and businesses fronted directly on the main streets of town, existing roads are often squeezed and overwhelmed with the demands of modern traffic. Roadside parking only compounds the problem. For some communities, recreational vehicles and travel trailers are best left at campgrounds.

Road Markings

The state roadways are for the most part very well signed and mapped, with the junctions marked with a route number or destination and distance. But for some of the smaller routes, problems can arise. Because these routes change direction—sometimes in defiance of what you would predict—and as junction signs have been known to disappear or have fallen victim to vandals, drivers should become familiar with the Department of Transportation's incremental signing system.

Look for the regularly placed 10-inch square or 18-inch-long rectangular white markers that indicate the highway number with "SR" and its two- or four-digit road number. These incremental markers can quickly confirm that you are still on the intended route or that you have strayed—both valuable pieces of information. In the event of the latter, knowing the errant road number and locating it on a map can help you plot your return to the intended tour or open a new door to discovery.

Waterway, bridge, and residential street signs are other valuable clues when touring. On formally designated drives, become familiar with the road tour's emblem and watch for it. On Pennsylvania's roadways, also watch for the blue-and-gold history markers placed by the Pennsylvania Historical and Museum Commission. These snippets from the past can bring added interest to a tour and suggest side trips.

Maps

Standard gear for any glove compartment would be the official Pennsylvania state road map. Secure one by dialing 1-800-VISITPA and requesting the map and Pennsylvania Visitors Guide. Another good basic source is the

Pennsylvania State Parks Recreational Guide and Highway Map, which not only contains road information but also has the state parks prominently featured. It also contains tables indicating the services at each park.

For a more detailed presentation of Pennsylvania's roadways, consult the *Pennsylvania Atlas & Gazetteer* that is put out by the DeLorme Mapping Company. It includes topographic maps for the state, indicates primary and many secondary roads, and identifies points of interest, recreational sites, museums, wineries, and more. One drawback with this source and others is that the road signs in the field often do not match the labels on the map. Where the atlas uses township road numbers, the actual road signs may feature street names alone or different road names may be featured on each. But these maps do help you piece together the puzzle of backroads travel.

Site-specific maps such as the individual state forest maps and county-specific maps that detail their own road systems are well worth seeking out. Often, they point out sidelights that may otherwise be missed.

While some people still view road maps as nothing more than unwieldy pieces of folded paper, the information they supply can mean the difference between carefree touring and a troubled drive of wrong turns.

Preparation

While the drives included in this book are highly "civilized" and do not pose much threat of travelers becoming stranded for long periods of time, some basic precautions can make for a more carefree, enjoyable tour. Carry road maps, water, blankets, a flashlight, and a usable spare tire, and start with a full gas tank. Snacks or the contents of a picnic basket seldom go unsampled, and parking meter change can ease a town visit. Binoculars, cameras, and perhaps a fishing pole will bring added pleasure when you take to Pennsylvania's roadways.

Courtesy of the Road

When sightseeing, it is easy to lapse into some careless road habits. So to make the trip safer and more delightful for both you and the other guy, make it a point to follow some basic rules:

Respect private property. Avoid blocking driveways, gates, barns, and mailboxes and do not trespass onto private land in search of wildlife or a preferred photo angle. Also, be courteous of other motorists who may be sharing the roadway. Regularly check your rearview mirror, and whenever possible, pull aside to let through traffic pass. Remember to signal before turning out and choose turnouts that will allow you to get safely out of traffic. When consulting a map, the travel guide, or brochure, pull aside. Reading and driving do not mix.

For your own protection, be sure to take your valuables with you and lock the doors whenever you venture away from the vehicle.

Using This Book

We have assembled 30 drives of varying length and locale to represent Pennsylvania and have structured this book to aid in the selection process. A summary heads each write-up to present the drive at a glance for a quick measure of its overall interest. Information bullets identify the drive's length and highlights, its general location in the state, the key routes traveled, attractions both along and near the driving tour, seasonal considerations, campgrounds, and services. At the back of the book in the Appendix, you will find a listing organized by drive number of the key agencies and organizations to contact for additional information.

You may note that we did not specify the number of days that each driving tour would take. The reason for this is that much depends on your individual interests, the side trips taken, your personal driving style, the weather, road construction, level of traffic, and other factors. Too, readers should feel free to edit the tours at will.

"The drive" component of the write-up describes the progress of the tour, drawing attention to special features and outings, while alerting readers to unusual or potentially confusing driving conditions. Mentions of seasonal surprises, festivals, and events help flesh out tours and may suggest when to visit. Where appropriate, we have mentioned flaws.

For private and public facilities and attractions, mentions of seasons and hours should be viewed as approximate, since both can change due to budget, staffing, or weather. A phone call may prevent disappointment and help you schedule your day.

Distance measures within the text represent odometer readings and may differ somewhat from the mileages on road signs passed along the way. Although odometer readings can vary from one vehicle to another, the listed mileages should provide you with a good sense of relative distance between landmarks and help confirm that you are still on the described route.

Within the drive descriptions, you may sometimes see a directional tag attached to a route number; this is done to help keep everyone on the same described tour. Routes run north-south or east-west. You will typically find a directional reference where you start out on a new route, where you come to a side-trip spur, where you return to the main route from sightseeing, or where it is necessary to clarify a junction. If there were no landmarks for awhile, we may have added a directional tag, simply as a reminder of which way you should be traveling.

For the most part, side trips to area attractions are indicated as specific-length detours that may be taken at the driver's discretion (the mileage reflects the distance off the main tour; for the total round-trip distance of a linear spur, double it). The text's running mileage typically excludes the side-trip mileages unless the side trip is essential to the tour, such as the official elk-viewing site on Elk Country Scenic Drive, drive 10.

The maps within the text are not intended to replace the more detailed agency maps, road maps, state atlases, and/or topographic maps, but they do indicate the driving tour and its side trips and attractions, and help readers visualize travel.

Glossary

Bank barn. This type of barn is built against a bank or slope, so that the terrain provides a natural ramp to the upper barn reaches. Bank barns are huge and scenic structures.

Covered bridges. These bridges have several different types of construction beneath their protective roofs:

Burr bridges have arch-truss supports that reinforce the structures and allow them to span broader waters.

Kingpost bridges have the oldest and simplest kind of beam support—a reinforced triangle; the longer the bridge, the more triangle supports.

Queenpost bridges are supported by a truncated-triangle truss reinforced by angled side beams and are typically longer than the kingpost bridges.

Green way. This is a thin strip of park lawn and shade trees. Greenways are often found along roadways or rivers and intended for beautification and light recreation. Many include pedestrian paths and benches.

Hexes. Hexes are a Pennsylvania Dutch folk art commonly used on barns. The decorations are round and painted with geometric designs, swirls, birds, hearts, and other emblems. The combined images and rich colors weave a request for rain, good health, love, fertility, or other good fortune.

Midstory. This is the middle level of vegetation in a multistory forest; it includes shrubs and young or low-growing trees.

Pumping jacks. These nodding drills draw oil from reserves beneath the ground.

Understory. This is the ground-level vegetation of a multistory forest.

1

Seaway Trail–Presque Isle Drive
New York to Ohio Border

General description: This driving tour explores nearly 46 miles of the southern shore of Lake Erie, passing through wine and Concord grape country and the port city of Erie. A 15-mile round-trip side excursion to Presque Isle completes the regional snapshot.

Special attractions: Access and views of Lake Erie; Presque Isle State Park; the U.S. brig *Niagara;* Erie Maritime Museum; lighthouses, piers, and waterfronts; charters and dinner cruises; wineries and vineyards; historic walking tours, hiking, fishing, swimming, birding.

Location: Northwest corner of Pennsylvania, edging Lake Erie.

Drive route numbers: Pennsylvania Highways 5 and 5-Alternate, U.S. Highway 20, and Presque Isle Peninsula Drive.

Travel season: Year-round, when free from snow. Expect brisk winter conditions, with lake winds common anytime.

Camping: No public campgrounds serve this travel corridor, but private campgrounds may be found near the entrance to Presque Isle State Park or between PA 5 and Interstate 90.

Services: Find a full complement of traveler services in Erie, with a helter-skelter offering of services along the route.

Nearby points of interest: Dickson Tavern, the Cashier's House, Erie Art Museum, and Erie Historical Museum and Planetarium (all in Erie); Lakeshore Railway Museum (North East); Sturgeon House (Fairview); Battles Museum of Rural Life (Girard).

 The drive

This drive follows PA 5 (the Purple Heart Highway) and PA 5-A west across the northwest limit of Pennsylvania from New York to the Ohio border. The route is an extension of the Seaway National Recreation Trail that begins in New York. It is also part of the Lake Erie Circle Trail.

The linear tour celebrates the Lake Erie region, with its broad blue horizon, bustling port, mild terrain, and rural backdrop. Even when the great lake is not visible, its influences on habitat and settlement can be seen. The War of 1812 and a nautical subchapter—the heroic naval battle for control of the Great Lakes—figure prominently in the region's tale. Look for

Drive 1: Seaway Trail–Presque Isle Drive
New York to Ohio Border

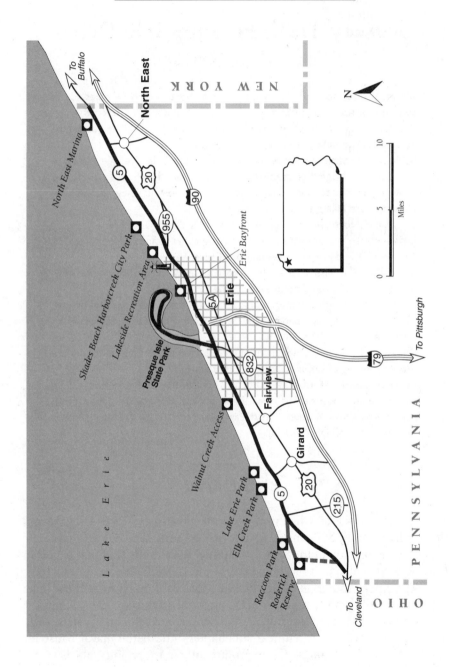

monuments to Commodore Perry and even the reconstructed victory flag-ship, the U.S. brig *Niagara*.

Presque Isle State Park puts a fine stamp on the tour. Its 3,200 acres protect a 7-mile-long spit that curls into Lake Erie. The isle has unique environments and a tendency for walking. In the past century, it has logged an eastward migration of nearly half a mile. Recognized as a National Natural Landmark, Presque Isle captivates with its beach and bay shores and dune and woods habitats and is considered one of the ten best birding sites in the United States.

This drive begins at the New York/Pennsylvania border, where PA 5 West takes the baton for the Seaway Trail after its 454-mile New York sojourn. The tour mirrors part of the historic Lake Shore Path used by Indians to travel between what are now Sandusky, Ohio, and Buffalo, New York. Less than 0.1 mile to the north, Lake Erie glimmers blue—a watery realm of power and beauty. The lake derives its name from an ancient tribe of Native Americans, the Eriez, who were eradicated by the Iroquois in the 1600s.

Beautiful barns, orchards, and vineyards become familiar backdrops. Elsewhere, residences and pocket stands of hardwoods pop into view, and ribbony creeks drain to the great lake. At just under 2 miles, you pass the first marina and public lake access—**North East Marina**.

Without a boat, this is strictly an access for lake views. The lake's oceanlike vastness stretches to a landless horizon. Breakers roll to shore as brisk winds invigorate water and onlooker. The marina itself is a big protected square more serviceable than scenic, but the moored boats are attractive and Canada geese commonly seek out the harbor's protection.

Along the Seaway Trail, rows of grapevine plait the undulating terrain. In fall, when the vineyards turn golden, the harvest of grapes begins. Destined for winery vats are Pinot Noir, Niagara, and Chardonnay grapes; the Concords ride in open-bed trucks to be processed for juice and jellies. The Victorian town of North East (south of the tour on US 20) marks the heart of one of the primary growing areas for Concord grapes, with the first vines put out in the late 1800s.

Mazza Vineyards and Winery and Penn Shore Winery both lie along the eastern portion of the Seaway Trail. They, along with two wineries on US 20, Heritage Wine Cellars and Presque Isle Wine Cellars, open their doors so guests may view the operation and experience the wine. The vintner image is richly woven across the property, with various grape motifs and oak barrels. The settings are crisp, clean, and warm like the vintage wine produced.

Also, in season, roadside produce stands offer just-picked apples and pears and orchard-fresh cider. Coloring the road shoulder are sumac, goldenrod, and wild berries. Elsewhere, cultivated sunflowers nod consent to the tour. Storm fronts that roll down from Canada and across Lake Erie raise the visual ante and stir hearts.

On the right at 11.7 miles is the entry to **Shades Beach Harborcreek City Park.** Be alert when turning into the park, as cyclists share the national recreation trail. A 100-yard walk from the ample paved parking lot puts you on the Lake Erie shore at the mouth of Eightmile Creek, but keep your shoes on as you tag the rugged, cobble and driftwood strand because this is no bathing beach. It does, however, extend an engaging look west at the eroded bluff curvature, Erie waterfront, and Presque Isle. Gulls sparkle white on the water. A picnic shelter and tables, playground, and restroom complete the amenities.

As the tour advances west, you will find more residential areas and blocks of woodland. The junction with PA 955 (15.6 miles) announces the start of a meridian-divided four-lane road, with street lights and traffic signals now part of the tour. If you look to the right here, you can also view an attractive 1830s-built stone house.

At Harvey Street 0.6 mile farther west, a short detour right leads to a small greenway park atop a bluff, with a boat launch and narrow beach below, all part of the **Lakeside Recreation Area** of Lawrence Park Township. It offers a contemplative stop with limited parking preserving the quiet. From a blufftop bench, you can admire black lines of cormorants flying low over the water, bobbing fishing and pleasure boats on the bay, and Presque Isle's treed profile.

The Seaway Trail then clings to PA 5 for another 0.2 mile to Franklin Avenue, where PA 5-A takes over as your westbound guide. Ahead stretches a city setting with attractive lawns, trees, and sidewalks gradually giving way to the more industrial aspects of Erie—the third largest city in Pennsylvania. Later, side-by-side homes of an older, front-porch community line the street.

A detour right at 17.5 miles to the foot of either Lighthouse Street or Dunne Boulevard leads to **Old Land Lighthouse** (1867). This is the third lighthouse to occupy the bluff. The original one constructed in 1818 was the first U.S. lighthouse on the Great Lakes. The stone tower rises 100 feet, but its beacon has been dark since 1885.

At **Perry Square** at the center of downtown Erie (19 miles), a prominent statue of Commodore Oliver Hazard Perry greets oncoming motorists. Look for PA 5-A to wrap around the memorial greenway as State Street halves the park. To visit Erie's renovated waterfront, the art museum, Cashier's House, and the dual attraction of **Erie Maritime Museum** and the **U.S. brig** *Niagara,* detour north on State Street. The maritime museum and flagship are on the waterfront off Bayfront Parkway; the other attractions are just off State Street.

4

Lake Erie, Shades Beach Harborcreek City Park.

Old Land Lighthouse, Erie.

Housed in a rehabilitated 1917 waterfront powerhouse, Erie Maritime Museum holds an exciting line-up of displays, exhibits, and film that unfold the origins of the War of 1812 and the drama of the sea battle. The museum also introduces you to the natural history of the Great Lakes. A unique and vivid "live-fire" display shows the chaos and destruction cannonball fire can deliver. When not on cruises, the U.S. brig *Niagara*, a sailing museum, caps off your visit. The maritime museum is the latest endeavor of the Pennsylvania Historical and Museum Commission; hours are Monday through Saturday 9 A.M. to 5 P.M. and Sunday noon to 5 P.M. An admission is charged for the dual attraction; when the *Niagara* is at sail, ticket prices are reduced.

The Battle of Lake Erie on September 10, 1813, began with Commodore Perry at the helm of the U.S. flagship *Lawrence*. After the *Lawrence* was badly damaged, Commodore Perry then abandoned her, boarded her twin square-rigged, two-masted warship, the *Niagara,* and continued the fight. On the *Niagara*, he brought the three-hour sea battle to an end with a decisive U.S. victory over the British fleet, winning control of the Great Lakes. Perry's curt message to General William Henry Harrison echoes through American military history: "We have met the enemy, and they are ours."

Some years after the sea battle, the *Niagara* was scuttled (sunk) in Misery Bay by order of the government, but was resurrected for the 1913 Perry centennial. Reconstructed between 1989 and 1990, the U.S. brig *Niagara* is once again fully seaworthy and from time to time sails the Great Lakes. She still sports some original timbers and sails with a complement of 40 crew members, one-quarter of the number of the original warship crew.

Dobbins Landing, a recreational dock at the **Erie Bayfront**, honors the shipmaster who built the *Niagara*—Captain Dobbin. At the landing, the 187-foot **Bicentennial Observation Tower** (a fee attraction) overlooks the city, port, lake, and isle. A ferry service between Dobbins Landing and Presque Isle offers an alternative means to add an isle visit. Eating, fishing, strolling, feeding ducks, and sunset romancing are other waterfront pastimes. Away from the waterfront, historic walking tours present the city.

West of Perry Square (19 miles), the Seaway Trail/PA 5-A pursues West Sixth Street through **Millionaire Row**, with its historic brick and frame mansions and looming churches. Afterward, pass the lawn and trees of Gridley and Frontier parks to enter Erie's modern commercial district. Seasonally, you may wish to visit a farmers' market at West Erie Plaza (22.2 miles).

At the drive's midway point, reach PA 832/Peninsula Drive, which heads north for **Presque Isle State Park** and its 15-mile scenic drive. (Note: A round trip on the isle's West Fisher Drive adds another 2 miles to this distance.) Visit the isle now or backtrack later in the day to top off the excursion with a Presque Isle sunset.

Mallard family, Presque Isle State Park.

Presque Isle's offerings are many: visitors can hike, bicycle, rollerskate, sunbathe and surf-swim at the guarded beaches, and fish, picnic, and bird watch. Birders proclaim the isle rivals Point Pelee National Park in Canada for springtime sightings of warblers, flycatchers, rails, and shorebirds. Acquire park information and maps at the interpretive center (2 miles into the park) or at the park office (3.3 miles into the park).

A divided park road explores the length of the isle, with beach, bay, and inland attractions and numerous watery views; the attractions are all well marked. Cottonwood, locust, silver maple, honeysuckle, and wild grape lend shade, color, and fragrance to travel. Landlocked ponds wear caps of water lily. The speed of 25 miles per hour and frequent turnouts allow for leisurely discovery.

The long, arcing beach on the open lake has both protected bathing beaches and natural strands. Intended to slow the isle's migration, regularly spaced white rock breakers fashion a dashed line 100 feet off shore. At Beach 7, a boardwalk and ramp provide lake access for wheelchair users.

Semi-buried in the cottonwoods east of Beach 8, visitors may spy the beacon of the still-active **Presque Isle Lighthouse** (1872), now a private park residence. Nearby lies the marked **Sidewalk Trail**, which spans the breadth of the isle. This straight-arrow path is the old trail used by the

Vineyard grapes, Erie County.

lightkeeper to access his boat on Misery Bay. Altogether, some 20 miles of trail explore Presque Isle; several depart from this easy path.

The park's most popular trail is the family-oriented **Presque Isle Multi-purpose Trail**. This paved trail parallels the isle's shore serving up exceptional views of Presque Isle Bay, the Erie Bayfront, wetlands, and the watery neck between Marina Lake and Long Pond.

Gull Point, a recent evolution to the isle, is another popular path, although one that can be wet. In 1903, Presque Isle ended at Budny Beach, but wind and wave have changed all that. An observation platform and wildlife viewing recommend this walk. Peak bird migrations occur between May 10 and May 25 and again in September. At the far end of Gull Point, you must heed a Special Management Area closure, April 1 through November 30.

Piers, boat ramps, and a marina call to both the nautical and wistful seagoer. **Perry's Monument** (a stone-block tower and water fountain), Misery Bay, and Graveyard Pond recall the 1813 Battle of Lake Erie and the hard winter that followed.

West on the Seaway Trail from its junction with PA 832 at 23 miles (38 miles with Presque Isle Drive), you will bypass an extensive cemetery and tree-shaded residential district to return to PA 5 (now West Lake Road) in about 3 miles. The drive then inches out of greater Erie, with speeds between 25 and 45 miles per hour. A full mile now separates the Seaway Trail from the lake.

At 28 miles, Manchester Road heads right to the **Walnut Creek Pennsylvania Boat and Fish Commission Access** on Lake Erie. At the access, find a marina, restrooms, picnic tables, and boat ramp. Bait anglers line the marina outlet, while the shallow waterway of Walnut Creek entices fly fishermen to cast dancing lines.

The Seaway Trail then returns to rural-suburban settings of cornfields, farm stands, nurseries, vineyards, orchards, and residential areas. Vultures may dip and soar above the fields and deer may be seen. Travel grows relaxed.

At the forked junction at 35.3 miles, you may detour west on Old Lake Road for one block, then turn north on West Park Drive to reach **Lake Erie Community Park** at road's end. This small park offers oak-, maple-, and cherry-shaded picnic tables, a restroom (open seasonally), and a steeply descending woods path to a spirited Lake Erie shore. A precariously thin beach, clapping waves, backwash of cobbles, and sharply eroded cliff, all contribute to the strand's wilderness soul.

As an alternative, a right turn off PA 5 at 36.2 miles leads to **Elk Creek Park Access**, with its wooded bluff picnic area, boat ramp, Elk Creek fishing, and several worn 0.25-mile trails branching through the woods to the

Erie lakeshore. Elk Creek yawns to Lake Erie, and although dredging and storm can make the water milky, locals tell us it is normally as clear as gin. Night herons, ducks, and clicking insects distract eyes from fishing lines. During October's steelhead run, when parking and shore frontage are prized, nothing distracts anglers.

Beyond the Elk Creek turnoff, the Seaway Trail passes the blue-and-gold historical marker for the old state line. Views now embrace cornfields and woods, signs point to private campgrounds, and the auto tour drifts farther from the lake.

At the PA 215 junction, you may opt to detour 3 miles north and west via Holliday and Old Lake roads to reach **Raccoon Park**, which has a tree-shaded picnic area, restroom, children's playground, and a sunbathing beach on Lake Erie. Monarch and swallowtail butterflies flit between the ushering blooms of tall joe-pyeweed.

At 44.2 miles, PA 5 ends at US 20, which carries the Seaway Trail west to the Ohio border in less than 2 miles; from there, the Lake Erie Circle Trail proceeds across the border. Where PA 5 tags US 20, you will also find the last call to detour; a turn north on dirt Rudd Road passes through **David M. Roderick Wildlife Reserve and State Game Lands 314** to a bluff overlook in 2.6 miles. This viewpoint punctuates the tour with a farewell look at the inland sea, but keep well back from the unstable edge.

To shape this detour into a 6.2-mile closing loop, turn east where Rudd Road crosses Old Lake Road (you will find the intersection just before reaching the bluff, 2.5 miles into the detour). The dirt and paved segments of Old Lake Road will then take you east past Raccoon Park (mentioned above) to Holliday Road, which returns south to PA 5 at the PA 215 junction, for a pleasant and picturesque backcountry-road sign off.

2

Wildlife Drive/Birth of the Oil Industry Tour

Circuit through Meadville, Titusville, and Corry

General description: This 103-mile boot-shaped tour passes through four mostly rural northwest Pennsylvania counties to visit some prized wildlife lands and recall the oil boom of the 1860s. Meadville, the toe of the boot, marks the tour's start.

Special attractions: Erie National Wildlife Refuge; Oil Creek State Park; Drake Well Museum; historic Meadville and the Baldwin-Reynolds House; state game lands; Amish communities; farm stands; a train excursion; walking tours, hiking, cycling, canoeing, fishing, birding.

Location: Northwest Pennsylvania.

Drive route numbers: Pennsylvania Highways 27, 426, and 77.

Travel season: Year-round, when free from snow.

Camping: Colonel Crawford Park, managed by Crawford County, has 111 campsites (some with electric hookups), showers, and dump station. It is open Memorial Day through Labor Day; take Pennsylvania Highway 198 West off PA 77 to Woodcock Creek Lake. Private campgrounds near Meadville, Corry, and Oil Creek State Park also serve tourists.

Services: Find a full range of services at Meadville and Titusville, with many traveler services available at Corry.

Nearby points of interest: Pit Hole City (a ghost town), Tamarack Lake, Conneaut Lake Park, Pymatuning Reservoir.

 The drive

This drive starts at Meadville, the toe of the boot, and travels counterclockwise toward Titusville and Pleasantville, which shape the heel. From Pleasantville, the tour swings north to Garland and Brokenstraw Creek (the top of the boot) before racing back from Corry to Meadville. On this drive, you will explore a rural and wooded countryside. Much of the area is comprised of donation lands awarded to soldiers of the Revolutionary War. Erie National Wildlife Refuge, Drake Well Museum, and Oil Creek State Park are highlights along the way.

The drive skirts within an easy distance of both parcels of Erie National Wildlife Refuge. Together, the Sugar Lake and Seneca divisions make up nearly 8,800 acres of critical birdlife habitat. Wetlands, ponds, creeks,

Drive 2: Wildlife Drive/Birth of the Oil Industry Tour

Circuit through Meadville, Titusville, and Corry

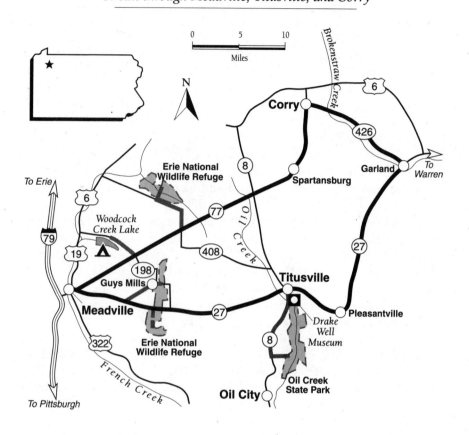

meadows, upland woods, cultivated cropland, and grassland weave the mosaic.

South of Titusville, the adjoining properties of Drake Well Museum and 7,100-acre Oil Creek State Park introduce the oil era from the first drilled well to the oil barons to the boom-and-bust petroleum towns. Today, the steep-walled canyon of Oil Creek presents a first-rate natural area with superb opportunities for outdoor recreation. Just a few ghosts and rusting relics recall the heyday of black gold.

To begin, from French Creek Parkway (U.S. Highways 6 and 19) at Meadville, take the off ramp for PA 27 East/Reynolds Avenue and follow PA 27E as it heads south on Terrace Street. In a matter of feet, locate the **Baldwin-Reynolds House Museum** on the left.

This stately four-story nineteenth-century mansion on the National Register of Historic Places was home to a U.S. Supreme Court Justice and two town mayors. It occupies an attractive 3-acre grounds looking out to French Creek. Beautiful old shade trees, rhododendron, and laurel complement the exterior. The mansion interior and a relocated country doctor's office may be toured for a fee, afternoons, Wednesday through Sunday, May 30 through Labor Day.

More of historic Meadville awaits. Follow signs for PA 27E through the narrow streets of this vibrant small community, which blends historic elegance with modern enterprise. Founded by David Mead in 1788, Meadville was the first permanent settlement in northwest Pennsylvania. A brief detour south via Main Street leads to the history at **Diamond Park.**

Bounded by Walnut and Chestnut streets, this central park boasts a walking tour that explores the surrounding historic district and identifies the park monuments. Diamond Park itself occupies the original common where drovers kept stock and the local militia trained. In the park vicinity are gothic stone churches, the Tarr mansion built by an oil-rich family, the 1885 Academy Theater, and the brick Market House—a vital farm market for more than a century, open Tuesday through Saturday.

Southwest of Diamond Park on the bank of French Creek sits the replica **David Mead Cabin** at Kenneth A. Beers, Jr. Bicentennial Park. The log structure is actually two cabins linked by a breezeway. One side depicts life during David Mead's time, the other an early-day schoolroom. His second wife, Jeannette Finney, started the region's first school.

If instead you keep to the main drive following PA 27, you will reach the loop junction with PA 77, at the eastern edge of town at 1.1 miles; stay PA 27E for the counterclockwise tour. The drive now draws up and out of Meadville into an area of rural landscapes. Amish buggies may share the curving two-lane roadway. The curves and buggies suggest caution and slowing.

At 7 miles, a 4-mile detour east through Guys Mills on State Route 2032 and PA 198 leads to the headquarters for **Erie National Wildlife Refuge**, where visitors may acquire maps and brochures and walk the **Tsuga Nature Trail**. The refuge is open from a half hour before sunrise to sunset, with office hours from 8 A.M. to 4:30 P.M. Monday through Friday.

Nine interpretive stations mark the nature trail that passes through mixed habitats and travels wetland boardwalks. Bullfrogs, turtles, and redwinged blackbirds enliven cattails and rush. Seasonally, enjoy dogwood, honeysuckle, hawthorn, and other flowering shrubs. Mature hemlocks suggest the trail's name: "Tsuga" is from the scientific name *Tsuga canadensis* for eastern hemlock, the state tree.

Forgoing the headquarters detour, motorists on PA 27E soon enter the refuge lands of the **Sugar Lake Division**, passing through the picturesque small community of Frenchtown. Travel is now between wooded stretches

Tsuga Nature Trail boardwalk, Erie National Wildlife Refuge.

and cultivated acres. At 10.9 miles, a detour south on dirt Boland Road leads to Pond K, with its fishing platform for the disabled in 1.1 miles and a wildlife observation blind in 1.6 miles.

Hiking trails (including the 3-mile Deer Run Trail, which starts at Pond K) explore the multitextured refuge lands. Geese, ducks, and herons occupy shore and shallows. Waterfowl migrations from March to early April and again from September to November swell bird numbers and suggest times to park and hike the 0.2-mile path to the observation blind. Wood ducks nest at the refuge, and bald eagles and osprey make appearances. The blind overlooks Reitz's Pond, which can be either marsh or meadowlike. Birding lists are available at the refuge headquarters.

Eastbound from Boland Road, PA 27 continues to carve through the sundry habitats of the refuge to enter the rural village of Mount Hope. Stay PA 27E all the way to Titusville (27.8 miles). The winding, rolling tour presents country images of horses and cows, Amish children tending to chores, and enormous barns—an emblem of Pennsylvania. Small residential villages dot the tour, but most have no services.

PA 27 crosses Oil Creek to enter Titusville, a town that owes its place in history to the oil boom of 1859. As an oil exchange, it became the "Queen City" of the region. Although oil barons built their mansions here, you will see few as the great fire of 1866 took many of the town's original structures.

Canada geese, Erie National Wildlife Refuge.

Pass City Center Park and the Titusville historic district before PA 8 breaks away south. A detour south along PA 8 leads to both Drake Well Museum and Oil Creek State Park. For Drake Well Museum, go 0.2 mile and turn left on East Bloss Street to reach the museum in 1.5 miles. Proceed south the entire way on PA 8 for Oil Creek State Park; the main entrance is at Petroleum Centre on the left in about 6 miles.

Drake Well Museum is a Pennsylvania Historical and Museum Commission site. An admission is charged, and the museum is closed Mondays. Along Oil Creek, the site has a parklike grounds, a first-rate museum devoted to telling the story of the oil industry, and full-scale outdoor exhibits, which include a replica of Colonel Edwin Drake's 1859 derrick and engine house. At the museum, revisit the Great Flood and Fire of 1892 and view a safe robbed of a quarter million dollars, a nitroglycerine wagon, and the world's first refinery.

Outdoors, the outrageously loud "Hrrmph" of an oilfield barker may make you jump. Each well was fitted with a different-sized pipe (or barker) for a different pitch so oilmen could quickly single out a problem well. As you wander amid the collection of old tanks, pumps, trucks, gears, and 65-foot-tall derricks, beware of the overhead cables that grind to and fro, linking the pumping jacks. Woodchucks scamper between the shadows of trees and machinery sheds.

Oil well exhibit, Drake Well Museum.

Also, at Drake Well Museum, visitors may access the northern terminus for the Oil Creek State Park **Bike Trail** or board the **Oil Creek and Titusville Railroad** (a separate fee attraction). The train travels the creek canyon, with the ride enhanced by narratives about the oil discovery, boom towns, explosions and fires, and people of the day. Its regular season runs weekends mid-June to late October, with added excursions Wednesday, Thursday, and Friday in July and August.

At the heart of **Oil Creek State Park** (Petroleum Centre), visitors can surrender to the tranquil beauty of Oil Creek and walk or bicycle past woods-reclaimed boom towns and overgrown cemeteries. Oil Creek is a gently bending canoe-water with rainbow and brown trout. Maple, tulip, hemlock, and big oaks clad the canyon, while deer, squirrels, wild turkeys, and even black bears may be encountered. Such natural bounty belies that the canyon hills were denuded of trees in the 1860s and choked in a black cloud of refinery smoke. Only the faded black-and-white historical photographs capture that image.

Thick woods along the yellow-blazed **West Side Trail** cradle rusting artifacts; the paved 9.5-mile Bike Trail travels back in time via interpretive panels. Near the rustic Petroleum Centre train depot, you will find the **Boardwalk Interpretive Trail**. Its pictorial and verbal panels identify the layout of Petroleum Centre as it looked in the 1860s—just another of the canyon's quicksilver cities, but it gained fame as a gambling center when a $64,000 bet rode on a roll of the dice.

If signaled, the excursion train will make a flag stop at Petroleum Centre Station. Near park headquarters, a seasonally open bicycle rental suggests another way to go. Elsewhere are shady lawns for picnics. Along the canyon trails, Adirondack shelters serve backpackers; a fee and reservations are needed.

Opting to stick to the primary drive alone, from the junction of PA 8 South and PA 27 in Titusville (27.8 miles), continue east on PA 27. The drive passes through woods and suburban areas en route to Pleasantville (33.4 miles). Crisp, clean, and orderly, Pleasantville lives up to its name.

In contrast to the open landscapes at the start of the drive, a shroud of woods narrows views for the tour northeast. Throughout this stretch, keep to PA 27E. The blush of fall, dancing aspen leaves, brief interruptions of meadow, and the rolling ribbon of roadway contribute to windshield viewing.

A water tower stands guard at Garland, where the tour departs PA 27 to follow PA 426 north to Corry. Sunlight passing through the leafy arbor animates the roadway with light and shadow. Attend to your driving because of the minimal road shoulder. Where the drive tracks Brokenstraw Creek upstream, tangles of grapevine attract notice, and homemade signs shout out "goat milk fudge." Ahead, steeply sloped fields alternate with woods until the terrain flattens.

Reach PA 77 in Corry at 65.6 miles for the loop's return southwest. Residential streets draped by sugar maples and a business district flying American flags mold first impressions of this working-class town. Corry, an early producer of tools for oil rigs, houses a number of old factory buildings. At many of the factories, the lights of business still burn. A walking tour best introduces this town.

Beyond the outskirts of Corry lies a rolling return to Meadville through fields and woods. Barns, silos, and dairy cows contribute a pastoral signature. The roadway itself is generally fast—55 miles per hour, with slowing for road bends.

At 72.6 miles, cross East Branch Oil Creek into Spartansburg, which is known for its old-order Amish society. The now-retired Old Sparta Mill sells Amish furniture and goods, while across the way, Platts Mill still serves the farm community. Graceful old homes and handmade billboards for home-based trades are among the town's farewell images.

PA 77 then slices a long rolling, straightaway across the region, drawing more through-traffic, although you may still spy straw-hatted Amish farmers bent over their toils. Tastes of the tour include maple syrup and blueberries. At 84.3 and 84.8 miles are means for accessing **State Game Lands 199**. Such chances to pull off the road are rare. Overall, the PA 77 leg of travel is one reserved for windshield viewing.

As the route crosses Muddy Creek, which drains from Erie National Wildlife Refuge, you enter the quaint farm village of Little Cooley. Produce stands may beckon you aside with bins of sweet corn, lugs of ripe tomatoes, and bottles of maple syrup.

Upon meeting PA 408 West (91.1 miles), you may choose to detour along it to view the **Seneca Division of Erie National Wildlife Refuge**. Go 4 miles and turn right on Swamp Road to view this less-developed refuge section; a kiosk with pamphlets sits at the Swamp Road corner. Swamp Road presents the refuge's many faces, including the serene wetland of Dead Creek.

Wildflowers dress the road's edge, meadowlarks add notes of cheer, and thousands of geese browse mowed fields. Turnouts are few, but by continuing to bear left, motorists will reach the unmarked trailhead for the 1-mile **Muddy Creek Holly Trail** (the trailhead is on the left, 3.3 miles from the Swamp Road kiosk). You will hike woods path and boardwalk through young forest and past wetland and meadow to the bank of Muddy Creek.

Ignoring the refuge's call, PA 77 motorists continue on the arrow-straight course through rural countryside. Go past an old cemetery and a Pennsylvania history marker for **John Brown's Tannery**. Look for the tannery foundation ruins in New Richmond (east off PA 77 via State Route 1033). John Brown was a Civil War abolitionist who won fame with his raid at Harpers Ferry; his tannery was a stop on the secret Underground Railroad.

Fruit stand, Little Cooley.

At 97.4 miles, reach PA 198 West; a 2.5-mile detour along this highway leads to **Woodcock Creek Lake** (a U.S. Army Corps of Engineers project), Woodcock Wild Area, and **Colonel Crawford Park**, which offers camping, picnicking, swimming, fishing, and boating. Colonel Crawford lends his name to many sites in northwest Pennsylvania, including Crawford County. A friend of George Washington, he served in the French and Indian War and was burned at the stake by a band of western Ohio Indians.

Colonel Crawford Park is on the south shore, reached by taking Huson Road over the narrow, 2-mile-long reservoir. For the dam site and Resource Manager's Office, continue on PA 198W to the far northwest shore of Woodcock Creek Lake. Area trails explore the lake canyon and cross the dam.

If you bypass PA 198W, PA 77 carries you southwest all the way back to Meadville. Fruit stands and barns bearing faded advertisements for chewing tobacco eventually give way to residential Meadville. Complete the boot-shaped tour at the PA 27 intersection at 103.2 miles.

3

Allegheny River–Old Growth Tour

From U.S. Highway 6, passing through and back to Tidioute

General description: This 56.1-mile doubling-back tour through Tidioute offers a lazy look at both banks of the Allegheny Wild and Scenic River, its wilderness islands, and the prized old-growth forest stands in its Allegheny neighborhood. The tour may be shortened for a 31.8-mile river loop alone or for a 40.3-mile river-and-forest loop if you eliminate one of the shoreline drives.

Special attractions: Allegheny River access and views; overlooks of Allegheny River Islands Wilderness; Hearts Content National Scenic Area; Anders Run Natural Area; Victorian Tidioute; canoeing, hiking, fishing, cross-country skiing.

Location: Northwest Pennsylvania, at the western perimeter of Allegheny National Forest.

Drive route numbers: U.S. Highway 62 and State Routes 3022, 3007 (Dunns Eddy Road), 2012, 3005, and 2002.

Travel season: Spring through fall. During winter, parts of drive may be closed to travel.

Camping: Buckaloons Campground (0.3 mile from the US 6 - US 62 junction) has 51 family campsites (some with electricity) and running-water facilities. Chapman State Park (a 4-mile detour off SR 3005) has 83 campsites (some with electricity), drinking water, and vault latrines with sinks. Hearts Content Campground (off SR 2002) has 26 sites, vault toilets, and pumped water.

Services: Warren (6 miles east of the tour's start) and Tidioute offer full services.

Nearby points of interest: Hickory Creek Wilderness, historic Warren, Chapman Lake, Tionesta.

 ## The drive

This drive starts west of Warren and tours the banks of the Allegheny River before sashaying the backroads of Allegheny National Recreation Area and Allegheny National Forest to visit Hearts Content National Scenic Area. Recognized as a wild and scenic waterway in 1992, the Allegheny River is a

Drive 3: Allegheny River–Old Growth Tour

From U.S. Highway 6, passing through and back to Tidioute

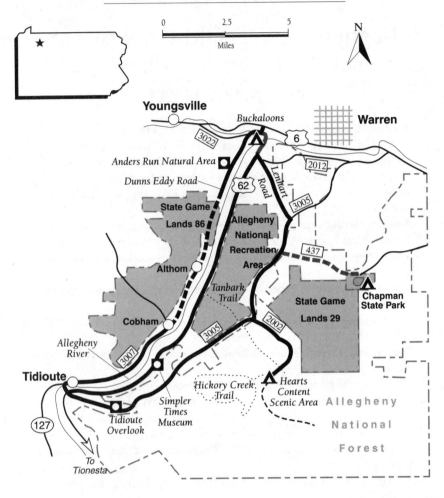

popular recreation corridor. Although much of the river's shore and many of its islands remain private, road travelers still enjoy captivating river views and ample roadside stops. At Hearts Content, the towering old-growth trees and jagged-crown snags swell respect. The lightly traveled dirt, oiled, and paved roads of this tour lend themselves to slow, quiet travel.

From the junction of US 6 and US 62 (6 miles west of Warren), follow US 62 south for 0.2 mile and just before the highway bridge over the Allegheny River, turn west on SR 3022 for Irvine and **Buckaloons Recreation Area.** On the left in another 0.1 mile is the entrance to Buckaloons, which rests on the west bank of the Allegheny River at the one-time site of a Seneca village called "Buckaloons." A campground, picnic area, boat launch, and 1-mile interpretive trail suggest a visit; a day-use fee is charged.

Beautiful old sycamore, silver maple, oak, and hickory dress the river's bank and shore, while benches look out at the water. The Allegheny is a placid river punctuated by islands, seven of which make up the **Allegheny River Islands Wilderness**. Strung between Buckaloons and Tionesta, these public islands entice canoeists to island hop, with 368 acres to explore. The islands wilderness is one of only two federal wilderness areas in Pennsylvania; the other is Hickory Creek Wilderness near Hearts Content.

Buckaloons and one of the wilderness islands occupy a page in American history. In 1778, ongoing Indian and Tory raids prompted George Washington to order a campaign against the Six Nations of the Iroquois. Major General John Sullivan received the command; Colonel Daniel Brodhead led the advance up the Allegheny River. It was one of four waves of the assault. All of the villages in Brodhead's path, including Buckaloons, were razed, and at Thompson's Island, a skirmish between Brodhead's forces and some 30 Iroquois marked the lone battle of the Revolutionary War in northwest Pennsylvania.

Back on the drive, proceed west on SR 3022 away from Buckaloons and past a forestry sciences laboratory and a heritage marker about General William Irvine, who surveyed the donation lands here. On the left, as you cross the bridge over Brokenstraw Creek, you will view a protected archaeological dig where excavations have supplied clues about a prehistoric Native American settlement. Then, at 0.9 mile, turn left at the sign for Dunns Eddy (River) Road for the west shore tour.

Full forest shapes a roadway cathedral. On the left at 1.9 miles is a turnout for **Anders Run Natural Area** and its 2 miles of trail. The linear natural area spans both sides of the road and boasts 200-year-old white pines and hardwoods that rival old-growth trees in stature and presence. The silver thread of Anders Run complements the dark forest gallery, while sunbursts add a mystical quality.

Stay Dunns Eddy Road through the natural area to pass through a small riverside community where old-growth maples line the fronts of homes, and black locust trees claim the riverbank. Where you win an open river view, discover the southern extent of Crull Island, the northernmost wilderness island. At 3.6 miles, it is Thompson's Island of Revolutionary War fame that contributes to viewing.

The first public turnout is within 14,000-acre **State Game Lands (SGL) 86**; find it on the right at 3.8 miles. As the river road snakes away, it becomes dirt and gravel riddled by a few potholes, and travel slows to 20 miles per hour, which is just fine for looking. Residences continue to dot the way, with broken parcels of SGL all the way to Tidioute.

White pines and hemlock, Anders Run Natural Area.

At the SGL turnouts, informal angler paths branch to shore. Beware of poison ivy as you step away from the vehicle to admire the glassy, steady river flow; cast for muskellunge, walleye, and smallmouth bass; or search for fossils amid the sandstones. Other shoreline rocks reveal the ripples of an ancient sea, while the wet mud records the footprints of last night's wildlife. The Allegheny River presents its finest face along these undeveloped shores—a glistening band piercing the state's prized northwest forest.

The canyon ridges alternately cast looming shadows or parade sungraced flanks. When autumn's multicolored leaves rain onto the road, beware of slippery driving conditions. Almost anytime, deer may divert your eyes.

At 6.7 miles, the village of Althom counts down travel. At the stop sign in Cobham (10.1 miles), bear left on SR 3007 to pursue the river. The route is now wider and once again paved, with an occasional turnout. Be alert for falling rocks along the fractured road cuts. Before long, you will enter the quiet, riverside community of Tidioute, site of the Pennsylvania State Fishing Championship.

In town, SR 3007 becomes Main Street. Travel past Victorian homes with gingerbread siding, scrolled eaves, and sculpted trims. Also, travel past historic churches that date to the oil boom of the 1870s; Triumph Hill above

Tidioute was a chief oil producer. Within the small business district, you will find gas pumps, a grocery store, bed-and-breakfast, and boutiques selling antiques and collectibles.

At 15.6 miles, a left on Johnson Street descends to **Riverside Park and the Tidioute River Access.** The riverside site offerings are a boat launch, the Baldwin Gazebo, a children's playground, and picnic tables, but no toilet facilities or other amenities.

The primary drive continues south another 0.1 mile on Main Street before turning left on Buckingham Street/PA 127 to cross the Allegheny River to US 62. From the bridge, admire the broad river, a couple of downstream islands, and perhaps a few white pelicans along with their shimmery reflections. On the east shore below the bridge is a monument to the world's first "flowing" oil well.

Now turn north on US 62 for the east shore tour and speedier travel. Upstream travel presents a different river perspective. Where hemlocks appear in the forest, the result is a deeper shade. At 18.2 miles, locate the **Tidioute Pennsylvania Fish and Boat Commission Access.** This parking turnout provides shoreline access and a single-lane boat ramp, but no other amenities. The open lawn allows for unobstructed river views.

On the right at 20.2 miles is Simpler Times Museum, which is billed as a "local interest museum of: Oil, Gas, and Lumber." A fee site, it may be viewed by chance or by appointment between 8 A.M. and 6 P.M. spring through fall.

The museum, an impressive, private, working collection, is a testament to the heart and dedication of two men—Mr. Ziegler (the owner) and his caretaker. Together, they do it all from acquisition to refurbishing to the display and conducting of tours. Antique Fords from 1913 to 1946, porcelain gasoline signs and early-day gas pumps, a working oilfield model, a railroad bicycle, and Pennsylvania license plates as far back as 1906, all salute Americana. Some of the collection dates to the 1800s. Even the bricks on the museum floor have a history, recovered from an old oil refinery.

In a blink, as the drive resumes north on US 62, you will pass the heritage marker for Painted Hill, located across the river and the site of an ocher mine. Native Americans used pigment from the mine for war paint. A long straightaway of river now complements travel, making the canoe rentals up ahead seem all the more tempting.

Where the tour enters **Allegheny National Recreation Area**, look for the 9-mile **Tanbark Trail** on the right at 24.7 miles. It heads uphill, eventually joining the **North Country National Scenic Trail** for long-distance discovery. Travelers with itchy feet and a desire to explore will find trailhead parking on the left side of US 62, north of the trail sign.

River views continue to be a siren, especially on hot summer days, but turnouts are notably absent. Oak, maple, birch, beech, sassafras, and aspen

Allegheny Wild and Scenic River, Allegheny National Forest.

add to woodland viewing. At 30.3 miles, you have a choice: to the right via Grunderville Road/SR 2012 lies Hearts Content and the full tour; north on US 62 completes the shorter river-loop tour at US 6 in another 1.5 miles.

For the full tour, turn right (east) on Grunderville Road, bearing right on Lenhart Road in 0.1 mile. Signs mark the way to Hearts Content. Ascend through forest on narrow, unlined paved road that can be rough but is generally quite good. Wildflower and fern shoulders often push back the forest of hardwoods and pines. A few homes and cabins dot the tour.

Reach SR 3005 at 33.7 miles and turn right, still chasing the signs for Hearts Content. This too is a fine road, allowing for speeds of 45 miles per hour. Beyond a residential area, you come to a junction with dirt and gravel Forest Road 437, which offers a back-door route to 805-acre **Chapman State Park.**

Centerpiece to the park is a 68-acre manmade lake on the West Branch Tionesta Creek. Camping, picnicking, hiking, swimming and sunbathing, fishing, and quiet boating headline recreational pursuits. Find a canoe and paddleboat rental at the lake. Chapman State Park also offers a full line-up of winter recreations with ice skating, sledding, cross-country skiing, snowmobiling, and ice fishing, but winter entry is strictly a front-door affair—enter via Clarendon off US 6.

The 4.2-mile twisting descent on FR 437 to Chapman State Park is itself an eye-pleasing extension to travel. On this quiet road, admire the arbor effect of the forest; the heady, sweet perfume of hay-scented ferns; picturesque rock slabs; and the seasonal floral display of mountain laurel and rhododendron. The laurel blooms in mid-June, while the rhododendron delays its show until early July. A whiff of natural oil may direct your eyes to pumping jacks in the woods.

Without the FR 437 spur, the drive proceeds along SR 3005. A fuzzy fern floor complements the spatially open woods. Reenter Allegheny National Recreation Area and at 38.5 miles, veer left on improved-dirt SR 2002 for **Hearts Content National Scenic Area (NSA).** You will later backtrack to this junction to complete the tour.

SR 2002 travels 3.6 miles to the NSA and Hickory Creek Wilderness, 3.7 miles to Hearts Content Campground. It traverses a low plateau clad by hardwoods and mountain laurel before coming to the 121-acre scenic area on the left. Hearts Content NSA won National Natural Landmark distinction in 1977. Trees tower 100 to 150 feet above the forest floor and boast diameters of 4 feet or more. Sky-piercing snags hint at natural catastrophes— events necessary for forest succession. A severe drought in 1644, followed by years of fire, gave the giant white pines of today their start.

Two interlocking interpretive loops meander the grove, inviting a neck-craning stroll among the 300- to 400-year-old trees. View white pine, eastern

Ancient Forest, Heart's Content Interpretive Area, Allegheny National Forest.

hemlock, American beech, black cherry, and sugar maple. Signs identify tree species, compare bark, and explain succession; benches bid pause.

The initial 0.25-mile loop of this 1.25-mile trail is suitable for wheelchair and stroller access; an audiotape may be checked out at Bradford Ranger District or from the summer host at Hearts Content Campground. A vault toilet and drinking water are available at the trailhead picnic area.

Along the entrance road to the NSA is a parking lot for **Hickory Creek Wilderness.** An 11.1-mile foot trail explores this 8,663-acre roadless area. Bounded by East and Middle Hickory creeks, the loop probes a quiet, rolling realm of hardwood and hemlock forests and broad meadows. The wildland is shared by deer, raccoon, fox, pileated woodpecker, turkey, and black bear. Intentionally faint yellow blazes (sometimes far apart) mark the way; secure a map before starting. Faint skid roads and an abandoned railroad grade hint at logging camps that predated the wilderness. As in any federal wilderness, no bikes are allowed.

After returning to the junction of SRs 2002 and 3005 at 45.7 miles, turn left on SR 3005 to complete the tour. Pass another access to the Tanbark Trail and leave the national recreation area. The two-lane paved road offers moderately fast travel through mixed-age forest and replanted woods; keep to SR 3005.

On the right at 54.7 miles is **Tidioute Picnic Ground and Overlook,** where two short, adjoining trails tag superb clear-day vantages. River View overlooks the glassy Allegheny River, its treed islands, forested canyon, and the alternating woods and cultivated acres of the valley floor. In autumn, a barrage of vibrant reds and golds confronts the eye. At the overlook, an interpretive board identifies the islands of Allegheny River Islands Wilderness.

At Town View, you will find a vista bench and picnic table and take in a 90-degree view. From here, overlook the crisp, clean river village of Tidioute and its frame of rolling hump-backed ridges. Side canyons extend looks to the back wall.

The drive then descends to US 62 and the river valley at 56 miles. Turn right (north) to revisit Tidioute in 0.1 mile; south on US 62 is Tionesta.

4

Longhouse National Scenic Byway
From Warren to Allegheny Reservoir

General description: This 37.7-mile lasso-shaped drive travels upstream along the Allegheny River from Warren past Kinzua Dam to encircle the Kinzua Bay arm of Allegheny Reservoir. On this drive, you will explore the wooded realm and rocky outposts of Allegheny National Forest and enjoy the wet fun and beauty of the harnessed river.

Special attractions: Allegheny Reservoir overlooks and access; Kinzua Dam; Jake's Rocks; Rimrock Overlook; nature and hiking trails; autumn foliage; fishing, boating, swimming, and winter sports.

Location: Northern Allegheny National Forest, northwest Pennsylvania.

Drive route numbers: Pennsylvania Highways 59 and 321, Forest Road 262.

Travel season: Spring through fall, for the entire tour. In winter FR 262 is a snowmobile trail.

Camping: Dewdrop Recreation Area (on Kinzua Bay's west shore off FR 262) has 74 family campsites, with flush toilets, showers, and dump station; to its south, Kiasutha Recreation Area offers similar services and 90 family campsites. Red Bridge Campground (on the east shore off PA 321, north of its junction with FR 262) has 55 campsites, a dump station, and running-water or vault toilet facilities, depending on season.

Services: Warren offers full services. Food and gas are seasonally available at the private Kinzua-Wolf Run Marina.

Nearby points of interest: Allegany (New York) State Park; historic Warren; North Country National Scenic Trail; Chapman State Park; the Knox, Kane, Kinzua Railroad excursion train.

 ## The drive

This postcard-pretty drive explores the Seneca Highlands of Allegheny National Forest and the Kinzua Bay arm of Allegheny Reservoir and received national scenic byway distinction in 1990. "Longhouse" refers to the large, communal log dwellings that housed the area's Seneca Indians centuries ago—what they called *"kanohsaas."* It also stands symbolically for the alliance of the Six Nations of the Iroquois. The Mohawk, Oneida, Onondaga, Cayuga, Tuscarora, and Seneca tribes were collectively the "people of the longhouse," with the Senecas being keepers of the west gate.

Drive 4: Longhouse National Scenic Byway

From Warren to Allegheny Reservoir

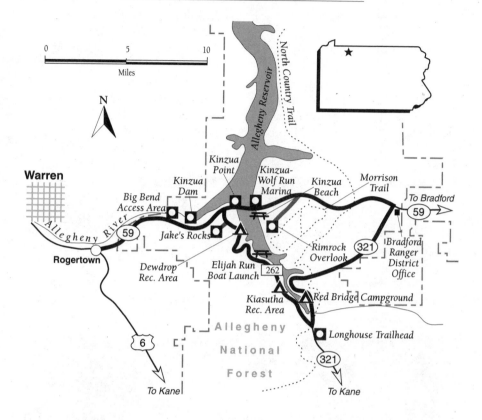

This drive starts 3 miles southeast of Warren at the junction of U.S. Highway 6 and PA 59 (at Rogertown). From here, you go east on PA 59, paralleling the Allegheny Wild and Scenic River upstream to Kinzua Dam. Gradually, residences disappear as the tour enters Allegheny National Forest. Beyond the roadside trees, glimpse river and forested ridge to the north, unbroken forest to the south.

In 6 miles, come to **Big Bend Access Area**. Situated below the dam, this landscaped site has a visitor center (open Memorial Day through Labor Day), a boat ramp, two short nature trails, a river overlook, and a paved walkway above the river. The 0.25-mile half-moon-shaped **Little Boulder Trail** travels a tree-shaded, rocky domain above the day-use area to tag 12 interpretive stations. The 0.3-mile **Smorgasbord Forest Trail** leaves the east end of Big Bend for a walk to Kinzua Dam that parallels PA 59. With the tailwater off the dam arriving fast and turbulent, Big Bend shore anglers may bank fish but not wade, and swimming is prohibited. Watch for ospreys in the air and mergansers to negotiate the fast water.

The next stop east on PA 59 is **Kinzua Dam**, in about 0.5 mile. View the imposing 1,900-foot-long river barrier, the enfolding forested Allegheny ridges, the reservoir, and the flowing Allegheny River. Gulls circle over the green quonset huts of the National Fish Hatchery below the dam on the north shore.

As you study the dam, you may notice the high-water mark from tropical storm Agnes in 1972. During this storm, engineers estimate that Kinzua Dam earned its cost many times over. The water came within 3 feet of the dam's top and threatened billions of dollars of downstream flood damage.

Built for the purpose of flood control, Kinzua Dam captures the Allegheny River and its headwaters, shaping a 24-mile-long reservoir at the New York–Pennsylvania border. In 1966, the newly formed reservoir swallowed the nearly 800-acre Chief Cornplanter grant (awarded the chief in 1791 for allaying tensions after the American Revolution), as well as many lands granted the Seneca tribe. The descendants who resided here and were dislocated by the dam represented the last surviving Native American community in all of Pennsylvania.

Just a bunny hop east is **Big Bend Overlook**, which offers a slightly different vantage on the reservoir landscape; farther east on PA 59 is **Kinzua**

Allegheny Reservoir, Allegheny National Forest.

Kinzua Dam, Allegheny National Forest.

Point Information Center (open summers only). Along this highway section, the stratified rock of the road cut cradles shell fossils and twig impressions. By searching the loose rubble, even amateur rockhounds can uncover fossils. A few wider turnouts allow for sightseeing or rockhounding stops; use caution when crossing the road and when searching through the rock debris below the road cut.

At the information center, you have a fine view north of Allegheny Reservoir, with the descending wooded ridges meeting its shores. Over Kinzua Bay to the east stretches Casey Bridge (sometimes referred to as Cornplanter or Kinzua Bridge). Kinzua is the Seneca term for "place of many big fishes." Reservoir angling is legendary, with trophy-sized walleye, muskellunge, trout, bass, catfish, and more. Views vary with the season and time of day; fog, autumn's palette, frost, and snow, each recast the reservoir image.

At the junction of PA 59 and FR 262 (10.6 miles), turn south for the designated byway on FR 262 for a counterclockwise tour of Kinzua Bay, exploring first the west bank. FR 262 is a picturesque two-lane, 35-mile-per-hour road, with mowed shoulders and wildflower embankments that give way to a dense broadleaf forest. Often the trees close ranks along the drive, creating a scenic bower. After just 1.2 miles on FR 262, turn right on FR 492 for a worthwhile side trip to **Jake's Rocks**.

Forest Road to Jakes Rocks, Allegheny National Forest.

This 3.6-mile round-trip detour offers both drive-to and hike-to vantages overlooking Kinzua Dam and the main reservoir stretching north. For this detour, you will enjoy a slower-paced drive through beautiful woods, with natural topiaries of wild grape, lichen-etched rocks, and showings of mountain laurel. At the gravel turnout in 0.5 mile is a forest window to Casey Bridge. After taking a right at the T-junction, you will reach a one-way circuit with a marked spur to the right for Jake's Rocks vista trails, picnicking, and restroom. Beyond the Jake's Rocks turnoff, two drive-to vistas then complete the side-trip circuit.

But Jake's Rocks is a don't-miss stop. Earthen footpaths fan to picnic tables, while a narrow, paved footpath explores the brink of the rim to snare two vantages: North Overlook and South Overlook. South Overlook peers out toward Kinzua Dam; North Overlook applauds the reservoir, with its rippled surface, scalloped shoreline, and even-height ridges. Some mornings, wind-whipped veils of mist ride across the reservoir's surface like a phantom fleet of sailing ships. The chance for viewing such a magical image recommends awakening to the alarm clock. Pitch pines grow amid the rim sandstone; laurel, huckleberry, sassafras, and sarsaparilla adorn the forest floor.

By avoiding the Jake's Rocks detour altogether at 11.8 miles, the scenic byway proceeds south on FR 262 to gather a few views of its own, mostly of

Kinzua Bay. Light filters through the forest. At 13.3 miles, locate the entrance to **Dewdrop Recreation Area** on the left. This is a campers-only facility, with campsites terracing the reservoir slope. Another 1.5 miles south is **Elijah Run Boat Launch,** with bank fishing, a paved shoreline trail, pier, and public dock; a day-use fee is charged.

The 0.25-mile paved trail at Elijah Run is wheelchair accessible and passes just inland from shore to deliver some exceptional reservoir views. Benches welcome nature study. Roosting vultures, some 20 or 30 in number, often command eyes skyward. Listen for their crash in the treetops as they exchange perches, staying just ahead of approaching hikers. Beech, hemlock, maple, basswood, birch, aspen, and silvered snags compose the trail's canopy. Wildflowers claim the reservoir banks. Partway, a fishing platform extends out across the rocky shore to the open water. The trail then halts at a striking sandstone outcrop.

From Elijah Run, Longhouse Scenic Byway proceeds south past additional mowed clearings to climb and contour the western bay slope. Travel through a U-shaped bend to enter a more mature forest setting before coming to **Kiasutha Recreation Area** (on the left at 18.1 miles). At Kiasutha, you will find one of the two beach areas on the tour, backed by a large, tree-shaded sloping lawn. You will also find a picnic area, launch, and full campground facility. Kiasutha takes its name from another prominent Seneca leader—Cornplanter's uncle.

Campground nature trails start at both Kiasutha and Dewdrop recreation areas. The 2.5-mile nature trail here and the 2-mile one at Dewdrop show a 600-foot elevation change and some difficult footing. Interpretive pamphlets (available at trailheads or Bradford Ranger Station) introduce the species of vegetation and explain their value to wildlife and humans.

The scenic drive resumes south on FR 262 and is intersected by the **North Country National Scenic Trail,** just as it meets PA 321 at 19.8 miles. The loop turns left, but less than 0.5 mile to the right is a small country business with cabin rentals, ice, groceries, bait, and fishing licenses. Just 100 feet to the right is **Longhouse Trailhead**; its winter snowmobile trail along South Branch Kinzua Creek is open to summer hiking, but generally overwhelmed by unruly vegetation.

For the scenic byway, turn left at 19.8 miles and follow PA 321 north along the east shore of Kinzua Bay, soon crossing Red Bridge over Kinzua Creek. Mudbars and feeding shorebirds can appear along the creek in summer. At 20.5 miles, reach the **Red Bridge Bank Fishing Access**, which utilizes part of an old road and bridge that predated the reservoir. Abutments, along with a small platform, allow anglers to cast across the riprap (rock reenforced) bank. The tiny access serves a handful of anglers, and despite being listed as fine for wheelchair users, conditions are rough.

To its north sits **Red Bridge Campground**, which occupies the site of a former Civilian Conservation Corps camp and later, a World War II German prisoner-of-war camp. Today, this reservoir-side campground draws only willing prisoners, and the sentence is relaxation.

At 21.7 and 22.4 miles are the last two primitive viewing accesses to Kinzua Bay before tree-shaded PA 321 veers away from the water. Travel is faster, but turnouts still welcome photographers and leisure travelers to pull out. Look for the North Country Trail to periodically cross or nudge the byway. A wetland wildflower meadow heralds Chappel Fork. Although unbroken greenway is the signature attraction of this byway stretch, travelers may spy the bobbing head of an oil pumper. Tucked in the woods is Mallory Lease Oil Field.

On the right, prior to the **Bradford Ranger District Office**, which is at 29.8 miles, you may also spy the metal building and tanks that remain from a **1920s oil field powerhouse**. Through a joint effort of the Pennzoil Company and Allegheny National Forest, this powerhouse is being restored as an interpretive site; inquire at the district office for more information.

Just past the ranger station, return to PA 59 and turn west to complete the Kinzua Bay circuit. Traffic is generally light to moderate, with speeds of 55 miles per hour. As woodland images blur past, you may sort out the branches of maple, oak, beech, and cherry. Where mountain laurel wins a stronghold, enjoy pale pink blooms mid-June to July.

Once again the North Country National Scenic Trail crosses swords with the auto tour route; some 87 miles of the North Country Trail explore Allegheny National Forest. Someday, the hiker interstate will span 3,200 miles from Lake Sakakawea, North Dakota, to Crown Point, New York.

On the left at 34.2 miles is **Morrison Trailhead**. From this trailhead leaves a popular, 12-mile forest-and-reservoir hiking trail. Its loop explores varied forest, effusive mountain laurel passages, and bouldery sites, with a spur trail to a shoreline camp on Kinzua Bay.

Next, mature forest lacking a midstory varies windshield viewing. Sometimes, shadowy deer may be spied moving between the tree trunks. At 35 miles, you may turn left for **Rimrock Picnic Area and Overlook**. Follow the ascending, paved forest road 2.5 miles to the parking lot and scenic woods-knoll picnic area. The path for the rimrocks descends from the lot.

Rimrock Overlook is a natural rock promontory explored by divided and winding stone stairways; it overlooks the Kinzua Creek arm of Allegheny Reservoir. Autumn visits (early to mid-October) prove especially popular because you have twice the color burst with the reservoir reflecting the flaming slopes. Gum, alder, sassafras, oak, maple, pine, laurel, and huckleberry dress and color the rim. Watch for squirrels to jump between branches and vultures to sail the thermals.

Rimrock Overlook, Allegheny National Forest.

Between the two viewing platforms, you may choose to take the spiral, pinched stairway that descends a fissure to the base of the cliff. While making your descent, watch both your head and your footing. At the base of the 100-foot cliff, you can admire the sheer face of the outcrop and discover a spring.

By instead continuing west on the byway at 35 miles, you will soon reach the corner attractions at the east end of Casey Bridge: **Kinzua-Wolf Run Marina** (north) and **Kinzua Bathing Beach and Picnic Ground** (south). At the Kinzua-Wolf Run Marina (open May through September), visitors can rent the gamut of pleasure boats and houseboats or relax on an excursion boat; purchase bait, tackle, and fishing licenses; enjoy waterfront dining; or prearrange for a picnic basket to go. Often, bald eagles can be spied soaring above the vast blue or perched on a shoreline snag. Kinzua Bathing Beach has a sloped lawn and rectangle of sand addressing the bay, with restrooms and changing houses; a user fee is charged.

With the crossing of **Casey Bridge**, complete the tour back at FR 262 at 37.7 miles. The changing angle of the sun may suggest an encore visit to Jake's Rocks or one of the many other vantage points along the drive.

5

Grand Army of the Republic Highway Tour
From Kane to Wyalusing

General description: This relaxing drive follows a rolling, 164-mile segment of U.S. Highway 6 across the northern tier of Pennsylvania. The journey traces historic Native American paths to explore the wilds and settlements of Allegheny National Forest; the valleys of the Allegheny River, Pine Creek, and Susquehanna River; and the Endless Mountains.

Special attractions: Kinzua Bridge; Pennsylvania Lumber Museum; the Grand Canyon of Pennsylvania; Victorian homes and hotels; hiking, fishing, boating, picnicking, antiquing, winter sports; historic walking tours; stagecoach, horse, and bicycle tours.

Location: Northern Pennsylvania, slicing across McKean, Potter, Tioga, and Bradford counties.

Drive route numbers: U.S. Highway 6/Grand Army of the Republic Highway.

Travel season: Year-round.

Camping: Several private campgrounds serve this corridor along with the following public campgrounds: Twin Lakes Recreation Area (a U.S. Forest Service facility off Pennslyvania Highway 321, southeast of Kane) has 50 modern campsites, restrooms and showers. Find rustic facilities at the 50-site campground at Lyman Run State Park (west of Galeton off State Route 2002), the 25-site campground at Colton State Park (on the West Rim of Pine Creek Canyon, south of Ansonia), and the 30-site campground at Leonard Harrison State Park (on the canyon's East Rim, reached via Wellsboro). Hills Creek State Park (5.5 miles north of US 6, at the marked turn between Wellsboro and Mansfield) has 110 sites with restrooms/showers. All have dump stations.

Services: Find a full complement of traveler services at the larger communities: Kane, Smethport, Coudersport, Galeton, Wellsboro, and Towanda, with limited services elsewhere.

Nearby points of interest: Allegheny Reservoir; two excursion trains: the Knox, Kane, Kinzua Railroad and Tioga Central Railroad; Denton Hill Ski Area; Susquehannock Trail System; West Rim Trail and Pine Creek Canyon Rail Trail; Tioga-Hammond Lakes; Mount Pisgah and Hills Creek state parks; French Azilum.

Drive 5: Grand Army of the Republic Highway Tour
From Kane to Wyalusing

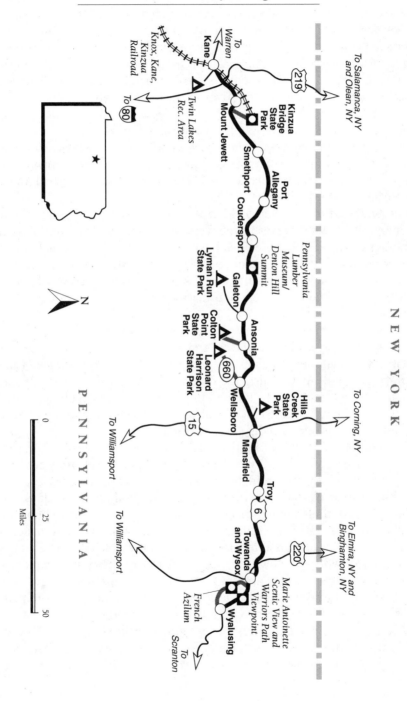

The drive

This vista-packed drive along transcontinental US 6 starts at Kane and travels west to east across the northern tier of Pennsylvania, revealing some of the state's finest forgotten wilds and paying visits to historic lumber, factory, and tourist towns. Native Americans, European explorers, and Revolutionary War soldiers previously took this path. Since 1948, US 6 in Pennsylvania has been called the "Grand Army of the Republic Highway" in honor of the Union Civil War veterans. The tour begins amid rich forests, wanes amid farmland. Serial mountain views are its hallmark.

The drive along US 6 brings back memories of the days before highways and thruways. The pace is fast then slow, passing from open country to small town streets, but overall travel is easy and relaxed. Hurried America typically opts for Interstate 80, to the south.

Snuggled in Allegheny National Forest in McKean County, the tiny community of Kane serves as the western gateway for this tour. Pass east through town, admiring the brick business district and charming frame and brick homes. At the east end of town, signs point the way to a station stop for the popular excursion train, **Knox, Kane, Kinzua Railroad**, which travels to Kinzua Bridge—the extraordinary high-rise railroad bridge of postcard fame.

Opting for road over rail, proceed east from Kane on US 6, entering a rolling tour across a broad plateau; train tracks are often viewed. At Lantz Corners, a small souvenir shop may coax you to spend a quarter for a Kinzua Bridge postcard. At 12 miles, the dramatic viaduct itself may be spied by motorists who take the 4-mile detour north on narrow State Road 3011. Watch for the turn at the east end of the crossroads community of Mount Jewett, which hosts a Swedish Festival each August.

On the side tour, locate the 1882-built bridge as it spans the gap of Kinzua Creek Canyon in **Kinzua Bridge State Park.** The record-sized bridge shoots 300 feet skyward from the creek and stretches 0.4 mile between rims. The most amazing statistic is that the bridge was built in just 94 days. Viewing platforms, trails along the rim and descending to the canyon floor, and a walkway across the vertigo-inducing bridge allow for a sizing up of this engineering feat and an appreciation of the natural setting. While on the bridge, you will peer down on treetops 200 feet below you, admire the structure's far-cast shadow, and spy beaver dams on tinsel-like Kinzua Creek.

For US 6 travel alone, the journey east from Mount Jewett pursues a curving forested aisle along Marvin Creek. The soothing route weaves between hill and ridge, gradually swinging northeast for the village of Smethport. Marvin Creek, like better-known Pine Creek to its east, entices trout fishermen in spring; a fly fishing access is on the left at 23.4 miles.

Kinzua Bridge, Kinzua Bridge State Park.

In 1.25 miles more, a sign for U-pik/We-pik blueberries may draw you aside to stain your fingers blue. Then, at 26.3 miles, Victorian Smethport rings in Christmas year-round. In 1932, local pharmacist Leonard Johnson first introduced the idea of an outdoor Christmas display. The idea sparked and flourished. Today, the cheery, multiroom **America's First Christmas Store** boasts a collection of Christmas ornaments, gifts, and decor that puts the North Pole to shame.

Also in Smethport, mansions from the oil boom dress West Main Street. During the Civil War, the town was said to have been a stop on the Underground Railroad that aided slaves in their escape to freedom. As secrecy was key to the network's success, documentation is nearly nonexistent.

As US 6 leaves Smethport, it crosses Potato Creek for a rolling tour east, passing over hilltops and through forested canyons, lowland swamps, and farmlands. Broadleaf forests clad the framing ridges. At 36 miles, travel slows to enter Port Allegany with its maple-shaded streets, town square, and lovely old homes. Port Allegany grew up at the historic Allegheny River ford, dubbed "canoe place" by Native Americans. During the early lumber era, the river transported logs to downstream mills.

US 6 then wraps around the forested ridges of Susquehannock State Forest. The Allegheny River, which carved this passage, remains for the most part a stranger. At 42.5 miles, near the river's headwaters, reach

Coudersport (population 3,000). This town retains much of its history dating to the lumber boom of the 1800s; its Victorian Main Street is on the National Historic Register.

The many wholesome communities that dot US 6, all seem to conform to a comfortable, formulaic town plan, with an ice cream parlor at the outskirts of town; an elegant, tree-shaded neighborhood of Victorian homes; the frozen-in-time brick business district; classic lunch counter diners and five-and-dime stores; and a fetching town common with memorials to the Civil War veterans. Each town carries the thread of déjà vu.

As you again trundle through the Allegheny Mountains, encounter the return of thick forest and enjoy a long business-free stretch. Atop Denton Hill Summit (elevation 2,424 feet) at 60.6 miles, locate the **Susquehannock State Forest District Office** and the northern gateway to the 80-plus-mile **Susquehannock Trail System.** Denton Hill Ski Area lies 3 miles east.

In autumn, a magnificent flourish of color grasps the mountains, but the forest of today is much different from that at the time the area was first settled. Then, old-growth white pine and hemlock covered much of northern Pennsylvania, and harvests went unchecked. The area's white pine produced some of the best "spar" timber in the world for shipbuilding, and tanning stripped the woods of hemlock. Although beautiful, the mixed hardwoods of today conceal the past.

To fill in the missing pages, you might consider a stop at the **Pennsylvania Lumber Museum,** north off US 6 opposite the ski area. This fee site of the Pennsylvania Historical and Museum Commission is open daily (except holidays) 9 A.M. to 5 P.M. Historic photographs help to recall the forest of old, while thousands of exhibits pay tribute to the mid-nineteenth-century lumber boom.

On the grounds, visit a rustic logging camp, complete with bunkhouse, mess hall, smithies, two-story mill, coal-powered Shay locomotive, and log loader. Indoors, wander about two rooms: one devoted to the Civilian Conservation Corps, the other to lumbermen. Each Fourth of July weekend brings the Bark Peelers' Convention, where woodsmen demonstrate their skills.

As the drive twists east through the Alleghenies, ample gravel road shoulders welcome sightseers to pull aside for a photo or a breath of mountain air. A few conifers lend their distinctive profiles to the mosaic of leaves. Galeton, a mill and rail town of the 1800s, next marks off progress. This town retains much of its historic district, best explored by a walking tour. Brochures are available from the Borough of Galeton office.

The walking tour strings past hotels, churches, cemeteries, mills, and lumberyards, as well as the infamous site of the town's "pigs-ear" pubs. These illicit pubs of the prohibition era catered to the rowdy "woodhicks," who drifted into town for Saturday-night entertainment. For a quiet picnic stop,

Sawmill exhibit, Pennsylvania Lumber Museum.

consider the quaint community park with its restored band house that overlooks the north shore of harnessed Pine Creek.

The drive now follows the canyon of Pine Creek east. Signs for outfitters tempt road travelers to trade seatbelts for lifejackets and the wet excitement of a float trip. The pristine waters of Pine Creek also bring anglers from all across the eastern United States—even herons may make it a stopover. Canyon wagon rides and bicycle rentals offer yet a different way to go, while gift and craft shops put in a bid for your travel dollar.

Despite this momentary retail blitz, north-central Pennsylvania boasts some of the most remote wilds in the state, with the **Grand Canyon of Pennsylvania** (Pine Creek Canyon) being the sterling prize. At Ansonia at 86.4 miles, the canyon's West Rim begs for a detour: turn south off US 6 onto Colton Road to find the northern terminus of the orange-blazed West Rim Trail (a 30-mile linear path) in 0.5 mile, Barbour Rock Trailhead in 3 miles, and Colton State Park in 5 miles.

For the **Barbour Rock Nature Way**, hike east on the blue-blazed foot trail to lasso the West Rim. Passage is amid a leafy woods of beech, birch, oak, hophornbeam, and witch hazel. In season, mountain laurel and mayflower dot the way with bloom. Tag the brink of the rim at a pair of vantages edged by low wooden rails at 0.5 mile. A few pines dress the rim.

Take in an unobstructed view, overlooking the twisting gorge of the Grand Canyon of Pennsylvania, which was sculpted over the ages by pristine

Barbour Rock view, Pine Creek Natural Area-Tioga State Forest.

Pine Creek. View the bulging and cupping 800-foot-tall canyon walls; pinnacles and protruding red rock pierce the tree cover. Far below, an abandoned stretch of Penn-Central Railroad travels the east bank of Pine Creek for a first-rate rail-to-trail. In summer, the canyon glories in green; in autumn, a multihued palette calls visitors back.

At **Colton State Park**, find additional easy-to-access rim views, many within its picnic area. Structures built by the Civilian Conservation Corps have won the park recognition as a National Historic Landmark. The enfolding canyon and bending Pine Creek captivate; fog may reveal and conceal the scene.

By keeping to US 6 at Ansonia, pass a Pine Creek canoe access and explore Marsh Creek east to the next whistle stop—Wellsboro, in about 11 miles. For a moment, break away from US 6 to discover the all-American, Main Street charm of this town: its gas streetlamps, classic courthouse, village green, and sprawling nineteenth-century homes. Or, pick up a walking-tour brochure at the visitor center or a town business and hoof the city. The **Lincoln Door House** at 140 Main Street still bears a red door given to the occupants in 1858 by a family friend—Abraham Lincoln.

West out of Wellsboro, the Grand Canyon of Pennsylvania may draw you back for an East Rim perspective from **Leonard Harrison State Park**. For this side excursion, take Main Street/Pennsylvania Highway 660 west out of town and follow signs. At the park, an easy walk-to vantage just beyond the breezeway of the visitor center and a hike-to overlook (Otter View) spotlight the stunning forested canyon threaded by Pine Creek. Bald eagles find favorable nesting habitat in the narrow wilderness.

If you resist the urge to explore at Wellsboro (97.5 miles into the tour), follow signs for US 6 through town and into the rolling countryside. In the distant shadow of the Endless Mountains, the tour now serves up broader views. You will travel past a glass company, spic-and-span dairy farms, rural residences, and gently rolling fields and pastures. The heavy, sweet scent of newly cut grass may hang in the air.

Once again, U-pik farms invite with strawberries and blueberries, while produce stands display an array of tempting vegetables and fruits. Mansfield with its historic university on the hill, tiny Troy with its farm museum, Towanda with its Riverfest in August, and Wysox with its Masonite mill count off distance; the broad Susquehanna River divides Towanda and Wysox.

Two side trips occur along this stretch. Between Troy and Towanda in Luthers Mills village (140.2 miles), a 1-mile detour north on Covered Bridge Road (paved and then potholed and graveled) halts at a now-closed **covered bridge** that spans the tree-shaded waters of Browns Creek. Along Covered Bridge Road, yellow warblers commonly flit between sumac and goldenrod. At Wysox, PA 187 heads south for **French Azilum**; the first of two spurs to the historic site (an 8-mile detour).

By keeping to US 6 as it ascends and skirts Rummerfield Mountain, pass a pair of prized roadside viewpoints: **Marie Antoinette Scenic View** (6 miles southeast of Wysox) and **Warriors Path Viewpoint** (another 3 miles farther). From this direction, it is a blind approach to the first overlook— upon emerging from a manmade canyon of road-cut cliffs at 159 miles, hook sharply right to find the stone castle-like viewing pavilions of Marie Antoinette Scenic View.

Below, an arc of the Susquehanna River cups the pastoral setting of French Azilum, which once supported an agricultural colony of 250 French aristocrats—refugees from the French Revolution of 1793. Story has it that the French settlers hoped to provide a safe haven here for their beleaguered queen, Marie Antoinette. The refugees erected a log mansion for the queen, but meanwhile she was beheaded. Word did not reach the colony for another year. Sometime after 1803, financial setbacks and changes in French politics brought about the colony's demise.

Despite areas of tall sumac, the Warriors Path Viewpoint serves up another grand Susquehanna River panorama. Historical markers on US 6 introduce Lime Hill Battlefield (1782), Warriors Path (the historic Native American route between the Six Nations country in New York State and the Catawba lands in the Carolinas), and farther east, Sullivan's March in 1779.

Dairy barn on US 6, Bradford County.

At 163.7 miles, Victorian homes and businesses with attractive 1890s facades signal the tour's end at Wyalusing.

Most famous of the town structures is the **Wyalusing Hotel** (111 Main Street). A former stagecoach stop, its older portion dates to 1860 and bears the architectural signature of J. Morgan Brown. He was noted for his use of elaborate gingerbread siding, decorative facades, dormers, and Mississippi riverboat porches. As the hotel front indicates, the establishment has been known as the Wyalusing Hotel since 1894, and it still welcomes overnight guests and serves meals.

At the east end of Wyalusing, travelers hear the last call for a side trip to French Azilum. From here, it is about 14 miles to the fee site of the Pennsylvania Historical and Museum Commission. Five reconstructed log cabins recall life at the French colony, while a model shows the original lay of the town. Due to irregular hours, phone before visiting.

Farther east, US 6 progressively grows more congested.

6

Pocono Mountains Loop
Circuit swings north from Honesdale

General description: This 66.3-mile circuit travels quiet mountain high-ways through the Pocono Mountains of Wayne County. From historic Honesdale, the leisurely route swings north, pinches to the Upper Delaware Scenic and Recreational River, travels past secluded lakes and ponds, and ventures through sleepy villages and leafy forests for a meandering return.

Special attractions: Remnants of the Delaware and Hudson Canal; the Stourbridge Line excursion train; Dorflinger Glass Museum; Upper Delaware River; a fish nursery; autumn foliage and winter bald eagle watching; fishing, canoeing, boating, skiing and other winter sports, shopping, antiquing.

Location: Remote northeast corner of the state.

Drive route numbers: U.S. Highway 6; Pennsylvania Highways 191, 370, and 670.

Travel season: Year-round.

Camping: Private campgrounds serve travelers along the route. On Lake Wallenpaupack (12 miles southeast of Honesdale, along US 6) is the Pennsylvania Power and Light's Wilsonville Campground with 318 modern sites.

Services: Find full services in Honesdale and in Hawley (to its south off US 6). Otherwise, services are limited.

Nearby points of interest: Zane Grey Museum and Roeblings Aqueduct (in Lackawaxen), Lake Wallenpaupack, historic Hawley, Shohola Falls Recreation Area, Claws and Paws Animal Park (Lake Ariel).

 # The drive

This drive celebrates the remote, laid-back beauty of the Pocono Mountains and the shining waters that divide the ridges and reflect the calm. The highways have a backroads quietness and round up a variety of unhurried stops: family picnic areas, historic society museums, an old mill, fishing spots on ponds or river, a fish hatchery, and farmstands. In fact, what most recommends this tour is its continuous, winning signature of simplicity and naturalness.

Seasonal changes suggest repeat tours. The month of May typically heralds the arrival of shad in the Delaware River. In September, the leaves

Drive 6: Pocono Mountains Loop
Circuit swings north from Honesdale

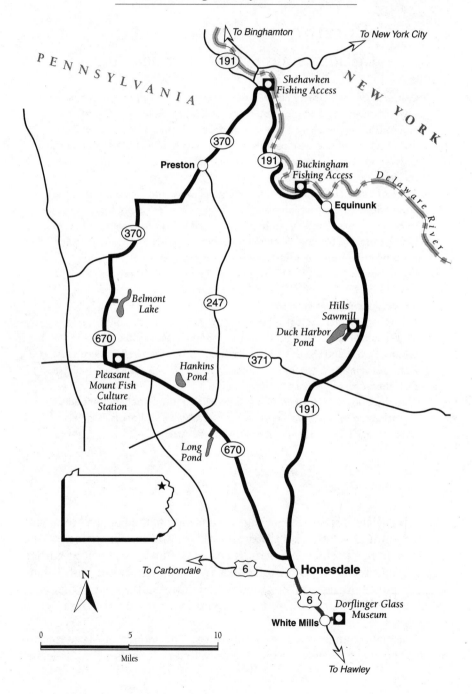

To Binghamton

To New York City

191

PENNSYLVANIA

NEW YORK

Shehawken
Fishing Access

370

191

Preston

Buckingham
Fishing Access

Delaware River

370

Equinunk

247

Belmont
Lake

Hills
Sawmill

Duck Harbor
Pond

670

371

Pleasant
Mount Fish
Culture
Station

Hankins
Pond

191

Long
Pond

670

N

To Carbondale

6

Honesdale

6

Dorflinger Glass
Museum

White Mills

0   5   10
Miles

To Hawley

on the trees and shrubs stop synthesizing their chlorophyll and change color, becoming a full-blazing kaleidoscope by the second week in October.

Next up, December through March sounds the arrival of the wintering bald eagles. Then, ice skates, cross-country skis, and horse-drawn sleighs offer alternative conveyance. When ice, frost, and snow brush the Pocono landscape, it is easy to become inspired. Therefore, it should come as no surprise that a Honesdale resident penned the song "Winter Wonderland."

Start this drive at Honesdale, 32 miles northwest of Interstate 84, Exit 10. On Main Street, which advances both US 6/PA 191 through the center of Honesdale, locate the **Wayne County Historical Society Museum** (810 Main Street); it signals the start of the tour. The museum occupies the old brick office of the Delaware and Hudson Canal Company and has a fine collection of area history (an admission fee is charged; hours vary).

Out the office's back door stretched the 108-mile, privately owned and operated Delaware and Hudson Canal (1828–1898), which transported anthracite coal from Carbondale, Pennsylvania, to New York ports. The first leg of the journey between Carbondale and Honesdale required a 16-mile gravity railroad to haul the coal up and over the obstinate Moosic Mountains west of town.

For what accomplished this task, see the pride of the historical society collection—the replica **Stourbridge Lion**. You will recognize it by the fierce

Pennsylvania Highway 670, Wayne County.

painted lion decorating the steam-engine boiler. In 1829, its namesake first conquered the tracks of the canal company's gravity railroad, sounding the birth of the railroad industry in America and giving Honesdale its slogan: "birthplace of the American railroad."

The tracks behind the museum today belong to the **Stourbridge Line** excursion train, which operates weekends June through Labor Day; tickets are sold by Wayne County Chamber of Commerce. The train runs to Lackawaxen or Hawley, with a stopover for sightseeing. Theme runs vary from old-time train holdups to oompah bands. Where the train follows along the Lackawaxen River, look for remnants of the old canal.

For the loop drive, follow US 6 West/PA 191 North through Honesdale, staying on PA 191 North in 0.3 mile. At the loop junction with PA 670 (at just under a mile), again stay on PA 191N for counterclockwise travel. Attractive homes from a bygone era usher you from town.

On the left, at the outskirts of Honesdale is **Apple Grove Picnic Area,** accessed by a rough dirt road. It occupies the bank of Dyberry Creek. Wooded hills overlook the site, while crickets drown out the sounds of PA 191. The grove's small playground can distract fidgeting youngsters.

Next, pass Wayne County Fairgrounds, while pursuing Dyberry Creek. A turnout at 2.7 miles overlooks the countryside and a flood-control dam. Unbroken forest swallows much of the route. Over 100 species of tree

Courthouse square, Honesdale.

contribute to the flamboyance of fall. Maple, oak, beech, gum, sassafras, aspen, birch, and conifer contribute to the richly woven tapestry. Hay-scented ferns and laurel patch the woodland floor.

A few cabins and lodges serve travelers. Gradually, sprawling farmhouses, barns, and cultivated fields create openings for extended mountain views. Traffic along PA 191 typically advances in pulses; stay attentive to the road and await proper turnouts to pull over for photographs or leaf collecting.

The Poconos were first inhabited by the Delaware, Iroquois, Lenape, Minisink, Shawnee, and Paupack. Their influence lives on in the area names—*Pocono* means "stream between two mountains." Since the early 1800s, these stream-carved mountain plateaus have attracted the city weary, and to this day, the appeal remains untarnished.

A small cemetery with a mix of old and new markers and Rileyville Grange Hall next mark off distance. At the hall, PA 371 East suggests a detour to the Upper Delaware River, but proceed north on PA 191. Where the route rolls atop rises, you will discover broader Pocono perspectives. Dairy cows and horses contribute to the tranquil backdrop.

Past the small, white St. Josephs Church, a left turn on Creek Road at 14.7 miles, followed by a right on Duck Harbor Road leads to **Duck Harbor Pond** in 1.5 miles. En route, pass **Hills Sawmill and Pond** on the left. This rustic, waterpowered mill was built just after the Civil War and operated until 1974. A national historic site, it is presently being restored by the Equinunk Historical Society as a piece of living history. Duck Harbor Pond is a long, beautiful pool cradled by the treed plateau of the Poconos and the white fences of private farms. At the Pennsylvania Fish Commission access, find a boat launch, dock, open shoreline, and vault toilets.

For the loop alone, stay north on PA 191. Drive past State Road 1016, which travels 7 miles east to Callicoon and the Upper Delaware River, postponing your river visit until points north. The drive now passes a general store and small cemeteries before plunging through a forested corridor to meet the **Upper Delaware Scenic and Recreational River**, a National Park Service recreation corridor.

At 23.1 miles, enter the tiny village of Equinunk, with its 100-year-old general store, the Calder House Museum, scenic Methodist Church, and the river for your first acquaintance. Equinunk Historical Society runs the **Calder House Museum**, which sits opposite the general store. Old photographs and documents; exhibits on early industry, farming, and textiles; and Native American artifacts take you through the building. A donation is requested; hours vary.

From Equinunk, you will view the Delaware River below to the right, the steep forested canyon slope to your left. The leafy aisle of the narrow road filters views. Although guardrails deny turnouts, primitive **Buckingham Fishing Access** is just ahead at 25.7 miles; be alert for the brown sign marking the turn. A thin roadway leads to the boat launch. Parking is roadside.

Here, the Delaware River flows broad and glassy, twisting through the tree-clad Poconos that tower 800 feet above; New York State is across the way. Viburnum and other flowering shrubs and wildflowers grow along the banks and river bars. This part of the river is noted for its trout fishery and its May-to-June shad run. In places, inch-long fingerlings darken the river shallows. Canoeists have front row seats for the tranquil river discovery.

Winter brings the bald eagle watch, when some 100 of the majestic birds escape the harsh Canadian cold and settle along the Delaware River. The river's fish population and ample roosts attract the birds. If you look for eagles, minimize your presence; watch quietly from a remote area and never give chase to the birds. Use binoculars and scopes to better your vantage.

Northbound, PA 191 hugs the Upper Delaware, now touring the wooded canyon bottom. Where the floodplain broadens, it often conceals the river, but deer may be spied as they make their way to the water. Where the slope to the river again builds, you still have filtered looks at the Delaware.

At 31.7 miles, the loop turns left (west) on PA 370, but just 0.1 mile north on PA 191 is another primitive river access—**Shehawken Fishing Access.** It overlooks the narrowed West Branch Delaware River, with areas of big willows and banks of joe-pyeweed, milkweed, and goldenrod. Opposite the entrance to the fishing access, a farm produce stand tempts travelers with tastes of the season.

As you take the turn west on PA 370, view an attractive dairy farm. Rolling, meandering travel along Shehawken Creek Valley follows. More ranches and farms dot this narrow valley. An ice cream parlor, general store, bed-and-breakfast, and historic country inn bring touches of life to this otherwise natural or pastoral segment.

At 39.7 miles, Preston extends limited traveler services. Beyond town, a private marsh to the left varies viewing. As the tour climbs, you will encounter a younger, bushier forest. At 45.1 miles, reach PA 670 and follow it south to return to Honesdale. This country highway lacks a road shoulder, but enjoys a wonderful arbor. A few rough patches may slow travel, while openings to the west provide a window to Mount Ararat.

After going about 3 miles on PA 670, a left turn on paved road leads to **Belmont Lake Pennsylvania Fish Commission Access**, where a large gravel parking area, boat launch, and vault toilets serve lake visitors. Dammed at its south end, Belmont Lake is a good-sized water body, with a symmetrical hill rising opposite the access. The water is ideal for small fishing boats and canoes. The tree-shaded slope between the lakeshore and parking area invites the spreading of a blanket.

Monarch butterfly, Wayne County.

Past the Belmont Lake access, turn left on PA 670/PA 371 East, bypassing a couple monuments to early-day residents of Wayne County. In 0.5 mile, **Pleasant Mount Fish Culture Station** (established 1903) and its associated picnic area straddle the quiet highway. Joe-pyeweed and cattail adorn the banks of the West Branch Lackawaxen River, which threads through this fish-rearing facility. Kingfishers dart along the creek-sized water.

At the station, a large fish tank with porthole windows permits a look at the common Pennsylvania game fish: catfish, bass, trout, and pickerel, while stairs mount the tank's side to a top-of-the-tank vantage. The fish culture station is an extensive operation with a series of stucco buildings, fish pens, and ponds. While it is unlawful to fish the hatchery waters, drooling is still acceptable for all you anglers.

Just beyond the station, at Pleasant Mount, PA 670 and PA 371 part company; bear right, staying PA 670. The rolling tour again dishes up fine mountain-country views. At 54.3 miles, a 12- to 15-foot-tall rockwork dam contains the fish-rearing basin of **Hankins Pond**. The reflective water and precise lay of the stones, now etched by lichen, contribute to viewing. Again, anglers must curb the temptation to cast.

Ahead, woods and farms grace the rolling tour. Picturesque country churches and the shimmery platters of private ponds add to windshield viewing. At 58.5 miles, a dirt access road heads right and then left to reach

Long Pond in about a mile. Find a public launch for canoes and fishing boats. Arrowhead grows in the shallows, and private residences dot the far shore.

Rural life and woods settings complete the tour. A painted line now divides the two-lane road. Days of humidity give the landscape an aura of mist and muted images. South of Bethany is an orchard with U-pik blueberries, apples, and peaches in season, as well as fresh honey. At the north end of Honesdale, the loop comes to a close at PA 191.

Turn right to revisit the history and visitor attractions at the center of Honesdale. Or, proceed southeast out of Honesdale on US 6 for White Mills and the Dorflinger Glass Museum, Hawley, or Lake Wallenpaupack.

For the combined attractions of **Dorflinger Glass Museum** (closed Monday and Tuesday), 600-acre **Dorflinger-Suydam Wildlife Sanctuary** (open daily, no pets), and **Wildflower Music Festival** (held summers, outdoors), go 5 miles southeast on US 6 to White Mills, turn left on SR 2006, and proceed 1 mile. Some 5 miles of nature trail explore the grounds of Dorflinger manor, while the manor/museum artfully displays the antique glass amid period pieces. Sunlight dances off the facets and prisms in rainbow spectrums. The collection exceeds 600 pieces: etched, cut, gilded, colored, and engraved. During its heyday, Dorflinger cut glass was the finest in the country.

If your drive occurs on a summer Saturday, evening concert tickets for the Wildflower Music Festival can put a fine cap on the day. Unfurl a blanket at the open-air amphitheater, watch the sunset, and commune with nature and a musical score.

7

Lakes Arthur and Wilhelm Loop

Clockwise circuit between the two lakes starting from
the intersection of U.S. Highways 19 and 422

General description: This 101-mile rural tour travels the west-central Pennsylvania lakes region, with visits to three state parks, two nature centers, and two of the large, manmade recreational waters. Cultural stops add to travel.

Special attractions: McConnells Mill, Goddard, and Moraine state parks; a relict wildflower prairie; neighboring old-order Amish communities; an 1860s cemetery for runaway slaves and freedmen; a working forge; bison ranch; picnicking, shopping, hiking, fishing, boating, swimming, and winter sports.

Location: Western Pennsylvania, between Pittsburgh and Meadville.

Drive route numbers: U.S. Highways 19 and 422; Pennsylvania Highways 285, 173, and 528.

Travel season: Year-round.

Camping: Private campgrounds located along the route serve overnighters. There are no public campgrounds, although Moraine State Park does rent 11 family cabins on Lake Arthur, available year-round; reserve in advance.

Services: Mercer, Sandy Lake, Grove City, and Slippery Rock, all have a full offering of traveler services, with many services available along the route.

Nearby points of interest: Pymatuning and Shenango lakes, Oil Creek State Park, Volant-New Wilmington Amish Country, Living Treasures Animal Park (New Castle), Pymatuning Deer Park (Jamestown), historic Meadville, the Pittsburgh metro area, Beechwood Farms Nature Reserve (Fox Chapel).

 The drive

This generally quiet drive draws a rectangle around the lake core of west-central Pennsylvania, passing through rural settings, rolling woodlands, and Victorian communities. In its 101 miles, it brings together an exciting boulder-riddled creek gorge, a remnant prairie ecosystem, wetlands, woods, delicate waterfalls, and vast recreational reservoirs. Echoes to the past enrich the journey: a water-powered grist mill, a covered bridge, a Civil War-era African-American cemetery, and stagecoach taverns.

Drive 7: Lakes Arthur and Wilhelm Loop

Clockwise circuit between the two lakes starting from the intersection of
U.S. Highways 19 and 422

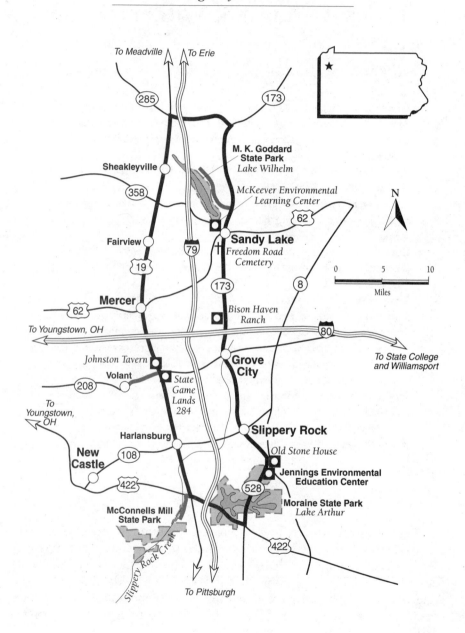

At Moraine and McConnells Mill state parks, you will read clues to the region's glacial past. Today, the centerpiece of Moraine State Park—manmade Lake Arthur—reclaims part of the basin of a much larger glacial lake that occupied this site 10,000 years ago. When the ice dam retaining the ancient lake retreated, it unleashed a torrent of rock and water that scoured the 7-mile-long, 400-foot-deep Slippery Rock Creek Gorge in McConnell's Mill State Park. Elephant-sized boulders deposited in the fury's wake still adorn the gorge.

Start the lakes drive at the junction of U.S. Highways 422 and 19, some 40 miles north of Pittsburgh. From there, head north on US 19 for a clockwise adventure that reserves the lake visits for later. From the onset, a detour calls.

Visitors may choose to start or end their excursion with a stop at **McConnells Mill State Park**, a National Natural Landmark, (0.1 mile west on US 422, then south on McConnell's Mill Road). Picnic areas and a fine network of trails allow for an appreciation of the gorge, the whitewater of Slippery Rock Creek, a couple of small but elegant waterfalls, and a rustic 1868 mill (open 10:30 A.M. to 5:30 P.M. Memorial Day through Labor Day, with variable spring and fall hours).

The 2-mile loop of the **Kildoo Trail** spotlights much of the park offering. It travels between the 1874-built covered bridge at the mill area and Eckert Bridge downstream; interpretive brochures for the trail are available at the park office. The path travels at the lower reaches of the richly forested gorge to gather rapid-fire views of Slippery Rock Creek. Discover pocket sandy beaches, boulder realms, and side drainages with cascading chutes. Turbulent, rock-squeezed rapids on Slippery Rock Creek bring amplified excitement. Keep toward the creek.

If saving your visit to McConnells Mill State Park for the finale, follow US 19 north away from US 422 and into the rural countryside. Wooded stretches, attractive barns, cornfields, hay bales, and farmstands soon work their spell of calm. US 19, however, remains a fast two-lane highway, counting down the mileage.

At the crossroads with PA 108, view the privately run **Harlansburg Museum of Transportation**, neatly housed in retired railroad cars, and the historic Village Inn, built 1845. Continue north. You will find this stretch along US 19 more forested than the parallel return south on PA 173.

At 12 miles, you will come to the next side-trip options. Here, PA 208 travels west a couple of miles to **Volant**, a small grist mill community within an old-order Amish settlement. PA 208 East leads to **State Game Lands 284** in 0.4 mile, where an abandoned railroad grade at the corner of PA 208 and Brent Road serves as a hiker path. When mosquitos are absent, the retired grade invites a relaxing walk through mixed woods and along marsh.

Volant's "Main Street" appeal and charming shops and eateries invite a stroll. The waterwheel still turns at the 1812 Volant grist mill, but indoors, Amish furniture and crafts now replace the gnashing millstones and bags of grain. Nearby flows Neshannock Creek, suggesting an ideal picnic setting. To see aspects of Amish life, you might consider driving the backroads between Volant and New Wilmington (6.5 miles west of Volant).

For the basic drive on US 19, go a mile north from the PA 208 crossroad to view **Johnston Tavern** on the right. Built in 1831, this stone tavern served early travelers on the Pittsburgh-Mercer Road. Today, it holds an antique, floral, and gift store. A beautiful old maple still graces its grounds. As the tour rolls north, pass a restaurant, inn, and campground. At the Interstate 80 on ramps, you will find a momentary blitz of fast foods, gas, and chain hotels.

Rural travel is quickly re-established though, and 2 miles north, enter the genteel spell of Mercer (18.4 miles), where hitching posts replace parking meters. As is true elsewhere in western Pennsylvania, Mercer has a familiar town blueprint, with a centrally placed courthouse and Civil War Memorial, its brick business district, surrounding neighborhoods of stately Victorian homes, prominent brick and stone churches, and, of course, an ice cream parlor at the edge of town.

From the outskirts of Mercer, again pick up the tour's rural thread, driving past produce stands, grazing geese, cornfields, pastures, and barns. In the distance loom wooded rises. Where unkempt fields host wildflowers, goldenrod parades its showy color in late summer. Briefly, a railroad track parallels US 19, before it crosses over the highway and disappears west. Cheese becomes an important product near the village of Fairview (25.1 miles). There, too, signs entice with Amish quilts and wood furniture.

At 30.4 miles, pass Long Cemetery on the left with its many old tablets. Next to several markers fly small American flags. The "GAR" emblems indicate the dead were soldiers in the Grand Army of the Republic during the Civil War. Next up, Sheakleyville has a few traveler services and a backdoor entry to Goddard State Park; stay US 19 North. Picket signs announce "peaches," "corn," "tomatoes," "cukes," and "potatoes" as you approach the next vegetable stand.

Where the route passes a state game lands parcel at a large creek, admire a wildflower-adorned marsh. Stay on US 19 to its junction with PA 285 at 40 miles. Now turn east on PA 285 to continue the lakes tour, crossing over Interstate 79 at Exit 35. Drive amid fields and woods, through villages, and past country churchyards for a quiet sojourn. Later, glimpse the broad band of French Creek to the north. At 47.3 miles, you will tag PA 173, which takes the tour south.

On this two-lane country highway, share in the quiet easiness of rural life. Hand-lettered signs now advertise the trades performed by neighbors:

knife sharpening, meat cutting, carburetor repair, hair cuts. At 54.9 miles, reach the turn for **M.K. Goddard State Park**; it lies 5 miles west via New Vernon Road.

This is the first of the lake attractions along the tour and the less developed of the two. Between wooded rises, narrow manmade **Lake Wilhelm** stretches between I-79 and PA 173. The lake's western extent, enfolded by State Game Lands 270, is more primitive. Picnic areas, boat launches and a marina, and hiking and nature trails present the area; canoe and boat rentals are available. Motors are restricted to a 10-horsepower maximum in keeping with the natural backdrop.

At the causeway, near launch 3, find the **Wilhelm Trail**, which explores the eastern two-thirds of the lake. Herons, ducks, geese, cormorants, and gulls animate shallows and shore. Warm-water fish species provide angler sport. At Rounded Point, near the marina parking lot, is a wheelchair-accessible fishing pier. In winter, the lake invites your return, with ice fishing, ice skating (near launch 3), sledding (area is near the dam), and marked cross-country ski and snowmobile trails.

For the loop drive alone, PA 173 continues south into the community of Sandy Lake. There, find another entry to Goddard State Park, via the quiet lakeshore route of Creek Road. At the center of town (59.4 miles) is the intersection of PA 173, US 62, and PA 358. Short detours right on US 62 South or PA 358 West beckon.

A 1.2-mile side trip on US 62 South leads to the **Freedom Road Cemetery**, on the left opposite Stoneboro Fairgrounds; a Pennsylvania history marker indicates the site. Exit your car and top the small wooded knoll to view the dignified wooden crosses (placed by Boy Scouts) and a few original stones. The graves belong to freedmen (ex-slaves), Black Civil War veterans, and escaping slaves. Several of the crosses bear the epitaph, "Ex Slave known only unto God."

Many African-Americans who escaped from slavery via the Underground Railroad (also known as Freedom Road) or who fought in the Civil War came to settle in nearby Stoneboro. Stoneboro was first established by a colony of freedmen in 1825, and for 37 years, it was a key station on the network to freedom.

A nearly equidistant side trip west on PA 358 leads to **McKeever Environmental Learning Center**. The center primarily has outdoor programs that cater to groups, but it also has a 5-mile nature trail system that is open daily to the public. Each of the trails offer tranquil woodland discovery. Brochures and information are available at the site's Discovery Building; all walks begin at the Information Shelter kiosk. The leg stretch brings a welcomed change from the bucket seats.

Without the diversions at 59.4 miles, PA 173 proceeds south from Sandy Lake, registering more rural images: cornfields, Christmas tree farms,

Freedom Road Cemetery, Sandy Lake.

and country cemeteries. Woods are seldom absent from the West Pennsylvania mosaic, but are now seen in the distance.

At 69.1 miles, an 0.8-mile detour west on Elliott Road and south on gravel Straub Road leads to the private **Bison Haven Ranch**, where the owners will take guests out to see the beasts of the western frontier. There is a fee and about a quarter of a mile walk to where the animals range; tour availability depends on staffing. Bison meat and authentic Native American crafts are sold at the gift store. The friendly, woolly-faced owner seems appropriately paired with his chosen herd.

Keeping to PA 173 South, motorists cross over I-80 to enter Grove City, where signs point the way to **Wendell August Forge** (a 0.6-mile detour). Visitors may journey to the back room of the gift shop, with its sounds of ringing metal and the artisans bent over their craft, turning aluminum, bronze, and pewter into fine pieces. Earplugs are available and make a visit more enjoyable. Draped in grapevines, the brick forge building is listed on the National Register of Historic Places.

The tour along PA 173 weaves south through the attractive town and past Grove City College, founded 1876, to return to the rural landscape. As PA 173 enters Butler County, the road grows wider and invites faster speeds. At 79.8 miles, view the town of Slippery Rock and its university. To the

Old Stone House Historic Site.

south, where the road crosses Slippery Rock Creek, you may watch anglers scramble over the rocks to dunk their lines in inviting holes.

At 84.8 miles, PA 173 ends at PA 8, and PA 528 starts up just to the south. Overlooking the busy intersection from atop its grassy knoll is the **Old Stone House.** This two-story tavern was built by John Brown in 1822 at the crossroads of the Pittsburgh-Franklin and Butler-Mercer pikes. The former stagestop and drovers' inn is now a museum. In 1825, Lafayette stopped here. Tales of drink, murder, counterfeiters, highwaymen, and scandal haunt the hall and color its tours. The historic furnishings inside and posted tavern rules outside provide a sense of time and tavern hospitality. An admission is charged; hours vary.

For the lakes drive, go south on PA 8 for a couple hundred yards to take PA 528 south. In shy of 0.1 mile, you will pass the education center building and woodland offering of **Jennings Environmental Education Center** (EEC) on the left; the site's acclaimed prairie is just a quick hop south on the right. The office is open 8 A.M. to 4 P.M. weekdays. You will find tables for a picnic lunch at the EEC's prairie component.

A web of short trails explores the habitats of this 320-acre EEC. A 0.5-mile interpretive loop visits the prehistoric prairie, which is similar to those of the Midwest. About 2000 B.C., the prairie ecosystem spanned between

Forest boardwalk, Jennings Environmental Education Center.

Lake Arthur, Moraine State Park.

the Rockies and Appalachians. However, when climatic changes ushered in forest succession, all but a handful of the eastern prairies were lost.

A wildflower—the prairie blazing star—drew the attention of botanist Otto Emery Jennings and now lends its name to the EEC grassland. In early August, look for the rose-purple radial blooms on a 4- to 6-foot-tall stalk. Much of the vegetation grows knee to waist high and parades forth blooms. A hawk moth, which hovers like a hummingbird, may draw study, and although the endangered Massasauga rattlesnake resides here, the recluse is rarely spied.

PA 528 next takes the tour south into **Moraine State Park**. Woods embrace the meandering route, which delivers a bouncing, curvy ride. On the left at 88 miles is **Frank W. Preston Conservation Area**; its entrance spur offers a one-way loop drive along a large arm of the park's **Lake Arthur**. View wooded rims and peninsulas, lilypad shallows, and cattail shores. A small boat ramp accesses the water, and a 10-horsepower limit on motors is enforced.

On the right, opposite the turn for the conservation area is the park's 14-mile **Glacier Ridge Trail**, part of the North Country National Scenic Trail. Next, traverse the bridge over the eastern extent of Lake Arthur—a ragged-arm 3,225-acre reservoir. Wild shores and wide-open expanses recommend this more remote area of the park; side roads spur to more launches and trails. Stay PA 528 south to meet US 422 at 93.5 miles.

Turn west on this fast, divided highway to reach exits for the developed **South and North Shore recreation areas of Moraine State Park**, at 96.9 and 99.2 miles respectively. A stop by the park office on the south shore is recommended. There, pick up a park map and trail flier to gain your bearings—Moraine State Park is enormous. Areas serve picnickers, birders, boaters, sailors, sailboarders, anglers, swimmers, cyclists, and even equestrians. Winter introduces a new catalog of recreations and recreationists. On weekends and hot summer days, expect a bustling lake crowd. Sunset sounds the departure.

To end the drive, stay US 422 west past the park. At 99.5 miles, the on ramps to I-79 suggest a speedy return home; the loop itself is completed at US 19 at 101 miles. For those who resisted the initial straying, McConnells Mill State Park and Slippery Rock Creek await.

8

Tionesta Creek Scenic Drive
From Ridgway to Tionesta Lake

General description: This drive carves a 66.5-mile arc through the heart of Allegheny National Forest, following the twisting course of pretty Tionesta Creek nearly two-thirds of the way. It is well suited for leisurely travel, with ample calls to stop and stretch your legs. In October, the flamboyant autumn foliage particularly recommends travel. Due to its width and hairpin turns, the portion of the drive along Pennsylvania Highway 666 is not recommended for large trailers or recreational vehicles.

Special attractions: Tionesta Creek and Lake overlooks and access; Brush Hollow Trails; Minister Creek hiking trail and campground; a fish hatchery; hiking, fishing, canoeing, lake water sports, winter cross-country skiing and snowmobiling, relaxing.

Location: South-central Allegheny National Forest, northwest Pennsylvania.

Drive route numbers: Pennsylvania Highways 948, 666, and 36; U.S. Highway 62.

Travel season: Year-round, when cleared of snow.

Camping: Minister Creek Campground (on PA 666) has six family campsites with pit toilets and water pump. Tionesta Lake Recreation Area is a U.S. Army Corps of Engineers project, with four drive-to campgrounds: one at Kellettville and three along Tionesta Lake, for a total of 234 sites; facilities vary.

Services: Ridgway and Tionesta offer full services at either end of the crescent-shaped drive.

Nearby points of interest: Cook Forest State Park and Cook Forest Sawmill Center for the Arts; Clarion and Allegheny river attractions; Knox, Kane, Kinzua Railroad; Elk, Bendigo, and Oil Creek state parks; North Country National Scenic Trail.

The drive

This forest drive is one of the best yet-to-be popularized drives in the state. Along it, you will travel the beautiful, remote woodland of Pennsylvania's only national forest, be mesmerized by the sparkling waters of Tionesta Creek, and enjoy the backroads spell of the lightly-traveled, serpentine Triple 6 (PA 666). Then, after being completely lulled into relaxation, you can exit your

Drive 8: Tionesta Creek Scenic Drive
From Ridgway to Tionesta Lake

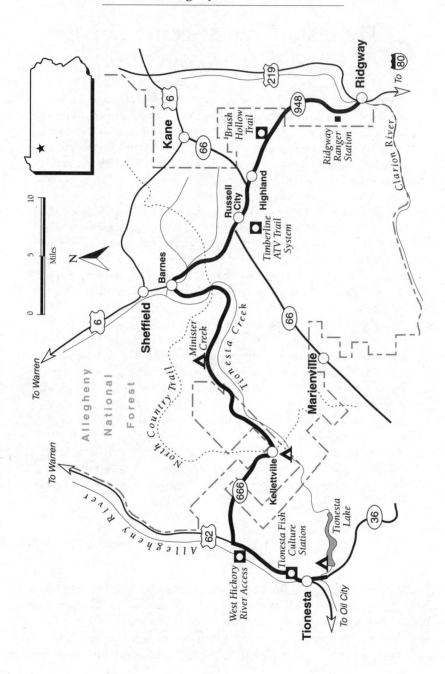

vehicle and jump wholeheartedly into the full-scale recreation of Tionesta Lake.

To set off on this journey, point your vehicle to Ridgway, located off US 219 at the southeast corner of Allegheny National Forest in the Clarion River Valley. From the stately 1880 **Elk County Courthouse**, with its clock-and-bell tower and sentry pair of Civil War cannons, follow Main Street/PA 948 North through the center of town. Tree-clad ridges enfold this whole-some, American-flag community.

Ridgway, a one-time leader in the leather industry, takes its name from a family of wealthy Philadelphia merchants who were major landowners here. For all of you baseball trivia buffs, Ridgway was also home to William Pearl "Bunker" Rhines (1869–1922), the major-league baseball player who perfected the underhand pitch.

As PA 948 approaches the Clarion River bridge in town, you will spy advertisements for outfitters and canoe rentals. The **Clarion River** stretches for 60 canoeable miles between Ridgway and the Allegheny River confluence. Throughout its journey, the Clarion courses broad, clear, and serene, pass-ing through gorgeous forest scenery; its waters are Class C, with an average flow of 4 miles per hour.

At 0.4 mile, PA 948N turns right to ascend out of Ridgway. On the left in another 2 miles is the **Ridgway Ranger Station**, where brochures and information are available. While at the station, view one half of a Bullwheel, a large wooden spool used in the oil industry. The oil industry had its begin-nings near here in the 1800s. You may also examine a fossilized trunk of an ancient fern, Lepidodendron.

As the tour advances north, signs for cottage industries shout out "rugs" and "quilts," while fields interrupt the woodland mosaic and expand views. Traffic is typically light, allowing sightseers to admire monarch butterflies on the roadside wildflowers or study the leaf patterns of draping trees. Along-side established fields, rows of sugar maple frame the way, their leaves a showy red in October.

At the intersection with Tambine Road, look for PA 948 to veer left for a more rolling, curving tour into Allegheny National Forest. On the right at 10.5 miles is **Brush Hollow Parking Area**, a developed trailhead for hikers and winter cross-country skiers; a vault toilet is the lone amenity.

Brush Hollow features a second-growth forest and other habitat to sus-tain bear, turkey, and pileated woodpecker. Mill Creek, which threads the area, is the clean and sparkling home to small, native brook trout. An 8.5-mile trail system passes alongside the creek and atop the forested plateau to tag tree-framed overlooks of the Mill Creek watershed. Old railroad grades from the logging days contribute to the trail system. The site's three inter-locking loops provide winter cross-country skiers with multilevel challenges.

Hay-scented ferns, Minister Creek Trail, Allegheny National Forest.

Back along PA 948, black cherry, maple, and beech contribute to the towering woods. The midstory varies from being shrub-congested to spatially open. Occasionally, a gas well may be glimpsed beyond the tree trunks. Beyond the village of Highland (14 miles), you will come upon the first of two marked trailheads for the **Timberline All-Terrain Vehicle (ATV) Trail**, a 38-mile system.

Before long, PA 66 South shares the way, and at the village of Russell City, you will find a snack hut and a general store/filling station, where fishing licenses may be purchased. After the departure of PA 66S, PA 948 follows a twisting, roller coaster course; groves of hemlock and plantations of pine and spruce alter the forest canvas.

Where the drive enters the Tionesta Creek drainage and follows alongside the South Fork at 24.1 miles, a right turn onto Forest Road 148 leads to a couple turnouts just before the forest road bridge over the South Fork Tionesta Creek at 0.2 mile. From here, you can enjoy a leisurely look at the clear, tannin-colored creek, its rocky bed, and flopping fish in the deeper pools beneath overhanging birch trees. Autumn leaves drift on the surface, collect to the sides, or sink to the bottom. Beyond the immediate shore, a dark hemlock-beech forest claims the creek flat.

Without the turnoff on FR 148, you will proceed north on PA 948 and cross paths with the **North Country National Scenic Trail**. When complete, this premier trail will span 3,200 miles between Lake Sakakawea, North Dakota, and Crown Point, New York. Where the South Fork Tionesta Creek again pairs with travel, admire its gentle bends and alternating riffles and quiet pulses. Brush sometimes snarls its shore.

At Barnes, the drive crosses the bridge over the joined waters of the East and South forks of Tionesta Creek, and the canyon begins to take shape. At 27 miles, PA 666 West takes the relay baton and for the first time crosses Tionesta Creek proper. The following ascent brings an attractive ridge-canyon view; a large dirt turnout allows for an unhurried look. Abundant sugar maples interweave the canopy of birch, beech, aspen, oak, and striped maple.

After dropping back down, the hooking Triple 6 tightly parallels Tionesta Creek downstream through its canyon. The road, the setting, and the periodic small village, all suggest a slow pace. At 30.9 miles, cross another Tionesta Creek bridge for grand up- and downstream views. A succession of creek-side turnouts now call motorists aside for a photograph, a cast of the fishing line, the unrolling of a blanket for picnic lunch, or simply to watch the day float by.

Tionesta Creek flows 80 feet broad, but shallow and glassy, with a changeable face. Unbroken forest houses much of the waterway. At the foot of the forest slope, rock slabs contribute to wavy reflections. Only the few wires that lace across the creek steal from the natural image. Tionesta is Iroquois for "it penetrates the land," but it also penetrates the spirit.

Before long, the North Country Trail makes another appearance, and leaf-filtered views of the creek alternate with open straightaway viewing. The profile of a canoe may complete the tranquil image; the best time for canoeing Tionesta Creek is early spring through May.

At 33.1 miles, you will come upon the **Tall Oaks Store**, billed as "the neatest little store in the woods." While not run by elves or fairies, as would seem appropriate for this out-of-the-way woodland store, it does offer an interesting collection of curios for hearth and home, handcrafted treasures, and seasonal specialties. During its autumn fest, the booths of artists and craftspeople expand the offering, and bright orange pumpkins and pale golden cornstalks dress the grounds.

Next up, the drive passes above a marsh and alder floodplain and by-passes private homes to enter a **windstorm site** at 35.5 miles. The storm of September 1994 struck this Georgia Pacific property with a fury, lifting trees up by their roots, snapping trunks, and flattening tons of foliage. Although the south slope has been salvage logged, the floodplain retains the chaos of the storm.

The selectiveness of the storm's intensity is dramatized because instantly the tour is plunged back into tranquil forest. Tionesta Creek remains closely paired with PA 666, which narrows, loses its dividing line, and becomes

Hikers on the Minister Creek Trail, Allegheny National Forest.

increasingly squirmy. To the right, beautiful boulder slabs erupt from the forest floor. Coated in moss and fern, some of the slabs appear otherworldly.

At 39 miles, enter the village of Truemans. Its general store is a landmark of long-standing. Afterward, the tour drifts a bit farther from Tionesta Creek. In another mile, you will come to **Minister Creek Campground and Trailhead**. Here, a popular circuit trail for family backpacks or day hikes explores along Minister Creek, meadow flat, forest, and rocky realm. Also, at this small recreation area, the wily trout entice anglers back and forth between Minister Creek and close-by Tionesta Creek.

White diamonds blaze the **Minister Creek Trail**, which later accesses the North Country Trail. On this trail, a 1.5-mile hike to **Minister Valley Overlook** provides a good area synopsis. Follow the closed-road section of trail to where it ends and the loop begins at 0.5-mile, and then hike the left fork. For the next 0.7 mile, a lazy, switchbacked woodland ascent carries the trail to the rocky upper slope.

At the rocks, watch for arrows to point the way through dark grottos, beneath overhangs, and along stone steps to the laurel-dotted plateau and a flat-topped, vertical rock at 1.5 miles. This dramatic promontory affords a natural view of the wooded ridges of Minister Creek watershed. By hiking 0.2 mile beyond the overlook, you will view a funhouse of rock features: boxy boulders, deep fissures, fern shelves, weeping mosses, and a broadened mossy fissure, 8 to 10 feet wide and 100 feet long.

Midweek and off-season visits to Minister Creek promise greater enjoyment. On summer weekends, the trail's parking lot often overflows. Despite the warnings against it, people still park roadside, so be alert as you take the turns leaving the area to continue west. Patchwork repairs on PA 666 likewise suggest slowing.

Just ahead, Tionesta Creek makes a reappearance, showing gravel-bar beaches, vegetated banks, and draping trees. A steep forested slope rises to the right, while private homes dot the banks; turnouts are now few. Ahead, PA 666 rolls through a couple of villages that are merely blips on the map; Balltown is where the first oil strike in Forest County took place in 1863. Past Mayburg, disturbed areas of goldenrod, grape, and an herb-forb tangle clear the way for open downstream views.

The drive now passes Allegheny National Forest lands and posted timber company lands that allow for public access; obey rules. By 46 miles, the U.S. Army Corps of Engineers takes the mantle of ownership and has posted turnouts for day use along the creek.

At 48.3 miles, you enter the village of Kellettville. During its heyday, Kellettville boasted regular rail service, two mills, a hub factory, wood kiln, and tannery. Now all is pretty well quiet. As PA 666 climbs away, look to your left for a road arriving at an angle from Tionesta Creek.

Although it is a bugger of a tight U-turn, you may want to take this side road down to the creek and across the bridge to the U.S. Army Corps of Engineers **Kellettville Recreation Site**; the best bet, though, is to proceed to a safe turnaround and backtrack to the junction. Stretched out along Tionesta Creek, this floodplain recreation site often receives visits from ring-necked pheasant, nut-gathering squirrels, and a curious buck. From the far end of camp, the **Kellettville to Nebraska Trail** parallels Tionesta Creek downstream.

As PA 666 continues away west, it grows wider and gains a dividing line. Woods frame the still twitching road. At 49.5 miles, encounter the North Country Trail for one last time. While negotiating the hairpin turns, pass a dude ranch at Whig Hill. At Whig Hill, you will also find a general store and gas pumps. Farms now intersperse the forest.

View a quiet country church at Endeavor and soon after, cross the Hickory Creek bridge in East Hickory to meet US 62 and the **Allegheny Wild and Scenic River** at 58.6 miles. Turn south on US 62 for both the town of Tionesta and Tionesta Lake. Travel is along the foot of the east canyon wall. History markers dot the tour, and the straighter, wider road welcomes faster progress.

On the right in about 1 mile is **West Hickory River Access**, where a large parking area, boat launch, and grassy shore serve Allegheny River users. The upstream view includes the PA 127 river bridge, the canyon ridges, islands, and shore. Downstream, the manmade levee of US 62 draws a sharp contrast to the shining waterway and natural canyon.

South on US 62, you will have unobstructed river views as you travel along the levee. Throughout history, the river has been a vital transportation corridor for Indians, trappers, soldiers, and local industry. Long ago, a path crossed the river's west ridge to Oil Creek, where Native Americans collected tar to waterseal their canoes. Today, the river's role has changed, with recreation becoming a primary value.

At 64.5 miles is the slightly more primitive **Tionesta River Access**, with the 1929-built **Tionesta Fish Culture Station** opposite it. Open daily (except holidays) 8 A.M. to 3:30 P.M., the fish hatchery has a modest visitor facility. Central to the offering is a freshwater tank with porthole windows and an open top for viewing common Pennsylvania game fish. Outdoors, visitors may view the rearing pens and trout display.

The hatchery raises muskellunge, walleye, and steelhead fingerlings for stocking the Commonwealth waters. The yellow-gold Palomino trout are particularly eye-catching. On approach to the pens, you may cause a surface-striking flurry as the small fish mistake your shadow for that of their feeder.

Next up, enter the river town of Tionesta, established 1856. It is another attractive, frozen-in-time community, with mature shade trees, old-time

Tionesta Creek, Allegheny National Forest.

storefronts, stone churches, and the Forest County Courthouse. The town hosts the Tionesta Indian Festival, a small-town street fair with Native American tributes, which takes place each August. It is believed that the Lawunakhannek village was located in the vicinity of present-day Tionesta.

To reach Tionesta Lake, take Colonel Drake Highway (PA 36) south off US 62 at 65.4 miles; an information center is near the junction. Between 65.8 miles and 66.5 miles, you will find a series of marked turns for the lake's developed recreation areas. At 66.5 miles is the left turn for **Tionesta Lake** (a day-use only area) and the **Forest County Historical Society**. Take this turn to end at the main open-water recreation area near the dam.

Completed in 1941 for flood control, **Tionesta Dam** rises 154 feet to harness the clear water of Tionesta Creek. It sits 1.25 miles above the Allegheny River confluence and shapes a nearly 500-acre lake that stretches for more than 6 miles to provide full-scale lake recreation. Its open waters are plied by high-speed boats with water skiers in tow; the quiet backwater coves attract canoeists and anglers in fishing boats.

At the **Tionesta Dam Visitors' Center**, the Forest County Historical Society operates a small museum with Native American, settler, and industry artifacts. The museum is open daily 10 A.M. to 4 P.M., May through October.

For a loop return to Ridgway that passes through the old-growth of Cook Forest State Park and along the Clarion River, follow PA 36 south and PA 949 east for a 126-mile tour.

9

Cook Forest–Clarion River Tour
Circuitous tour between Marienville
and the North Bank Clarion River

General description: This 53.7-mile circuit out of Marienville visits the virgin trees of Cook Forest State Park, pursues the curvaceous Clarion River, and makes a wildlife stop at Buzzard Swamp before it draws to a close.

Special attractions: A National Natural Landmark cathedral forest; Clarion Wild and Scenic River access and views; Cook Forest Sawmill Center for the Arts; a 1929 fire tower; Knox, Kane, Kinzua Railroad; wildlife ponds; rhododendron and laurel blooms; autumn foliage; winter sports, picnicking, hiking, fishing, canoeing, inner tubing, bird watching.

Location: Southern outskirts of Allegheny National Forest, western Pennsylvania.

Drive route numbers: Pennsylvania Highways 66 and 36, State Route 1015, River Road, and SR 3002/2005 (Loleta Road).

Travel season: Year-round, when free from snow.

Camping: Cook Forest State Park campground (on PA 36 north of its junction with SR 1015) has 226 family sites, with modern washhouses and a dump station. The park also has 24 rustic cabins for rent. Loleta Recreation Area along SR 3002/2005 has 38 campsites (some with electricity), water, vault toilets, and a beach bathhouse with running-water facilities.

Services: Marienville has the most complete service offering along the tour, but Brookville (16 miles south of Cook Forest on PA 36), or Ridgway (off PA 949) lie within reasonable reach.

Nearby points of interest: Clear Creek State Park and State Forest, Allegheny National Forest trails and attractions, North Country National Scenic Trail.

 The drive

This primeval forest and scenic river drive starts from the Marienville Ranger Station (just northeast of Marienville) and travels at a clip along PA 66, before slowing to a crawl upon entering the sylvan wonderland of record-sized trees. Hallmark of the Pennsylvania state park system, 6,668-acre Cook Forest, encompasses one of the largest virgin white pine and eastern hemlock

Drive 9: Cook Forest–Clarion River Tour

Circuitous tour between Marienville and the North Bank Clarion River

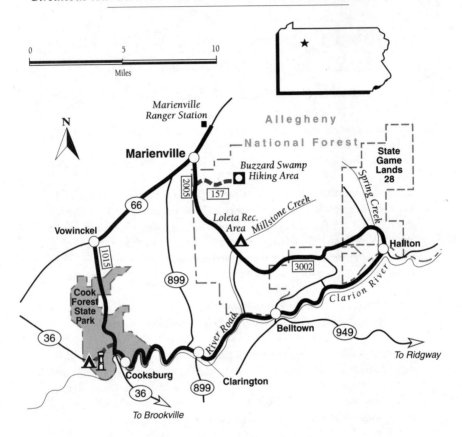

forests remaining in the eastern United States. Here, too, motorists meet up with the Clarion River, which in 1996 was designated a federal wild and scenic river.

For the next 24 miles, the Clarion River, a popular canoe water, engages travelers with twisting upstream canyon travel. Afterward, the scenic drive swings north and west, up Spring Creek and through the southern fringe of Allegheny National Forest to visit a prized wildlife area, Buzzard Swamp. Its open meadows dotted by ponds and potholes offers a striking contrast to Penn's woods and allows for fine nature study and bird and wildlife watching; bring binoculars.

Locate the **Marienville Ranger Station** west off PA 66, 1.7 miles north of Marienville. At the station, secure the brochures and maps to gain your bearings and plot your stops. As you leave, note your odometer reading and proceed south on PA 66. In Marienville, the tour's loop junction is at the

Giulfoyle Holiness Chapel, Marienville.

town common at 1.7 miles. For a counterclockwise tour, continue south on PA 66; the drive will conclude on South Forest Road.

A gateway to Allegheny National Forest, Marienville is a small forest community with a fresh-scrubbed look and basic services. It is also a station point on the **Knox, Kane, Kinzua Railroad,** which is perhaps the finest excursion train tour in the state for both length and scenery. If a rail trip figures into your plans, a 0.5-mile detour south on South Forest Road will lead to the historic train station, with a small museum devoted to railroading on the opposite side of the road.

For the drive alone, continue southwest out of town on PA 66 to enter the countryside, with its fields, woods, rural homes, and outlying businesses. Speeds range between 45 and 55 miles per hour, with traffic generally light to moderate unless a festival or the arrival of the autumn foliage swells numbers. Aspen often frame the road, with black cherry, maple, and oak growing deeper in the woods.

Where a richer forest, complete with pine and hemlock, enfolds travel, look for the **North Country National Scenic Trail** to cross PA 66. Then, at the crossroads community of Vowinckel (8.6 miles), turn left on SR 1015 (Vowinckel-Cooksburg Road), the main north-south artery through **Cook Forest State Park.** *National Geographic Traveler* has named this park one of the 50 best state parks in the United States.

Within a couple of miles, enter the park and discover the **Baker Trail**, as it crosses SR 1015 near the Browns Run bridge. This 140-mile foot trail that begins in Freeport, Pennsylvania, and travels through Cook Forest to Allegheny National Forest is actually a part of the North Country National Scenic Trail. It traverses the less-trafficked northern tier of the park for tranquil discovery.

Three tracts of virgin forest exist within the state park: Forest Cathedral, Seneca, and Swamp. The island of virgin forest east of here on the Baker Trail is the **Swamp Old Growth**.

As you continue the drive, a few private parcels still intersperse the park lands, with offerings of food, horse stables, and private camping. In the park, ample picnic areas along SR 1015 and River Road waylay visitors. Proceed south.

Up ahead, look for the Sawmill turnoff at 12.5 miles. The **Sawmill Center for the Arts** and the park's summer swimming pool are both popular attractions. At the rustic sawmill building that houses the arts center, view exhibits and demonstrations of traditional crafts such as quilting, basket weaving, wood and stone carving, or even dulcimer making. The showroom is open 10 A.M. to 5 P.M., except during the winter season. A gift shop sells the local artisan crafts. Next door, the 200-seat **Sawmill Theater** presents summertime musicals and plays.

Ancient forest, Cook Forest State Park.

By taking the dirt spur uphill from the sawmill entrance road, you will reach the park's wheelchair-accessible **Nature Trail**. This 0.25-mile paved circuit offers a first-rate window to what makes Cook Forest so special. Leisurely pass amid old-growth and second-growth trees, touring a dark eastern hemlock grove interspersed with huge beech, oak, and black cherry. Breezes whisper through the treetops, some 200 feet overhead. Amid the impressive big trees, stumps harken to bygone days. The logging officially ended in Cook Forest in 1915.

For a hike in the acclaimed **Forest Cathedral Natural Area**, a National Natural Landmark, start at the historic **Log Cabin Inn Visitor Center**. It is located near the bustling intersection of SR 1015 and Toms Run Road at 13.3 miles.

Occupying the slope above Toms Run, Forest Cathedral Natural Area boasts a piney woods that dates back to the time of William Penn, Pennsylvania's first governor. The ancient white pines and hemlocks exceed 300 years in age, 200 feet in height, and 3 to 5 feet in diameter. Along Toms Run, the birch also achieve uncommon size. Towering, straight evergreens and sky-scraping snags engage from the start.

A number of fine trails web the landmark grove allowing for round-trip, loop, or extended treks. On the **Longfellow Trail** (the gateway trail), pass the "Tree of Peace" (planted by the Mohawk Nation Council of Chiefs) and Memorial Fountain to enter the "windthrow area" of 1956. Here, a storm of cyclonic intensity leveled many of the giants within a 4-acre site. More of the neck-craning travel then follows before the trail halts at Toms Run at 1.2 miles.

South from the Log Cabin Inn Visitor Center, the drive along SR 1015 crosses over and then parallels Toms Run downstream. For a glimpse of the third virgin stand, the **Seneca Old Growth**, you may hike west on the **Hemlock Trail**, found at 13.9 miles; there is roadside parking along SR 1015 above Toms Run. If you continue 0.5 mile on the trail to where it crosses PA 36 and changes name, you can also view the legacy of the July 1976 tornado.

At 14.2 miles into the drive, meet PA 36. By detouring 0.7 mile north on PA 36, you will find the park campground and the 2.8-mile dirt **Fire Tower Loop Road**. This one-way interpretive forest drive offers exceptional woods views as it ascends to the Fire Tower parking lot. Riotous rhododendron and laurel adorn the plateau.

From the upper end of the parking lot, short, easy walks lead to two vantages. To reach them, hike uphill 80 strides to the plateau trail fork. For **Seneca Point**, hike 0.1 mile to the right to reach the fractured natural sandstone outcrop and a vegetation-framed view of the Clarion River. For the 70-foot-high **Cook Forest Fire Tower**, hike left 0.1 mile; the tower extends an overlook of the Clarion River and Toms Run, with Allegheny National Forest beyond. As the stairs spiral skyward, piece together the 360-degree view; heed the posted ten-person limit.

Upon returning to your vehicle, follow the descending Fire Tower Road through rhododendron-splashed hardwood forest to deep woods of hemlock, marked by impressively big trees. Deer offer a chance encounter. Locate a quiet picnic area prior to returning to PA 36 and proceeding south.

Without either the Fire Tower Loop Road tour or a campground visit, the primary drive immediately turns south on PA 36 at 14.2 miles. A quick left follows—near the park office and just prior to crossing the Clarion River bridge, turn left on narrow River Road to enter Cooksburg—compact, touristy, and hectic. Here, River Road is also labeled SR 2002. Throughout the next 24 miles, River Road will show frequent changes in road name and number, just keep toward the Clarion River.

The **Clarion River** drains a 1,200-square-mile basin and hosts river trips between 4 and 40 miles in length. Under usual conditions, the Clarion is ideal for family canoe or tubing adventures. In summer, the river is a veritable freeway of rented canoes. Stocked with trout and supporting smallmouth bass, the water also attracts its share of anglers. An October tour on either the Clarion River or its companion drive has the gilded endorsement of changing leaves.

Flat sandstones erupt from the riverbed and scatter its shores, while tannic acids give the clear water the appearance of ice tea. Native Americans referred to the Clarion River as "Tobecco," which means "dark brown water." Such derogatory names as Stump Creek or Mud River were applied to this waterway during the logging era, which brought with it heavy erosion. Finally, in 1817, surveyors who had remarked on the clarion-like sound of the lower river bestowed the present name.

River Road offers pleasant 25-mile-per-hour travel as it hugs the bending Clarion course. From the guardrail, a 10- to 15-foot bank initially drops away to the river. Picnic areas and a series of single roadside tables that overlook the river, turnouts aplenty, and historic overnight cabins contribute to the Cook Forest corridor. Hardwoods and hemlocks provide shade.

The river beckons visitors down to its shore to hopscotch over the rocks, cool their ankles, or watch the canoeists float by. A kingfisher may skim the water, while mergansers glide to the sidelines. When fall water levels reach uncommon lows, the canoes—normally the epitome of tranquility—bring comedy to the river. Then, scraping aluminum, high-centered crafts, and frustrated oarsmen become commonplace. But throughout the mischief, the placid Clarion with its rocky funnels and wavy reflections engages.

Sharing the roadway are the private shuttle services, with canoes stacked high on flatbeds and vans bursting with eager river-runners. A canoe launch

Canoeing on the Wild and Scenic Clarion River.

is located at 17.9 miles. Twisting River Road effectively presents the beauty of both river and forest. In late June and early July, rhododendrons color the road slope and spill to shore. Several big-diameter trees rise above the river.

At 19.4 miles, depart Cook Forest State Park and pass the Clarion River Lodge, which sits back in a side canyon. A few private cabins now blend into the deep woods; respect private property and the posted "no parking" areas. Gravel bar beaches still line stretches of shore. Outside the park, the river drive loses its congestion for more relaxed touring.

In 3 miles, look for River Road to climb to a stop sign. Here, bear right on what is signed "Greenwood Road" to cross the Maple Creek bridge. Soon after, reach a stop sign for PA 899. Stay on River Road/PA 899 South to continue upstream travel along the Clarion River. A fuller woods isolates shore.

The scenic drive then keeps to the north shore, with a left turn to enter Clarington where PA 899 crosses over the river. In the town of Clarington, follow the signs for Belltown Road; a right at the stop, followed by a quick left continues the river journey.

At 24.7 miles, cross-river views present Clear Creek State Park, with its campground, yurts, and cabins that overlook the Clarion River. Hemlock, ash, gum, beech, birch, wild grape, and rhododendron contribute to the roadway's forest. In another 3 miles, cross Millstone Creek and turn right at the T-junction for Belltown, which has a canoe rental and general store. Again, remain on the north shore, bypassing the bridge to PA 949 at 30 miles.

The tour continues to engage with natural merit, although private residences dot the way. Where river views are denied, the forest corridor picks up any slack. Often big boulders contribute to the river's character and shape deeper pools for fish. Within state forest lands, find more turnouts. Follow River Road all the way to Hallton (38 miles). There, cross the steel one-lane bridge over Spring Creek, drive past the state game lands **Hallton Canoe Launch**, and make a left turn at the stop sign onto paved SR 3002.

The tour now rolls and curves up and away from the Clarion River. Mixed-age forest clads the slope, while Spring Creek threads below on the left. In 1.5 miles, stay on SR 3002 as it crosses Spring Creek bridge. State Game Lands 28 often borders the tour, and a wide, vegetated shoulder opens up travel.

Atop the plateau, pastures, open and cultivated fields, and the occasional bank barn vary viewing. Keep to SR 3002, turning right for Loleta at the T-junction at 41.1 miles. Before long, you are in Allegheny National Forest, with its red-and-gold color palette in the fall. A few conifer plantations and aspen vary the tapestry as SR 3002 descends to road-straddling **Loleta Recreation Area** (48 miles).

This recreation site offers trout fishing on the East Branch Millstone Creek, with swimming at a dam-broadened part of the waterway. A 3-mile trail explores the enfolding woods. On this spot stood the logging boomtown, Loleta (1889–1913). At its crest, the town boasted 600 residents, a sawmill, shingle mill, broom handle factory, and regular rail service, but it sawed its way into extinction. Today's swimming area reclaims the old millpond.

SR 3002/2005 then winds north away from the recreation site and through tiny present-day Loleta. Next up, reach dirt Forest Road 157 at 52.3 miles, which heads right for **Buzzard Swamp Wildlife Viewing and Hiking Area**; look for the National Forest Service and Pennsylvania Game Commission sign at the turn.

Buzzard Swamp has 10 miles of interlocking trail that double as cross-country ski paths, and it lies on the Atlantic flyway, attracting migratory birds. The 15 manmade ponds and numerous potholes provide superb wildlife habitat. In spring, spy as many as 20 to 25 waterfowl species. Other times, turkey, osprey, and bald eagle number among the winged sightings. Look for snapping turtle and beaver near ponds, browsing deer or rabbit in the meadow, and the neighborhood predators: coyote and bear, as they slip into the shadows. Warm-water fish species provide angler sport.

Closed roads, re-seeded tracks, and foot trails explore the gentle, mostly open terrain. Hikers should carry a map (available at Marienville Ranger Station) and watch for the labeled field junctions. The off-limits 40-acre propagation area supplies the necessary wildlife cover and nesting habitat to keep this land vital and thriving with discovery. The site's 1.6-mile silver-diamond-marked **Songbird Sojourn Interpretive Trail** concentrates travel within an attractive hardwood grove.

Passing up the swamp detour, return to Marienville via SR 2005/South Forest Road at 53.7 miles.

10

Elk Country Scenic Drive
From Weedville to Emporium

General description: This 45.6-mile drive along a lightly traveled highway and backroads hugs the Bennett Branch Sinnemahoning Creek and twists its way through the prime elk habitat of Elk and Cameron counties. Here, Pennsylvania's lone elk herd ranges free and undisturbed—one of only two herds found east of the Mississippi River.

Special attractions: Bennett Branch Sinnemahoning Creek; a designated elk viewing site; Pine Tree Natural Area; overlooks; autumn foliage; hiking, fishing, relaxing.

Location: North-central Pennsylvania.

Drive route numbers: Pennsylvania Highways 555 and 120, Hicks Run and East Hicks roads, Township Road 310, State Route 3001.

Travel season: Spring through fall; PA 555 year-round.

Camping: Hicks Run Camping Area (on West Hicks Road at its junction with Hicks Run Road) offers a dozen primitive camping sites; an Elk State Forest camping permit is required and bring drinking water.

Services: Basic visitor services are available at both ends of the tour: Weedville and Emporium.

Nearby points of interest: Straub Brewery tours (Saint Marys), Bucktail State Park Natural Area Scenic Drive, Sizerville and Parker Dam state parks, the 19-mile Elk Trail.

 The drive

This off-the-beaten-track forest meander ventures into the heart of the open range for Pennsylvania's free-roaming but protected elk herd, which now numbers some 300 strong. The elk travel within a 227-square-mile area, with the four corners roughly prescribed by Weedville, Driftwood, Emporium, and Saint Marys. Out of Benezette is a designated elk viewing site that helps your chances for spying elk. Early morning and evening hours and the September to October rut and mating season bring out the elk in number. Come with binoculars or spotting scopes.

Between the upper Hicks Run drainage and Emporium, much of the tour follows unsigned roads. For that reason, it is a good idea to pick up an *Elk State Forest Public Use Map* beforehand or try to obtain one from Hicks

Drive 10: Elk Country Scenic Drive
From Weedville to Emporium

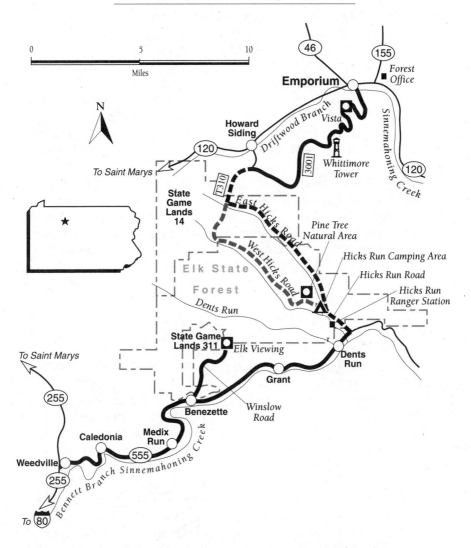

Run Ranger Station en route. A Pennsylvania atlas is likewise helpful when a junction poses doubt. But the quiet travel and chance for elk sightings or other wildlife encounters make the added effort worthwhile.

When elk are sighted, be sure to select a safe location to pull over and watch them. Respect private lands and driveways, and grant the elk a safe viewing distance. Remember that feeding the elk is a violation of Pennsylvania law.

From PA 255 in Weedville (16 miles north of Interstate 80 at Exit 17), go east on PA 555 to follow the Bennett Branch Sinnemahoning Creek downstream. A beautiful, steep wooded canyon houses the tour; the enfolding ridges carry the even-height signature of the Allegheny Plateau. Past town, find only a few scattered residences. Occasionally, you will win a glimpse of the Bennett Branch or of a lily-covered side pool. A few gravel turnouts allow for stopping.

In autumn, the maple, oak, gum, sumac, and sassafras introduce bursts of amber, yellow, gold, orange, and red. Stay PA 555 through the villages of Caledonia and Medix Run. By afternoon, vultures ride the thermals over the ridges. At 9.4 miles, arrive at Benezette. After crossing the Trout Run bridge, turn left, go one block, and turn right on paved Winslow Road; Benezette Hotel is at the corner.

Winslow Road twists through the tiny town to ascend the forested flank of Winslow Hill to the elk-viewing site. Pass Christmas-tree farms and private and state forest lands. Again, autumn treats eyes to a pleasing mesh of color. A large sign for the Rocky Mountain Elk Foundation tallies the funds raised for habitat improvement and confirms you are indeed in elk country. Atop a grassy knoll on the right, you may spy the private, 60-foot Winslow Fire Tower—no trespassing. The final 0.8 mile to the viewing site is on dirt road; avoid turns.

On the left at 13 miles, a sign "**Elk Viewing Area, Dents Run**" marks the State Game Lands 311 overlook and its parking area. As chemical toilets are the lone amenity, be sure to bring water, food, chairs, blankets, a shade source, and reading material to stage your watch in comfort. A low rock wall edges the shadeless vantage.

The view encompasses the rolling terrain of the Dents Run watershed, a mosaic of open fields, conifer stands, an abandoned apple orchard, and hardwood slopes. Enjoy a clear 180-degree field of view, panning down and across the countryside. The uncertainty of seeing elk makes a sighting all the more exciting and meaningful. A few regulars will attest to this.

While bull elks can weigh up to 1,000 pounds and females, 500 pounds, the animals will appear quite small in the distance, so keep your binoculars handy. A light-colored rump patch distinguishes the elk from the area's white-tailed deer. The elk seen today are Rocky Mountain elk, originating from the herd introduced to Pennsylvania soils in 1913. Pennsylvania's native eastern elk were eliminated by settlement and hunting, with the last elk dropped by gunshot near Ridgway in 1867.

From this Winslow Hill vantage, cows and calves are most often spied, with the bachelor groups tending to hang around the Saint Marys area. In fall, bugling may provide a clue to a bull's whereabouts or arrival. Impressive antler racks regally arc back from the heads of mature bulls. In the clash of battle, the locking and knocking of racks echoes from below.

When ready to surrender your watch, backtrack to Benezette (16.6 miles), and resume east on PA 555, which is still a quiet 45-mile-per-hour highway, with a few pullouts along the way. Mixed woods cloak both sides of the road. In places the canyon walls grow pinched. Even from a moving vehicle, small wonders of nature can be spied, such as an upside-down nuthatch on a roadside tree. By 18.5 miles, the roadway is paired with leaf-filtered looks of the Bennett Branch Sinnemahoning Creek—a classic, broad, smooth waterway framed by overhanging trees.

Where PA 555 enters the village of Grant (20.5 miles), a sign indicates "Elk crossing next 115 miles." Do not shrug off the caution. Elk sightings are common along this stretch of creek, so adjust your driving and keep an eye out.

At the village of Dents Run (don't blink), you will find back-to-back bridge crossings: first Dents Run and then Hicks Run. Upon crossing the latter, turn left (north) on gravel Hicks Run Road (25 miles); it is signed for Hicks Run Ranger Station.

Travel is now up the side canyon of Hicks Run. The managed state forest and state game lands along this run provide year-round habitat for elk, and benefit bear and deer as well. A special fish habitat/stream improvement project has enhanced the fishery along a 4-mile stretch of Hicks Run; in 0.5 mile pass the **Dents Run Game Feeding/Hicks Run Hatchery**. While not much to see from the road, the rangers explain that the hatchery is extremely successful and grows lots of fish.

Enter Elk State Forest at 25.7 miles to find the historic site of a Civilian Conservation Corps camp and **Hicks Run Ranger Station**. Stop at the station to pick up an Elk State Forest map, or to fill out the paperwork for a free overnight permit if you plan to camp at Hicks Run Camping Area farther up canyon. The station also has interpretive brochures for the Pine Tree Trail—a surefire attraction if you are going to camp or have time on your hands.

Resume the drive upstream on Hicks Run Road, a narrow, primary forest road. Besides the gravel road surface, the unexpected crossing of a flock of wild turkeys may dictate a slow speed. A hemlock-hardwood forest encloses the avenue.

At 27.2 miles, you will come to a fork. To the left on West Hicks Road is **Hicks Run Camping Area**, reached immediately upon crossing Hicks Run. Opposite camp is one of three trailheads for the **Pine Tree Trail**, which accesses the 276-acre **Pine Tree Natural Area**. To the right is East Hicks Road, the better quality of the two forest roads, and the choice for continuing the tour.

The camping area has a few tables and vault toilets and occupies the hemlock-shaded floodplain of Hicks Run. Pine, beech, and tulip poplar are

Pine Tree Trail, Elk State Forest.

the other trees of measure. A repeated hooty-hoot may betray an owl, roosting high in the treetops.

The orange-blazed, 2-mile Pine Tree Trail ascends the flank of Hicks Run Divide to explore the plateau of the natural area, which was set aside for its old field growth of white pine. The trail's interpretive features primarily sort out the many varieties of trees and explain their uses and significance. Where the tour points out a Juneberry, be sure to study the trunk for the claw marks and depressions left by a zealous berry-seeking bear; the imprints are some of the best you will find anywhere.

By instead keeping to East Hicks Road at the 27.2-mile fork, you will have two more chances to visit the natural area. East Branch Hicks Run is the new upstream guide. Hemlocks cling to the watercourse, while hardwoods mount the east canyon wall. Floodplain flats of fern, hornbeam, and other moisture-seeking species vary viewing.

Cross the East Branch at 28.4 miles to find roadside turnouts and the next marked trailhead for the Pine Tree Trail; it is on the left just as the road curves away. The bridge affords a pleasant overlook of the run. In autumn, leaves collect in side pools and catch on the rocks of the stream. Where the road crosses back over the East Branch at 29.1 miles, orange blazes near the south end of the bridge signal the final Pine Tree Trail access.

Cross into Cameron County in another 0.5 mile. The road offers a gently bending, 25-mile-per-hour ascent. Here, areas of low shrubs vary the cover of the slope. Later, lichen-and-moss-coated rock slabs punctuate the woods to the right. The road often enjoys a beautiful arbor effect, and the East Branch is never far from sight.

Open-field slopes (likely reclaimed strip mines), cattail marshes, and beaver dams complete the tour image. Across the floodplain, glimpse the divide. **State Game Lands (SGL) 14** now abuts the tour; its closed roads welcome exploration. Deer hunters need to be extra cautious, given that elk roam the area and are protected. At 33.9 miles, West Hicks Road converges on the left. As you bear right up yet another side canyon, the road becomes T-310 (a jurisdiction and map distinction only).

A wasp nest dangling from an overhead branch, grouse, and deer may number among the wildlife sightings. Atop the ridge, leave behind SGL 14 to find private lands. View Christmas tree farms, grassy slopes, and perhaps the tilled furrows of a prepared field, with a distant ridge disappearing in the blue haze. Elk, unaware of land ownership, still may be spied.

At 35.9 miles, come to a stop sign at a paved road (SR 3001, although no signs). To the left leads to PA 120 at Howard Siding; go right to continue the tour. Drive past a state game lands access, rolling pastures, and fields of hay and corn, with forest stretching beyond. The mosaic is rich in texture.

Whittimore Fire Tower, Elk State Forest.

Emporium, Pennsylvania.

In 5 miles, where the paved road curves left for the continuation of the tour, locate a gated, dirt state forest road angling uphill on the right (not to be mistaken with the drivable dirt road that heads hard right forming a T-junction at the curve). The closed road provides a hiker access to the 1921-built **Whittimore Fire Tower**, which rises 47 feet skyward. Although the structure is closed to the public, the grassy tower knoll affords a lofty vantage. A small parking turnout is by the gate, but check the ground first to avoid getting stuck.

For the hike to the tower, walk around the gate and follow the closed road for 0.9-mile, zigzagging uphill. Clover now colors the road's shoulder and center; showings of laurel add to June walks. White-tailed deer or acorn-bombing squirrels may be seen, as well as clues to bears; an electrified fence keeps browsing deer out of a revegetated area. The tower, still staffed during dry seasons, ascends seven stories and complements the view or suggests a picture. Views span west and south.

For the drive alone, remain on the paved road (SR 3001) as it curves left, wrapping around and down the forested hillside, working its way toward Emporium. Back-to-back curves slow travel. At 42 miles, come to a paved T-junction and turn left to remain on SR 3001, still twisting downhill; again, there are no signs. Aspen, gum, oak, sugar maple, and red maple contribute to the collage of leaves. On the left at 43.3 miles is a **vista turn-out** at the nose of a ridge.

From this vantage, overlook the Driftwood Branch Sinnemahoning Creek Canyon; its folded, serial ridges; and tidy Emporium (founded in 1853) nestled in the valley. White-painted houses, sugar-maple–lined streets, and church towers contribute to its wholesome image. Like dark specters, vultures and ravens soar through the view.

The town's peaceful demeanor seems to contradict that Emporium was once known for its manufacture of explosive powders and dubbed the "Powder City." The town was a primary supplier of blasting material for construction of the Panama Canal. Ruins of the old magazines, where powder and dynamite were once safely housed, still riddle the forested hills about Emporium.

From the viewpoint, complete the downhill journey, keeping right where the labeled side streets branch left. Cross over the Driftwood Branch Sinnemahoning Creek and a railroad track to meet PA 120 in downtown Emporium, ending the drive at 45.6 miles.

If your departure takes you west on PA 120 as far as Saint Marys, you may want to add a visit to the airport, where oddly enough the elk make regular appearances. Once in town, follow the signs to the airport.

11

Bucktail State Park
Natural Area Scenic Drive
From Lock Haven to Emporium

General description: This drive follows Bucktail Trail Highway for 73.5 miles, closely paralleling the West Branch Susquehanna River and its headwaters through an impressive, mostly forested canyon, designated a state natural area. From Lock Haven, the journey is upstream; side canyons extend the discovery with forest, reservoir, and vista attractions.

Special attractions: Bucktail, Sinnemahoning, Kettle Creek, Hyner Run, and Hyner View state parks; spectacular river and canyon views; hang gliders and bald eagles; small museums; fall foliage; contenders for the "Great Pumpkin"; hiking, fishing, picnicking, canoeing.

Location: North-central Pennsylvania.

Drive route numbers: Pennsylvania Highway 120, known as the Bucktail Trail Highway.

Travel season: Year-round.

Camping: Three state parks offer public camping within easy access of the tour: Hyner Run (2 miles north of PA 120 on State Route 1014) has 30 rustic sites; Kettle Creek (7 miles north of PA 120 on SR 4001/Kettle Creek Road) has 71 rustic sites (some electric); and Sinnemahoning (8 miles north of PA 120 on PA 872) has 35 modern sites (some electric) and offers showers.

Services: The tour's full-service communities are Lock Haven, Renovo, and Emporium.

Nearby points of interest: 32-mile Bucktail Path and 52-mile Donut Hole Trail, Bald Eagle and Sizerville state parks, Woolrich Outlet (village of Woolrich), William T. Piper Aviation Museum (Lock Haven), Tom Mix Museum (Mix Run), Elk Country Scenic Drive, Straub Brewery Tour (Saint Marys).

 ## The drive

This picturesque, nearly 75-mile-long canyon route has long been dubbed the "Bucktail Trail," in honor of the region's woodsmen who volunteered and valiantly fought during the Civil War. The local men, expert with rifles, gathered in Driftwood, where they boarded homemade rafts and floated

Drive 11: Bucktail State Park
Natural Area Scenic Drive
From Lock Haven to Emporium

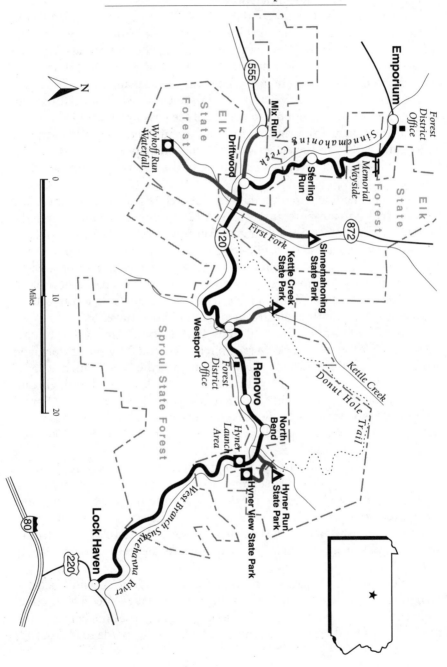

downstream to Lock Haven to travel by train to Harrisburg. There, they were mustered into the Union service, the bucktail their adopted insignia. Assigned to the Army of the Potomac, the "Bucktails" fought in such key battles as Gettysburg and Antietam.

But even before the days of the white settler, this river corridor served Native Americans. For them, what was known as the "Sinnemahoning Trail" led to the crossing of the eastern Continental Divide and passage between the Allegheny and Susquehanna river valleys. In the seventeenth century, the Senecas used this path to war against the Susquehannas.

For contemporary travelers, the tour is not so much about getting from one point to another as simply to marvel in the passing. Bucktail State Park Natural Area spans from rim top to rim top, enfolding the valley between Emporium and Lock Haven. Private holdings intersperse the public lands of Elk and Sproul state forests. Each twist of the waterway brings new discovery.

To start the tour, from the junction of U.S. Highway 220 and PA 120 southwest of Williamsport, go west on PA 120 to enter and pass through the charming West Branch Susquehanna River town of Lock Haven. Attractive tree-lined streets and a 2.25-mile-long river levee topped by a paved and lighted walkway help shape first impressions. A metered parking area on the right at 1.8 miles provides access to the levee exercise path. Views span river and canyon ridge. You will later drive past Hanna Park, a comfortable city park, as you continue upstream and out of Lock Haven.

At 4.8 miles, reach **Bucktail State Park Natural Area**; a turnout accesses the information kiosk. Maple, birch, oak, elm, Virginia creeper, and wild grape dress the roadside; below PA 120 flows the West Branch. Rhododendron may announce itself with profusion, as the 1,000-foot-high canyon walls cause heads to tilt. By 8.7 miles, you will have entered Sproul State Forest. A few private businesses still dot the corridor. The woods dominate, with the river's glimmer beyond the leafy mesh. Quiet PA 120 is conducive to leisurely travel.

The West Branch and all its feeding waters have a similar profile, flowing broad, clear, and shallow over muddy rock. At the rest area at 18.3 miles, a wide path descends from the picnic-area lawn to the West Branch shore for a closer look at the bending waterway and steep canyon wall. Here, beautiful, tall ash, maple, and locust grow toward the river, their trunks wrapped by skyward-inching Virginia creeper. As the rest area is dry, plan to bring drinking water.

North off PA 120 prior to the West Branch bridge at 21.5 miles sits the **Hyner Access Hand Launch Area**. At the turn, you may notice a hang glider club; cast your eyes skyward on the chance you might see the colorful aerialists as they soar the narrow overhead cathedral. A steep side road descends

Pennsylvania Highway 120, Bucktail State Park.

to the primitive river put-in; parking is limited to a few clearings amid the viburnum. Monarch butterflies often light on the muddy shore; insect chirrs blend with the river's whisper. As you admire the rolling upstream canyon, you may detect the skyline break of Hyner View (the hang glider launch) atop the north rim.

Another mile west in Hyner (where canoe rentals are available), turn north off PA 120 onto SR 1014/Hyner Run Road for both **Hyner Run and Hyner View state parks.** At the road split in 1.7 miles, straight leads to Hyner Run State Park; right, to Hyner View.

Hyner Run State Park, 0.3 mile ahead, entices with its large picnic area and campground wrapped in the deep shade of planted red and white pines (a Civilian Conservation Corps project). In the summertime, the park raises its bid with the cool refreshment of a swimming pool. It also has a trailhead for the popular **Donut Hole Trail.**

Hyner View (open 8 A.M. to sunset) is reached by a narrow, snaking 4.3-mile road that is not maintained in winter. This cherished park occupies the rim plateau (elevation 1,940 feet) and delivers a vulture's eye view of the canyon. It, too, has a picnic area, although much smaller.

Originally, Hyner View was the site for the region's Flaming Foliage Festival, but with its growth in popularity, the October festival has since been moved to the town of Renovo, which can be seen below and to the west. Thermals that roll up the mountain flank carry hang glider and vulture aloft. Hang gliders launch from wooden platforms just below the vantage.

The graceful flight of man or bird adds to an already exciting view of the meandering West Branch Susquehanna River some 1,300 feet below, with its rural valley floor, forested canyon, and fingery side canyons. The yellow-red kaleidoscope of fall further enchants. Strong winds keep the summit flags flapping.

Forgoing the state park detours, continue west on the Bucktail Trail Highway. You will round the cliff of the road cut and cross Young Womans Creek to enter the village of North Bend with its complement of services. A left in town at 26 miles leads to the tiny **North Bend Fishing and Boating Access** (no visitor facility and for all practical purposes, no parking).

Next up is the working-class community of Renovo, a weary, depressed-looking historic brick town nestled in this fairy tale–pretty river canyon. While American flags still don the posts of downtown, the town generally only perks up at festival time, the second full weekend in October. Then the flame-colored trees of the cupping canyon infuse Renovo with renewed life. You will find a full range of visitor services, as well as canoe rentals and a canoe launch in town.

From Renovo, travel an open valley floor, keeping to PA 120. A trio of transportation routes thread the canyon: river, rail, and road. Canyon views come nonstop. On the left at 32.3 miles is the **Sproul State Forest District Office**, where brochures and information are available. At Westport (38.5 miles), reach the turnoff for **Kettle Creek State Park**, which lies 7 miles north.

Kettle Creek State Park occupies a narrow, forested side canyon, with a network of trails traversing the hillsides and with a 160-acre lake impoundment, part of the area flood-control system. Trout and bass fishing are popular pastimes. The wildness of the canyon is sometimes dramatized by the sighting of a black bear. Near the park office, a modest but alarming sign indicates the height of the water during tropical storm Agnes. The remoteness of the picnic and camping area appeal to guests.

But for PA 120 travel alone, maintain your tunnel vision. West of the Kettle Creek turnoff, the wooded floodplain often isolates river and road, while wild turkey may surprise. At 38.6 miles, teaser signs announce **Waltz's Farm Market**, growers of the giant pumpkins.

In autumn, you may be dazzled by the road-shoulder array of bright orange, backbreaking pumpkins. In 1997, the Waltz family brought in 12.5 tons of these Halloween pleasers, with the largest weighing more than 200 pounds. The rarity of the big pumpkins brings buyers from as far as New Jersey. Gourds, apples, cabbage, and Indian corn are other offerings of fall.

Farm market pumpkins along Pennsylvania Highway 120.

Near Keating, PA 120 skirts the base of Little Roundtop and bids farewell to the railroad alongside and hello to the upstream waters of Sinnemahoning Creek. Road-cut cliffs, steep forest flanks, and squeezed side canyons vary views. Woodpecker and squirrel may be spied from the moving vehicle. Enjoy stretches of gentle bends and open straightaways along the creek, but the straighter pairings of creek and road typically lack turnouts.

The drive passes from Sproul to Elk State Forest. The woods mix varies from creek shore to canyon slope; ash, sycamore, hornbeam, dogwood, and birch prefer the riverbank. Near the 50-mile point, PA 120 pinches closer to shore and a broad shoulder allows for stops to view Sinnemahoning Creek. At 52.7 miles, reach PA 872 North, which heads upstream along the First Fork to **Sinnemahoning State Park** in 7.2 miles.

At the south end of this linear state park, the **George B. Stevenson Dam** captures the water of First Fork Sinnemahoning Creek for flood control and creates a feeding ground for the bald eagle. At the dam site, a special viewing area has been set aside for eagle watchers; the spring return of the national bird is cause to celebrate. Watch the skies for the bald eagle's majestic flight or scan the treetops for where it roosts. The fishery of Sinnemahoning Creek not only attracts eagles, but anglers, too.

Sinnemahoning Creek drainage, Bucktail Natural Area.

From the lake-access area 1 mile north of the dam, the 5.5-mile one-way drive north along shore to **40 Maples Picnic Area** is a fine mini tour in itself. This park road journeys at the belly of the side canyon along the First Fork impoundment and free-flowing stream, traveling sycamore-meadow floodplain and woods. Twitching ears of insect-pestered deer often pierce the tall milkweed. Merganser, duck, and kingfisher are co-travelers. The picnic area's prominent row of shade maples provide an engaging reason to stop. Ahead lie more floodplain discoveries as this mini drive skirts the park campground and a few abandoned apple trees to return to PA 872.

Another popular Sinnemahoning State Park draw is the **pontoon boat ride** that introduces the 142-acre lake impoundment, the surrounding habitat, lake ecology, and wildlife. The pontoon also offers an alternative means for seeing the area's bald eagles. Preregister at the park office for a free trip. Pontoons run on alternate Sundays, Memorial Day to Labor Day, with tours at noon, 1:30 P.M., and 3 P.M.

By opting to stay on the Bucktail Trail Highway at 52.7 miles, the tour continues upstream, with Sinnemahoning Creek now reduced in size. In 0.1 mile, look for Wykoff Run Road, which heads south across the creek to a small community park. By staying on this side road and following Wykoff Run upstream some 10 miles, you will locate **Wykoff Run Waterfall**, the most photographed falls in Cameron County.

Without the Wykoff Run deviation from the PA 120 tour, you will pass through the villages of Sinnemahoning (53.4 miles) and Driftwood (56.4 miles). At Driftwood, a detour west on PA 555 leads to the **Bucktail Monument** in 0.1 mile. This statue of a frontier soldier looks out over the bank of the Driftwood Branch Sinnemahoning Creek. Plaques commemorate the event of the Bucktails' enlistment and the battles fought.

Fans of Western films may wish to continue on this PA 555 detour for 4.5 miles to the tiny village of Mix Run, the birthplace of the "king of the cowboys"—Tom Mix. **Tom Mix Birthplace** is a Pennsylvania Historical and Museum Commission fee site, open daily April through September. A small museum holds Mix family artifacts.

PA 555 then continues west to Benezette and Pennsylvania's elk country. Driftwood roughly marks the southeasternmost corner of the open range for the state's lone elk herd.

For the Bucktail Trail alone, remain on PA 120 through Driftwood, now following the Driftwood Branch of Sinnemahoning Creek upstream. Sycamores dominate the creek flat. The canyon walls retain their even-height and imposing presence, while cultivated fields sometimes claim the rich valley bottom.

Just inland from the Driftwood Branch, **The Little Museum at Sterling Run** (64.7 miles) occupies a former country schoolhouse and has exhibits on Cameron County history. Several exhibits are devoted to area

Little Museum exhibits, Sterling Run.

noteworthies: a four-star general, cowboy legend Tom Mix, and a prize fighter. Outdoor displays include a rebuilt coke oven and ore car. Coke, a residue from coal, provided a high-efficiency fuel for area iron furnaces. The museum is open in summer on Wednesday and Sunday afternoons (a token admission is charged). You can view outdoor exhibits anytime.

Farther west on PA 120, rugged footpaths descend from the turnouts to shore. The **Memorial Wayside** at 71.1 miles invites the weary aside with a refreshing sip from its freshwater spring and the cool shade of its trees. This peaceful roadside memorial honors eight Civilian Conservation Corps members who died while fighting the Lick Island Forest Fire of 1938. A springtime shower of rhododendrons decorates the site.

At 72.6 miles, leave Bucktail State Park Natural Area, and at 73.5 miles, enter the east gate of Emporium.

12

Pennsylvania 144 Scenic Drive
From Snow Shoe to Ole Bull State Park

General description: This 62.5-mile serpentine drive serves up a superb moving nature show, as it twists its way north through Sproul and Susquehannock state forests. Autumn's wand of color particularly recommends a tour. Midway along the route lies Renovo, host of the Flaming Foliage Festival.

Special attractions: Kettle Creek and Ole Bull state parks; vistas; a fire tower; mountain laurel and rhododendron blooms; fall foliage; hiking, fishing, boating, canoeing, swimming, picnicking, relaxing, winter sports.

Location: North-central Pennsylvania.

Drive route numbers: Pennsylvania Highway 144.

Travel season: Year-round.

Camping: Kettle Creek State Park (6 miles south off PA 144 on State Route 4001) has 71 rustic sites (some electric). Ole Bull State Park (the tour's northern terminus) has 81 rustic sites (some electric). The park's Ole Bull Lodge is also rented out.

Services: Along this remote Pennsylvania travel corridor, Renovo is the lone full-service community, although basic services are available at Snow Shoe, Tamarack, and Cross Fork.

Nearby points of interest: Bucktail Trail Highway; Bucktail, Black Moshannon, Bald Eagle, Hyner Run, Hyner View, and Cherry Springs state parks; Denton Hill Ski Area; Pennsylvania Lumber Museum; Chuck Keiper, Susquehannock, and Donut Hole trails.

 The drive

While many of the scenic drives in this book are propelled by the destinations along the way, the merit of this drive lies in the quiet beauty of the route itself. Although travelers will still find ample opportunity to pull over, stretch their legs, and catch a falling leaf, the view from the bucket seat is topnotch. The slow, wiggling, lightly developed passage of PA 144 discourages most through-traffic, leaving the roadway to sightseers. Enjoy rolling forest travel atop plateau and along creek canyon, with infrequent but prized panoramic views. Mountain laurel splashes spring-summer color to the plateau; rhododendron colors the drainages.

Drive 12: Pennsylvania 144 Scenic Drive

From Snow Shoe to Ole Bull State Park

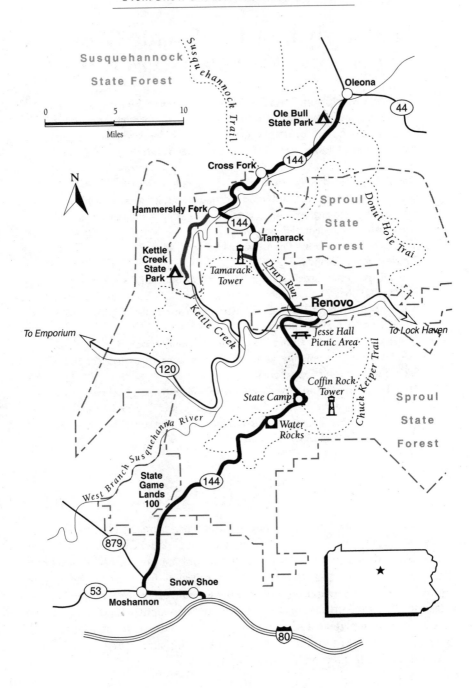

Start this drive at Interstate 80, Exit 22, and travel north on PA 144 to enter the tiny borough of Snow Shoe in about a mile. The 45-mile-per-hour narrow road then travels an aisle of hardwoods and pine, parading shades of red, yellow, and orange in fall. Where the road rolls to the tops of hills, you will gain ridge panoramas. Outlying businesses, homes, wooded plots, fields, and milling dairy cows complete the canvas. Small signs bid you aside with brown eggs and the like.

At the junction with PA 53 in Moshannon (4 miles), turn right to remain on PA 144 North and then continue past PA 879 to enter unbroken forest. Maple, oak, sassafras, gum, tulip, and aspen create an attractive arbor of mix-shaped leaves. As the chlorophyll declines and the leaves explore a new spectrum of color, ready yourself for stunning travel. The evergreen attire of young spruce lends a striking contrast to the autumn blaze, as does the black ribbon of the road.

By 7.9 miles, **State Game Lands 100** borders PA 144, with its abandoned woods roads to walk. Insects and tree frogs may enliven the canopy. Deer may bound across the road, appearing and disappearing as if by sleight of hand. In June, discover bountiful blooms of mountain laurel. A few meadow openings, thick with goldenrod and milkweed, vary the flashing images. At 9.5 miles, enter **Sproul State Forest**.

A few larger oaks now rise amid the dizzying array of dark, thin-trunked hardwoods. A beautiful cathedral graces the route. Look for bracken and hay-scented fern, as well as the mountain laurel in the understory. During bow-and-arrow season, which coincides with the arrival of fall colors, hear turkey calls both genuine and mock. In places, the open pattern of trees allows for deep woods views; the forest mix and arrangement can conjure up different moods.

At 15.6 miles, the replanted meadows that border the tour temporarily open up viewing before the woods again swallow the road. At 18.1 miles, encounter the southern extent of the orange-blazed **Chuck Keiper Trail (CKT)**, a 50-mile, dual-loop trail system through forest and wild areas. Laurel-deciduous woods dominate the terrain. Grouse may be spied roadside.

Where the route passes through a recovering fire zone, look for a turnout and kiosk on the left at 20.6 miles. From here, you may overlook the far-flung legacy of the **Two Rock Run Fire**. Careless burning on private land started this fire in 1990, and it swept an area measuring 9,656 acres. The hot flames licked across 10 miles in 10 hours, making it the largest wildfire in Pennsylvania in the past 50 years.

The fire zone creates its own mosaic of beauty with jagged white snags; vast sweeps of huckleberry, bramble, dogwood, sassafras, and young maple; and a multicolor wildflower array. Young pines hold the promise for the future. Western views stretch across Burns Run Wild Area, while the views

Drury Run, Sproul State Forest.

to the east and southeast overlook the drainages of Beech and Bald Eagle creeks, with Bald Eagle Mountain barely visible in the haze.

At the northern outskirts of the fire zone, look for large rock slabs to punctuate the young woods. This area is called **Water Rocks**. The huge slabs are picturesque despite some having been vandalized by spray-paint graffiti. Ahead, you will still travel the mildly rolling plateau. Exclusive areas of pine occasionally displace the hardwoods.

At 25 miles, again encounter the CKT, with road-shoulder parking near a small monument commemorating the first State Game Refuge (1905–1946). The hiking trail briefly follows the skyward twisting road as it delivers views west. In 0.3 mile, a turnout extends an open view northwest spanning Fish Dam Wild Area and Fish Dam Run to Bucktail State Park Natural Area.

At 25.7 miles, where the double-looped CKT splits, drivers may want to follow the orange blazes of the west trail segment left 100 yards to another vista turnout. It delivers a new perspective on Fish Dam Wild Area, broadening the look at the upper drainage. Afterward PA 144 dips below the top of the ridge, with speeds slowing to 25 miles per hour.

In about half a mile, look for the east loop of the CKT to depart PA 144 on the right at **State Camp**, today just a roadside clearing with a concrete foundation. Here, a quick duck into the woods on the CKT reveals the aftermath of a tornado blast.

Remain on PA 144N for rolling travel. Looks right may reveal the **Coffin Rock Fire Tower**, an area landmark rising 13 stories, but closed to the public. The descent along Hall Run to the canyon bottom begins at 27 miles. The aisle of travel now shows more statuesque trees and fuller forest, but forget looking for pullouts on this twisting descent.

At the foot of the hill, the drive re-tags the CKT. At Drake Hollow (31 miles), admire showings of rhododendron, the stonework bridge, and hemlock darkness. This narrow hollow offers a fine short sampling of the CKT, but safe parking is limited.

Northbound on PA 144, you will enjoy more of the roadside rhododendron and glimpse the small pool of South Renovo Reservoir, before reaching **Jesse Hall Picnic Area** at 33 miles. It occupies a conifer-hardwood strip alongside PA 144 and has three shelters, pit toilets, and a seasonal water pump.

From the picnic area, pursue the West Branch Susquehanna River downstream to South Renovo. The enclosing ridges shape an imposing corridor. Across the river bridge, you enter dreary Renovo and turn left on PA 120 West/PA 144 North to continue the tour.

Flood damage from tropical storm Agnes in 1972 dealt this river town a harsh blow from which it has never truly rebounded, but its river-canyon location remains idyllic. Each October, Renovo puts its best foot forward for the Flaming Foliage Festival, drawing tens of thousands of visitors. At the corner where the tour meets PA 120 is the **Flaming Foliage Canoe Launch**. In town, you can find canoe rentals.

The tour next backtracks on itself, tracing the opposite bank of the West Branch upstream out of Renovo. At the village of Drurys Run, PA 144N turns right to follow Drury Run upstream through its narrow canyon. A hemlock-hardwood mantle cloaks the steep-walled canyon, and bountiful rhododendron hugs the stream. Whereas mountain laurel reigned along the southern half of the drive, rhododendron takes charge for this half.

Travel is 45 miles per hour. Unfortunately, litter is a problem at turnouts on this otherwise unspoiled drive. Drury Run has considerable charm, with its trickling cascades, draping tree branches, and bold rhododendron shores. For this part of the excursion, run and drive remain closely paired.

At 42.6 miles, the red-blazed, 52-mile **Donut Hole Trail** meets and briefly follows PA 144, before it plunges right to cross Drury Run via the **Left Fork Sandy Run Trail**. At 43.5 miles, you may choose to veer left, angling uphill on dirt, dry-weather Tamarack Tower Road for the 1.7-mile detour to **Tamarack Fire Tower**. Park at the turnaround at road's end, where you will find a stonehouse, covered water pump, pit toilet, the Donut Hole Trail, and the nine-story fire tower. A communications tower shares the

Tamarack Fire Tower, Sproul State Forest.

view. Signs at the site read "Mary's Camp Welcome" and "BSA Troop 137 Renovo, PA."

Visitors may mount the tower at their own risk. Limit party numbers on the tower and exercise caution, as the landings are largely open, and they get narrower near the top. The upper landings lift visitors above the tree tops for a full 360-degree view. Survey the folded Allegheny Plateau, with ridge after ridge parted by drainages. The lone interruption to the forest panorama is the sparkling, white CNG Transmission Corp complex in Tamarack.

Skipping the fire tower detour, you will proceed north on PA 144 to enter the village of Tamarack, where basic services are available. At the village of Hammersley Fork (49 miles), cross the Kettle Creek bridge to come to a T-junction and the next detour opportunity. A left on SR 4001 leads to isolated **Kettle Creek State Park**, with its lake impoundment, natural runs, and steep canyon slopes traversed by trails. Reach the northernmost attractions in 2.7 miles, and the park core in about 6 miles.

To remain on PA 144N though, turn right at the T-junction to follow picture-pretty Kettle Creek upstream. The creek flows broad, sparkling, and shallow. Cross-canyon views present the ridge. Tulip, oak, sumac, pine, birch, grape, and gum shade the stream. The drive now passes from Sproul to **Susquehannock State Forest**; a few services dot the corridor.

At 55.4 miles, the drive enters the village of Cross Fork, through which the **Susquehannock Trail System** passes. Again find some engaging views of Kettle Creek, as PA 144 travels the rural valley floor. On the left at 58.3 miles as you approach a bridge across Kettle Creek is a **Pennsylvania Fish Commission access**. This site is open to catch-and-release fly fishing only. The clarity of the creek reveals various-sized trout, weaving through the water. Ahead, a few more fishing turnouts beckon. Private, rustic cabins along PA 144 display shingles with imaginative hideaway names.

A full forest with cathedral trees and fern floors hosts the closing distance. At 62.5 miles, arrive at **Ole Bull State Park**, a fine terminus to the excursion. The park offers picnicking, camping, swimming, and hiking along Kettle Creek and convenient access to the Susquehannock Trail System. Of historical interest, this park occupies the site of an unsuccessful Norwegian-American settlement (1852–1853) founded by the famous concert violinist, Ole Bornemann Bull.

From the beginning, the Norwegian-American colony was fraught with disappointment, with most of the tillable soils being excluded from the land sale. The site's isolation, the difficulty of clearing the land, and the lack of funds brought further hardship. Four communities were planned: New Norway and Valhalla at what is now the park; Oleona, which still exists 1 mile to the north; and New Bergen, 8 miles from Cherry Springs.

Picnic Shelter, Ole Bull State Park.

At the time the colony disbanded, some 20 log houses and a schoolhouse existed at New Norway, with a two-story log cottage—the castle—mostly complete at the mountain-shelf location of Valhalla. Today, all are gone, but a trail leads to the castle foundation and its canyon view for a chance to share in Ole Bull's vision.

For those who wish to continue the tour or to plot an alternative return, PA 144 continues north to meet PA 44 at Oleona in 1 mile, U.S. Highway 6 at Galeton in 18 miles.

13

Allegheny Plateau Scenic Drive
From Lock Haven to Sweden Valley

General description: This unhurried 65.5-mile drive explores the Pennsylvania Black Forest–Allegheny Plateau country, snaring rim views and visiting fire towers and remote forest parks.

Special attractions: Heisey Museum; Cherry Springs and Patterson state parks; mountain views; autumn foliage; mountain laurel; hiking, fishing, relaxing.

Location: North-central Pennsylvania.

Drive route numbers: Pennsylvania Highways 664 and 44.

Travel season: Year-round.

Camping: Ole Bull State Park (off PA 144, 1 mile south of the junction of PA 44 and PA 144) has 81 rustic sites (some electric). The park's Ole Bull Lodge is also rented out. Cherry Springs State Park (on PA 44, 11 miles south of Sweden Valley) has 50 rustic, informal campsites. Patterson State Park (on PA 44, 6.5 miles south of Sweden Valley) has 20 rustic sites that double for camping or picnicking.

Services: Find full services at Lock Haven and at Coudersport (4 miles west of the drive's northern terminus). Various traveler services are available at Oleona, Carter Camp, and Sweden Valley.

Nearby points of interest: William T. Piper Aviation Museum (Lock Haven); Woolrich Outlet (Woolrich); the Little League World Series (Williamsport); Ole Bull, Lyman Run, Hyner Run, Hyner View, Little Pine, and Upper Pine Bottom state parks; Pine Creek; Black Forest Trail; Bucktail State Park Natural Area.

The drive

This north-central Pennsylvania drive lazily curls between U.S. Highway 220 and U.S. Highway 6 for a superb woodland wander. It starts on the banks of the West Branch Susquehanna River in historic Lock Haven and swings north through and along the edge of three state forests: Sproul, Tiadaghton, and Susquehannock. Atop the Allegheny Plateau, the tour delivers fine views spanning the Black Forest, Pine Creek drainage, and neighboring ridges. Vertigo-inducing, open-cage fire towers and peaceful state parks complete the tour package.

Drive 13: Allegheny Plateau Scenic Drive

From Lock Haven to Sweden Valley

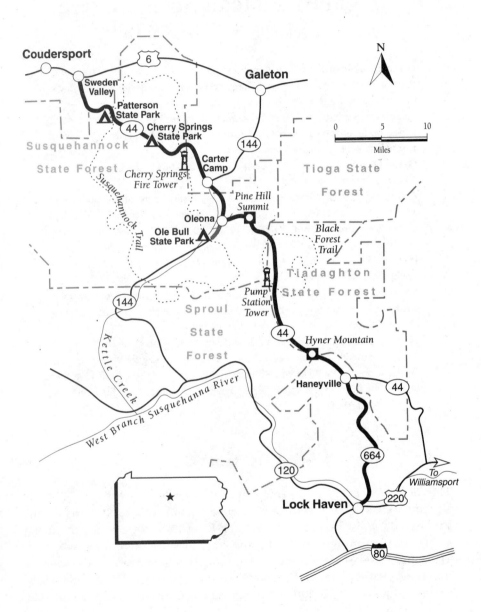

Start the tour at the junction of PA highways 120 and 664 in Lock Haven. Within this important river-canal town of the early 1800s, a National Register historic district encompasses nearly 350 buildings, including the business center, homes of lumber magnates, early churches, and original taverns. **Heisey Museum**, at 362 East Water Street (0.1 mile east of the tour's start), records much of the town's past from the early Native American river villages to the canal era to the devastating floods of the twentieth century.

The Victorian home that serves as the museum is furnished to reflect life in Lock Haven more than 100 years ago, with human-hair wreaths and horsehair chairs. Among the collection, look for the Jenny Reed teapot, which dates to the 1700s and carries an interesting legend of frontier life. A lithograph depicts Lock Haven in 1859, when a covered bridge spanned the West Branch. The museum is open Monday through Friday 10 A.M. to 4 P.M.; a donation is suggested.

Out the museum's front door stretches the 2.25-mile **River Walk**, inviting a stroll. The exercise path travels atop the hard-to-miss levee that protects Lock Haven from the river's swell. On East Water Street, not far from the museum, is a National Register Memorial Park at the site of a historic Native American village. For airplane buffs, a don't-miss attraction in town is the **William T. Piper Aviation Museum**, celebrating the birth of the Piper "Cub."

For the drive alone though, go north on PA 664, cross the bridge over the West Branch Susquehanna River, and bear right. In 0.3 mile, discover a greenway park, **Lockport Recreation Area**, with a boat launch, river access, and tables along shore. Cross-river views are of the levee.

PA 664 then winds its way out of Dunnstown and away from the river. Turn left at 0.9 mile to remain on PA 664/Swissdale Road for twisting, canyon travel. The lightly visited wooded canyon and residential area has an attractive arbor of young oak, maple, pine, sassafras, birch, aspen, and gum. On the narrow, two-lane, 35-mile-an-hour road, you will chase Reeds Run upstream to the plateau.

Atop the plateau, the road straightens for faster travel, with laurel and beautiful white-trunked birch adding to the forest. Gravel turnouts welcome closer looks at the natural setting; the leafy cathedral creates a fanciful shadow-and-light show. At 9.8 miles, enter the patchwork of Sproul State Forest; posted private lands alternate with public lands. Deer, skunk, raccoon, or porcupine may provide chance encounters. Classic, white country churches dot the quiet highway tour, while open fields reveal just how broad the plateau is.

Pass through tiny Haneyville to meet PA 44 at 17.5 miles; go north on PA 44 to continue the tour. On the right, a laurel-crowded shoulder distances the forest; on the left, trees closely edge the road. Travel the boundary between

Heisey Museum, Lock Haven.

Tiadaghton and Sproul state forests. Where milkweed grows profuse, look for monarch butterflies. Hay-scented ferns seasonally perfume the mountain air.

At 21.3 miles, you will top **Hyner Mountain** (elevation 2,107 feet). Openings now allow for long-distance views. The broad, even-height plateaus create a deceptively flat terrain. In less than a mile, look for Hyner Mountain Road to head left to Hyner Run and Hyner View state parks; stay PA 44.

Grassy fields and snag-opened woods briefly alter windshield views. Autumn explodes with warm colors: scarlet, red, burgundy, orange, lemon, and gold. Sunlight brings a heightened intensity to the color array; the dark trunks contrast. The rolling straightaway of PA 44 further engages the eye, while gravel turnouts and abandoned woods roads invite you aside for photography or leaf collecting.

On the right at 28.4 miles, reach the gravel turnout for the first **viewpoint**. Peer across a meadow of laurel, scrub oak, and huckleberry to the ridges parted by Trout Run. The Pine Creek drainage is visible in the distance. The geography of the Allegheny Plateau is boldly presented: broad plateaus divided by narrow stream-carved valleys. In another mile, meet the orange-blazed **Black Forest Trail (BFT)**. Engulfed in the sylvan splendor of Black Forest, it is one of the best long-distance hiking networks in the state, boasting wilderness solitude and multiple tour options.

Susquehanna River, Lock Haven.

On the left at 29.8 miles, a gated forest road leads to the **Pump Station Tower**. Park to the side of PA 44, being careful not to block the gate, and hike the road west for 0.1 mile. There, the tower shoots up nine stories, with the crow's nest still open to the public, although some of its windows are missing. As the tower has a scary bare-bones construction and minimal railings, ascend at your own risk; this is not a stop for young children. Planted pine and spruce rival the height of the structure and deny an open 360-degree view. Nonetheless, visitors can piece together the north-central Pennsylvania story; best views are to the northwest.

North on PA 44, the mountain laurel still abounds, suggesting return visits in June, when the shrubs reach full bloom. On the right at 30.4 miles starts the 5.6-mile circuit of the **George B. Will Trail**, which is part of the greater BFT network. Ferns dress the forest floor and parade shades of vibrant green in summer, golden ale in fall. A woodpecker-drilled snag or the telegraphing bird itself may cause heads to turn for a double take.

At 32.2 miles is the sleepy village of Black Forest. A mild descent then takes you into Potter County and Susquehannock State Forest. Still the drive rolls across plateau, tours forest, and rounds up hiking trails that can sidetrack. At 38.5 miles, top **Pine Hill Summit** (elevation 2,175 feet). On the right, a turnout offers an eastern view overlooking the upper Slate Run drainage and unbroken forest. The sturdy trunks of pine and oak partition the view.

With a few tight turns, PA 44 next wraps its way downhill as it parallels a Kettle Creek tributary downstream. At the bottom of the hill, cross the bridge over Kettle Creek to enter the village of Oleona and meet PA 144 (41.6 miles). One mile left on PA 144 is **Ole Bull State Park**, with its camping and picnic areas along Kettle Creek and its opportunities for fishing, swimming, and hiking.

For the plateau tour alone, turn right and proceed north on PA 144/44, contouring the steep eastern slope above Little Kettle Creek. Maple, witch hazel, hornbeam, cherry, and hemlock cling to the drainage, while maple and oak clad the upper slope. On this upstream tour, you have turnouts toward Little Kettle Creek, but only limited access to the tranquil water. The gently bending road allows for 45-mile-per-hour travel. A gust of autumn wind can unleash a flurry of tumbling leaves.

At 46.7 miles, the drive passes through the large block of private land around Carter Camp. Here, PA 44 proceeds straight, while PA 144 turns right. Stay PA 44 North. Seemingly out of character with the forest sojourn are signs for U-pik blueberries and fresh sweet corn. Again, PA 44 twists skyward to top the plateau, where a snag-punctuated, mature forest cradles travel.

On the right at 51.1 miles is another **viewpoint**. Admire the imposing north wall of the snaking West Branch Pine Creek. A shrubby slope opens

Pennsylvania Highway 44.

up the view. Once more, sassafras, laurel, and hay-scented fern adorn the plateau.

At 52.3 miles, the dirt state forest road on the left leads to **Cherry Springs Fire Tower** and the **Susquehannock Trail System (STS)** in 0.1 mile. Ringed by spruce, the tower rises eight stories. If you choose to ascend, do so at your own risk. Limit numbers on the tower and be attentive to your next handhold. Heavy wire now replaces some of the missing metal supports. Again, there are sizable openings in the structure. From the upper landings, overlook the Allegheny Plateau, with its broad, serial ridges fading to the horizons.

Without the tower stop, PA 44 serves up a roadside **vantage** on the left at 52.4 miles. This site actually presents a more open look at the immediate ridges than that attained from the tree-rimmed fire tower. View the rippled plateau country and mostly unbroken forest of Kettle Creek watershed. As PA 44 wiggles away, meadow shoulders open up the aisle.

Cherry Springs State Park then straddles the country highway at 54.2 miles for a quiet, "roughing-it" picnicking or camping experience. Three shelters serve picnickers; an arena for the annual Woodsmen Show (held each August) is also at the site. At the northwest end of the park stretches the grassy airstrip of **Cherry Springs Airport**, where sightseeing charters may be arranged.

Drive past a deer-browsing demonstration area and a number of private camps and cabins. Primitive signs identify the forest getaways; cabin names are often tongue-in-cheek or reveal a homespun philosophy. At 58.9 miles, you will find **Patterson State Park** and another segment of the Susquehannock Trail System. This forest park, too, has a rustic charm, with picnic shelters and open tables. A rolling meander follows.

On the left at 61.2 miles, tag the final **vista turnout**. This manicured view spans a sumac slope to overlook Prouty Run, part of the upper Sinnemahoning Creek drainage. Through the U-shaped canyon window of Prouty Run, view the far-off ridges. Afterward, descend from the plateau to the narrow valley bottom of Mill Creek to reach Sweden Valley and U.S. Highway 6 at 65.5 miles to end the tour.

14

Pine Creek Valley Scenic Drive
From U.S. Highway 220 to Morris

General description: This 42.8-mile drive up the acclaimed Pine Creek Valley crisscrosses Pine Creek, passes through Black Forest, and pays visits to quiet villages, creek accesses, prized trailheads, and state parks.

Special attractions: Pine Creek State Scenic Waterway access and views; Little Pine and Upper Pine Bottom state parks; Golden Eagle, Black Forest, Mid State, West Rim, and Pine Creek Rail trails; fall foliage; nesting bald eagles; blue-ribbon trout fishing, rafting, canoeing, winter sports.

Location: North-central Pennsylvania.

Drive route numbers: Pennsylvania Highways 44 and 414.

Travel season: Year-round, when cleared of snow.

Camping: Little Pine State Park (4 miles north of PA 44 on State Route 4001) has 104 family campsites with flush toilets and dump station. Private campgrounds also dot the valley floor.

Services: Find full services in the Jersey Shore–Williamsport area (east of the tour's start). The small villages along the route offer a variety of essential traveler services, including gas, groceries, and overnight accommodations.

Nearby points of interest: Historic towns of Lock Haven and Wellsboro; Woolrich Outlet (Woolrich); the Little League World Series (Williamsport); Ravensburg, Hyner Run, Hyner View, Leonard Harrison, and Colton Point state parks; Bucktail State Park Natural Area; Pine Creek Gorge; Oregon Hill area downhill skiing and winery.

 The drive

This drive follows the shimmery invitation of Pine Creek upstream from U.S. Highway 220 to the roadless Grand Canyon of Pennsylvania—Pine Creek Gorge. Settle back for a relaxing journey enfolded by steep canyon walls and tranquil forest. Ample stops allow you to establish a better acquaintance with the creek, valley, and canyon setting. The outdoor recreation afforded by the corridor is among the best in the state. The feeder drainages of Slate Run and Little Pine Creek add to the menu of beauty and recreation.

Originally, Pine Creek flowed north to the Tioga River, but during the glacial era its outlet was dammed and its waters forced south. The re-routed

Drive 14: Pine Creek Valley Scenic Drive
From U.S. Highway 220 to Morris

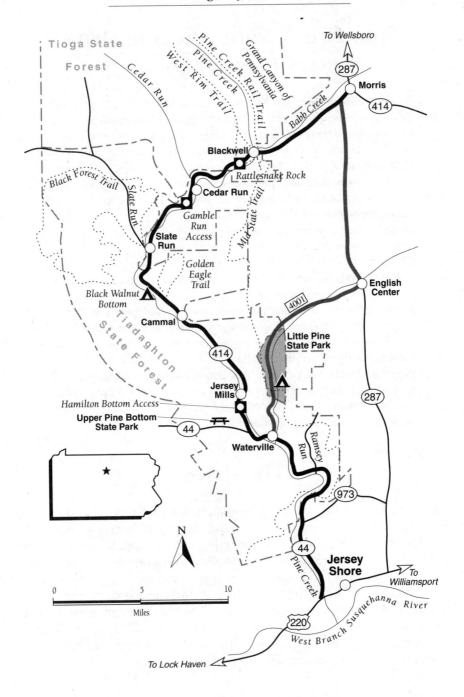

water swelled with the melting ice, then scoured out the dramatic, now-celebrated Pine Creek Gorge. The narrow wilderness attracts an appreciative audience to both rim and valley floor. Its natural merit has won it National Natural Landmark distinction.

Although the described drive is a linear route, loop returns to US 220 are possible. Motorists may choose a direct return south via PA 287 from Morris or make a lasso-shaped drive. This is done by following PA 287 south from Morris to English Center, and then SR 4001 along Little Pine Creek past Little Pine State Park to return to PA 44 at Waterville. From there, you would then backtrack the tour's first segment to US 220.

To begin the Pine Creek Valley scenic drive, from US 220 west of Jersey Shore, take the PA 44/Pine Creek Exit and head north. The white steeple and belltower of Phelps Chapel, valley cornfields, and canyon forest greet you at the start. At 0.2 mile, cross the first of a series of Pine Creek bridges for an introduction to the sparkling host, with its seasonally green or yellow-gold islands and perhaps a heron stalking its shore. Pine Creek is alternately glassy and riffling, and at this point, a vegetated levee contains its flow.

Ahead, PA 44 passes below the steep, forested East Rim, edging the valley patchwork of fields. Clouds cast changing shadows over the rounded rims. Sycamore, sumac, locust, and box elder claim the canyon bottom; oak, maple, pine, and aspen mount the slope. Travel is meandering and 45 miles per hour.

Where PA 44 approaches the base of Short Mountain, you may discover a few rhododendron. Gaps in the woods present creek bends. At 4.8 miles, proceed north past PA 973. A trading post offers one-stop shopping for ice cream cones, bait, and gas. Pine Creek is a premier trout stream, drawing ardent anglers from across the state and from neighboring states. Pass additional services before entering Tiadaghton State Forest.

For a spell, you may notice the orange blazes of the **Mid State Trail** as it follows along PA 44. At 7.5 miles, a turnout on the left overlooks a scenic Pine Creek bend. Upstream is a rusted railroad bridge that will one day be rehabilitated to carry the Mid State Trail as it lays its north-south sash across the state.

Private and public lands alternately border Pine Creek. Near Ramsey Run, a segment of abandoned railroad separates PA 44 from the creek. Although this stretch of railroad grade has not been improved for trail, it is open to walkers—just expect some overgrown spots.

Niches in the exposed shale of the road cut cradle white, red, and blue wildflowers. At 10.9 miles, cross Little Pine Creek and reach the junction with SR 4001 in the village of Waterville. You may detour north now on SR 4001 to reach linear **Little Pine State Park** in 4 miles. Or, postpone a visit until the return, if you backtrack or choose to add a closing loop.

Love Run Trail, Little Pine State Park.

Within its 2,158 acres, Little Pine State Park has a free-flowing stream and reservoir floodplain, steep forest flanks, and broad summit plateaus, all which welcome exploration. Outcroppings of sandstone and flagstone interrupt the forest mantle. Mountain laurel claims the upper slopes and plateaus.

Along its course, Little Pine Creek has a 94-acre impoundment which invites fishing, boating, swimming, and in winter, ice skating and ice fishing. The dam built for flood control has only been overwhelmed once, during tropical storm Agnes in 1972. The park floor still retains the storm's fingerprint.

For the drive alone, keep to PA 44 at Waterville, again crossing Pine Creek for up-and-down canyon views. At the 12.5-mile junction, PA 414 continues the Pine Creek saga. But a 2-mile detour north on PA 44 leads to **Upper Pine Bottom State Park**. Rhododendron complements this side trip, which twists up the narrow, forested canyon of Upper Pine Bottom Run. The state park has a small picnic area with just three tables and barbecues, but welcoming shade.

Although there are gravel turnouts above the creek, most have a breakneck slope down to the water. Cross-canyon views present the East Rim's Huntley Mountain. Roadside wild grape grows with abandon, creating topiary monsters. At 14.8 miles, you will come to the **Hamilton Bottom Access**, a primitive approach to Pine Creek for angler and canoeist that is reached by an eroded dirt road, no amenities. At 15.3 miles, the drive crosses Pine Creek a third time at Jersey Mills.

The abandoned railroad now lies to the right, waiting for the **Pine Creek Rail Trail** to be built south. The proposed trail will one day stretch some 62 miles between Wellsboro Junction and Jersey Shore. Enjoy open looks across the guardrail to the creek and floodplain. The deep pools entice fishermen to dance fly lines on them, while merganser and kingfisher animate the waterway. Pointy knolls bring variety to the West Rim skyline.

The railroad and road crisscross as the valley floor broadens and now supports cornfields. Trickling runs thread from dark hollows to join the waters of Pine Creek. Upon entering the village of Cammal (20.3 miles), you may spy a beaver dam that raises a side water. Cammal is a "don't sneeze or you'll miss it" village.

Briefly, PA 414 draws above the creek, passing pine plantation and open field. Upon the drive's return to Pine Creek level, you will find a vista trail duo: the orange-blazed **Golden Eagle Trail** and the blue-blazed **Bob Webber Trail**, which explore the 6,900-acre **Wolf Run Wild Area**. Their shared trailhead is on the right at 23 miles. In a little more than 1 mile is the Bonnell Run access to the Golden Eagle Trail; it lies opposite the Clark Access Area.

Frog, Little Pine State Park.

From **Clark Access Area**, a 0.5-mile trail heads north to the **Black Walnut Bottom Camping Area,** a walk-to/canoe-to campground with sites available by permit only; contact Tiadaghton State Forest. Mowed hiker paths part an open field of goldenrod, milkweed, and grass, with options to tour above the creek or directly through the field. Where the forks merge, proceed upstream to the tree-shaded camping flat.

By continuing north on foot through camp, you will reach **Black Walnut Bottom Access** in another 0.2 mile. Via vehicle on PA 414, you would reach this access at 24.8 miles, for a shorter approach to the campground. Black walnuts do grow here, and there is direct creek access.

On the left at 26.3 miles, you will pass the marker for **Slate Run Vista**, but find no turnout. From the moving vehicle, all you catch is a quick glimpse of a bridge, Pine Creek, and Mount Fern (elevation 2,060 feet). Next up, enter the village of Slate Run, where another one-stop store answers travelers' needs.

The bridge that spans Pine Creek at Slate Run leads to the 42-mile hiking network of the **Black Forest Trail.** This outstanding trail system celebrates the forest wild and quiet, and knits together sparkling runs, dark hollows, and summit views.

For the scenic drive, stay north on PA 414; Mount Fern still adds to windshield views. Before long, you will cross to the west shore of Pine Creek. As you exit the bridge, look left for **Algerine Wild Area**; it covers some 3,700 acres, north of Slate Run. The tour now passes above wooded floodplain, field, and private homes. At 29.1 miles, a look over your left shoulder finds a springtime waterfall; here, a gravel turnout does allow you to park for a better assessment.

As PA 414 narrows, you will enter an area where great sections of trees were toppled or ripped apart by the tremendous wind of August 1997. Although it was not classified as a tornado, it had all the earmarks of one. On the far shore, the trees were leveled like matchsticks.

Next find **Gamble Run Access**, set back from a volunteer fire department. This small public access occupies a grassy corner at the confluence of Gamble Run and Pine Creek. When you park, be sure you are nowhere near the fire department doors. Ahead, the drive enters Tioga State Forest. Tyoga is Seneca for "meeting of two rivers" and refers to the tribe of Senecas who inhabited this area.

At 31.7 miles, Beulahland Road descends right to the village of Cedar Run; bear left to remain on PA 414. The road narrows even more as it crosses Cedar Run and rounds below Cedar Mountain. Cedar Run, like Slate Run, is a large Pine Creek tributary. Beyond the bridge, travel is on oil-surfaced road, forest shades the route, and speeds slow to 25 miles per hour. Cliffs of the road cut measure 30 to 40 feet high.

Pine Creek Pennsylvania Scenic Waterway.

On the right at 35.7 miles is the paved **Rattlesnake Rock Parking Area**, with phone and toilet. It serves double duty as a trailhead—it is the southern terminus to the 30-mile **West Rim Trail** that explores the skyline of Pine Creek Gorge for views and tranquil woods strolling. It also occupies the southern terminus for the 20-mile **Pine Creek Rail Trail**. This comfortable rail trail, with a crushed-limestone surface, explores the belly of Pine Creek Gorge and is open to travel by foot, bike, horse, and cross-country skis.

Riding a mountain bike along the retired Penn-Central Railroad grade allows you to see more of the canyon, with its sterling images of forest, rock, and water. By hiking or cross-country skiing the grade, it opens the door to more wildlife encounters, including the possibility of spying a bald eagle. So park, attach a fly rod to your pack, and go.

For the conclusion of the drive though, keep to PA 414 as it crosses Pine Creek one last time, returning to pavement and entering Blackwell. In the village, you will find a bike/ski rental, hotel, and restaurant. On the east bank, just as you exit the bridge is the **Blackwell Boating and Fishing Access**, through which the Pine Creek Rail Trail passes.

Follow PA 414 through the tiny tourist-residential community, cross the one-lane bridge over Babb Creek, and follow Babb Creek upstream. The road weaves out of the canyon and through picturesque forest that displays a fruit basket of color in the fall. In Morris (42.8 miles), you will come to the junction with PA 287. Morris was the seat of an unusual 1940s enterprise that took place in Tioga State Forest—birch stills, where the harvested bark from birch trees was processed for its oil. The last still in Morris went silent in 1972.

You may now follow PA 287 south for the loop return options. Or, go north to reach Wellsboro and branch off to Leonard Harrison or Colton state parks for rim views of the Grand Canyon of Pennsylvania.

15

Loyalsock Creek Scenic Drive

From Montoursville to
U.S. Highway 6 near Russell Hill

General description: This 69.3-mile drive follows Loyalsock, Little Loyalsock, and Mehoopany creeks through the Endless Mountains of Pennsylvania, blending rural and wooded canyon-and-rim images. On its northeast-arcing way, it passes from the West Branch Susquehanna River to the upper Susquehanna River.

Special attractions: Creek views, but limited access; drive-to and hike-to vista knobs; covered bridges; fall foliage; hiking, picnicking, trout fishing, kayaking.

Location: North-central to northeast Pennsylvania, passing through Lycoming, Sullivan, and Wyoming counties.

Drive route numbers: Pennsylvania Highway 87.

Travel season: Year-round, when cleared of snow.

Camping: Worlds End State Park (3 miles southeast of PA 87 on PA 154) has 70 family campsites with modern restrooms, showers, and a dump station. The park also rents 19 rustic cabins.

Services: Find full services at Montoursville and Dushore, with a complement of traveler services along the route.

Nearby points of interest: Montour Preserve, Crystal Lake Ski Center, Worlds End and Ricketts Glen state parks, Loyalsock Trail, the village of Wyalusing, French Azilum historic site.

 The drive

This drive begins by following the curvaceous, sable beauty of Loyalsock Creek upstream through a spectacular canyon setting tucked away in the southwest corner of the Endless Mountains. The tour passes through state forest and private lands. As it continues northeast, it becomes progressively more rural and private. Little Loyalsock Creek hosts the middle leg of the journey before Mehoopany Creek takes the tour downstream to the Susquehanna River.

The 12.2-mile round-trip side tour to High Knob puts a fine addition on the scenic drive, providing an elevated look at the Endless Mountains–Loyalsock countryside. The view spans seven counties. Elsewhere, on the

Drive 15: Loyalsock Creek Scenic Drive

From Montoursville to U.S. Highway 6 near Russell Hill

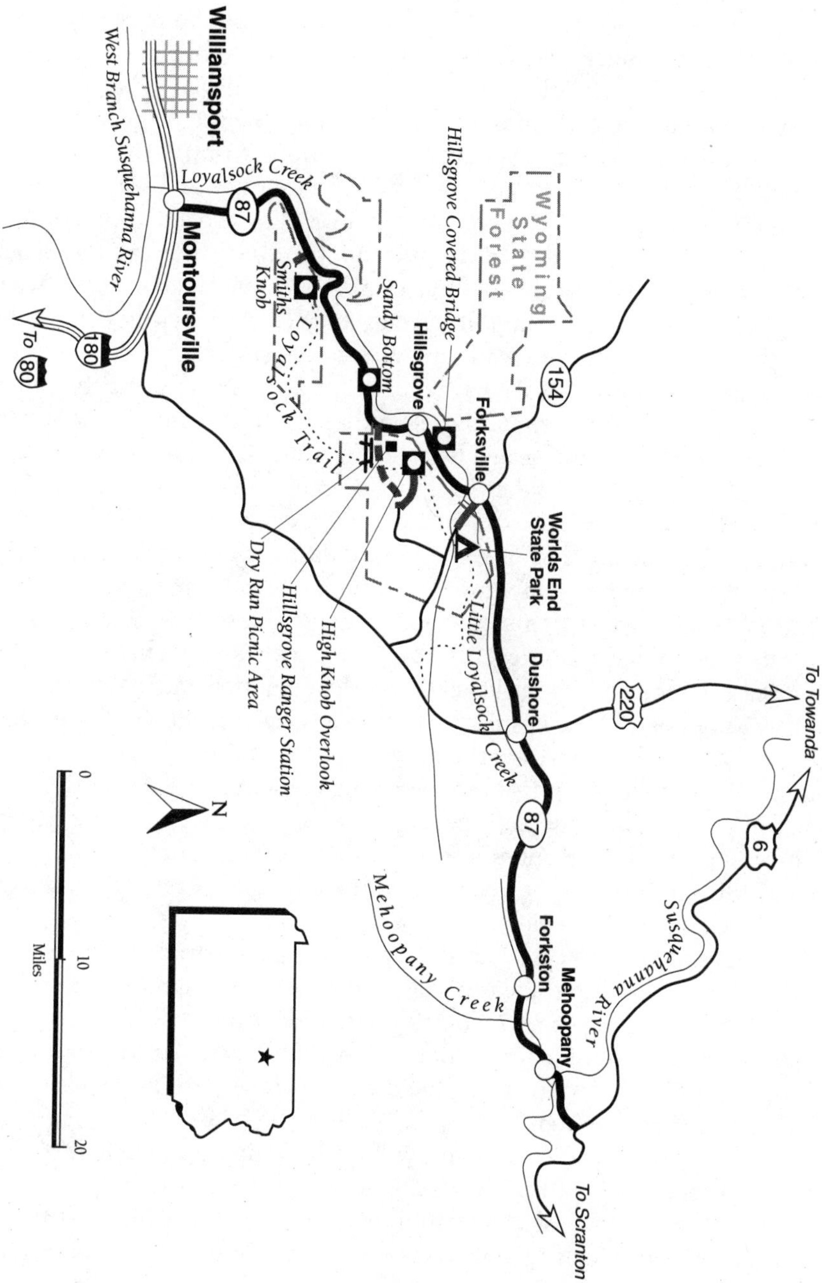
Williamsport
West Branch Susquehanna River
Loyalsock Creek
87
Montoursville
180
To 80
Smiths Knob
Sandy Bottom
Loyalsock Trail
Hillsgrove Covered Bridge
Wyoming State Forest
Hillsgrove
Forksville
154
Worlds End State Park
Little Loyalsock Creek
Dry Run Picnic Area
Hillsgrove Ranger Station
High Knob Overlook
Dushore
220
To Towanda
6
Susquehanna River
87
Mehoopany Creek
Forkston
Mehoopany
To Scranton
N
0
10
20
Miles

main drive, covered bridges conjure images of a more tranquil, bygone era. Late September to early October, leaf colors are engagingly presented as creek reflections, distant patchworks, and up-close displays.

To begin this drive, from U.S. Highway 220/Interstate 180 at Montoursville, go north on PA 87 to follow the east shore of Loyalsock Creek upstream. Trademark Pennsylvania bank barns, scenic old farmsteads, cornfields, pastures, and shade maples claim the broad valley bottom. Like welcoming arms, the canyon walls lure you into their scenic grasp.

Stay on PA 87 North, bypassing the junctions with PA Highways 864 and 973. Hand-lettered signs for homemade pies, honey, and ice cream may start stomachs to growl. Early on, tall trees mask Loyalsock Creek, but by 5 miles, you gain an open view of the graceful, bending waterway. Loyalsock Creek traces its name to the Wolf Clan of the Lenni Lenape Tribe. Their word Lawisaquik means "middle creek"; Loyalsock Creek is flanked by Lycoming Creek to the west, Muncy Creek to the east.

By now, the canyon walls have pinched together, narrowing the valley. Some farmhouses and outbuildings sparkle with fresh paint, while others are rustic, weathered, and scaled by creeping vines. The steep canyon walls wear cloaks of broadleaf and evergreen. Sycamores grace the creek.

At 8.8 miles, a broad road shoulder accesses the nearly 60-mile-long **Loyalsock Trail**, marked by its signature red dash on yellow blaze. Here, the trail streaks up the east canyon wall. As the drive continues, there will be additional meetings with this trail and its associated spurs.

In another 0.6 mile, reach Little Bear Creek Road. This forest road heads east 0.8 mile to the Little Bear forest headquarters and a trailhead for **Smiths Knob**, part of the Loyalsock Trail. It is a worthwhile, but fairly challenging 1.8-mile hike north to the knob. It passes through changing forest, mountain laurel belts, and summit showings of Mayapple. From the trail, you will gather manmade and natural views, before halting at the lichen-whitewashed sandstone outcrop of Smiths Knob. The natural window created by this knob allows for overlooks of the Loyalsock Creek drainage and immediate Smiths Knob cliff.

Motorists who keep to PA 87N will also pass a trailhead to Smiths Knob at 10.6 miles, but there is no easy parking in the vicinity of this hiker route. Maple and tulip poplar contribute to the woods, while hay-scented fern bring helter-skelter color to the road banks. Private lands deny access to Loyalsock Creek, but the windshield views parade forth frequent images of the serene mirror water.

On the left at 17.5 miles, you will find the first public creek access, **Sandy Bottom**, reached via a 0.2-mile gravel road. This Tiadaghton State Forest access consists of a primitive parking area on a forested flat of Loyalsock Creek; Sciate Knob rises opposite the access. A gated road

Alpine Falls–Loyalsock Trail, Wyoming State Forest.

Smiths Knob view, Tiadaghton State Forest.

welcomes an upstream walk amid the hemlock, pine, maple, birch, hickory, and beech. An island, however, isolates the old road from the main flow of the creek. About 0.2 mile into the walk, you will notice the disheveled leavings of a windstorm. Although the hiker path degenerates, it remains walkable, allowing for a 0.5-mile stroll along Loyalsock Creek. Where the path hooks toward PA 87, turn around. Deer, wild turkey, kingfisher, and squirrel may be among the wildlife encounters.

From the Sandy Bottom turnoff, PA 87N bends and rolls. The speedometer needle generally hugs the 45-mile-per-hour mark, as the canyon is well settled and has a regular, light-to-moderate traffic flow. Woods dominate as the canyon ridges fold together and drift apart.

At 21.7 miles comes the side tour to **High Knob Overlook**. Turn right on Dry Run Road to add this 12.2-mile round-trip diversion. In 0.2 mile, pass the **Hillsgrove Ranger Station** and the start of a trail to High Knob, and in 0.6 mile, skirt **Dry Run Picnic Area**, snuggled in a picturesque hemlock hollow. After 1 mile, a gravel, all-weather road advances the winding, 25-mile-per-hour forest ascent. Sunlight bathes the leaves. At 3.8 miles, go left for the overlook, now on its paved, one-way loop. Be alert, as alarmed deer with white tails raised sometimes bound across the road and down the slope. Flickers flit between summit snags, causing passengers to lean to the windows for a skyward glimpse. At 6.1 miles is vista parking.

From the open vantage, survey a ridge panorama of bumps, knobs, coffin mountains, and flat plateaus, punctuated by gaps and canyons. October paints the landscape in fanciful shades of red, maroon, orange, and gold; for an update on the progression of the fall color, phone 1-800-FALLINPA. Picnic tables and pit toilets are at the summit site. (For an alternative, fully paved approach to the overlook, drivers may access High Knob via Double Run Road (State Route 3009) out of Worlds End State Park; from the primary drive, reach Worlds End southeast out of Forksville, which is north of the 21.7-mile junction.)

By omitting the High Knob side trip and keeping to the Loyalsock Drive, you will cross Loyalsock Creek at the village of Hillsgrove to find a country store with post office and gas pumps. Travel is now along the west shore, passing below Round Top, for a new perspective on canyon and stream. Where PA 87 crosses back over the creek, admire the beautiful western knobs that loom over the valley.

You may glimpse **Hillsgrove Covered Bridge**, prior to reaching the turn for it at 26 miles. To visit this bridge, turn left on Splash Dam Road (at its south end), go 0.1 mile, and again turn left on Covered Bridge Road to pass through and admire the attractive wooden bridge.

Hillsgrove Covered Bridge (circa 1850) is a 186-foot single span over Loyalsock Creek, with Burr-truss supports and weathered wooden sides.

Hillsgrove Bridge, Sullivan County.

Awning-covered windows and safe interior walkways to either side of the driving lane suggest unhurried views of Loyalsock Creek. As the enclosure of the bridge performs much like a wildlife blind, heron and geese often are spied. While stopped and exploring the bridge, take a moment to read the original use and speed rules that are posted at the entry.

From the windows of Hillsgrove Covered Bridge, some of the best views of Loyalsock Creek are found. Downstream, a splash dam spans the breadth of the creek as the hillsides fold together for a pleasant frame. Upstream, the waterway curves away. In each direction, the clear water holds breathtaking reflections, with a cobble streambed contributing to the beauty.

Without this detour, PA 87 continues its journey north, with farmland ushering in views of the west canyon wall—a long, curving ridge plateau. At 30.8 miles, the drive crosses Loyalsock Creek to enter the borough of Forksville and meet PA 154. A detour right on PA 154 South leads to **Forksville Covered Bridge** on the right in 0.2 mile, just past a picturesque white chapel; the core of **Worlds End State Park** is in about 3 miles.

Built in 1850, the Forksville Bridge (or Sadler Rogers Bridge) is a 146-foot single span over Loyalsock Creek. Hidden supports help this bridge withstand contemporary traffic. Pass through the bridge to reach a general store, which sells sandwiches and ice cream. Picnic tables at the back of the store overlook the creek and allow for side views of the covered bridge.

Painted red, this covered bridge likewise has awning-covered windows. Views downstream are dominated by the PA 87 road bridge. Upstream stretches a natural stage with the rocky bed, rounded boulders, and shimmering water. The rocks lend character and give the creek voice.

By keeping to PA 87N at 30.8 miles, you bid farewell to Loyalsock Creek and hello to the quiet of Little Loyalsock for more upstream pursuit. Dairy farms engage with green pastures and milling cows. Fruit-and-vegetable stands suggest snacks for the road. Next comes twisting travel through a narrow forested canyon. At 37.5 miles, the drive crosses over Little Loyalsock Creek. After crossing back, look for the valley to flatten and for a return of rural images.

At 43 miles, turn left on US 220 North/PA 87N to enter the charming community of Dushore. There, find services and the historic **Dushore Railroad Station**, where visitors rediscover the golden age of railroads. In another 0.7 mile, PA 87N turns right and soon after, bypasses PA 487.

Ahead stretches a rolling tour across the plateau, with its mosaic of fields and woods. Most of the land is in pasture, not tilled. Skeins of geese may cross the big, yawning sky. Below to the left at 47.7 miles, overlook private Saxe Pond. After the junction with SR 2007 (48.3 miles), PA 87 passes between Briskey and Tyler mountains.

Before long, woods scenery engages along North Branch Mehoopany Creek. Mountains rise to the tour's sides, and up ahead, hemlocks enfold the glistening stream. A few homes, a scenic country chapel, or a cabinet-maker's shop may push aside the woods. The quiet roadway after Dushore allows for leisurely travel.

Where PA 87 crosses the North Branch Mehoopany Creek at Forkston, to the right on State Route 3001 is **Creek Junction Park**. This quiet community park, with picnic shelter, ballfields, playground, and pit toilets invites road travelers aside for a breather. It sits on the bank where the North Branch and main stem Mehoopany Creek merge.

Bypassing Creek Junction Park, you will cross the bridge over Mehoopany Creek at 59.8 miles. The branch-swelled creek has an attractive, shady bower. Throughout the miles, the drive unfolds a symphony of familiar Pennsylvania images: prized woods, rich pastures, rolling cornfields, stylish barns, shallow waterways, and rural villages. For a short while, attractive stone walls retain the road.

Where PA 87 next crosses the creek, enter the village of Mehoopany, where basic traveler services are available. Then, in another 0.4 mile, turn right to remain on PA 87N as it crosses the Susquehanna River—a 0.25-mile-broad, smooth-flowing waterway. The industrial complex of Proctor and Gamble Paper Products signals an abrupt return to the real world, although the treed ridges continue to please.

Ascend from the river valley to meet US 6 at 69.3 miles, completing the tour. US 6 is a National Recreation Trail, with city/village offerings, history, natural assets, and parks calling in either direction.

16

Columbia County
Covered Bridges Tour

Loop swings north from Interstate 80 at Bloomsburg

General description: This drive makes a 51.7-mile, open-ended loop between Interstate 80 and Pennsylvania Highway 118 that can be extended by half a dozen side trips that range between 200 feet and 11.5 miles round trip for a tally of 11 covered bridges. An ideal complement to the drive is a visit to Ricketts Glen State Park, which boasts 500-year-old trees and more than 20 waterfalls.

Special attractions: Nineteenth-century covered bridges; ribbony creeks; a fish hatchery; Ricketts Glen State Park; the Covered Bridge and Arts Festival (held in October); hiking, fishing, swimming, boating, picnicking, winter sports.

Location: Northeast Pennsylvania.

Drive route numbers: Pennsylvania Highways 42, 118, and 487.

Travel season: Year-round, when cleared of snow.

Camping: Ricketts Glen State Park has 120 family campsites, with showers and flush toilets during the primary visitor season and dry camping in winter. The park also has 10 cabins for rent; advance reservations are needed. Private campgrounds along the loop also serve travelers.

Services: Find full services at Bloomsburg, with a smattering of visitor services along the route.

Nearby points of interest: Milton, Worlds End, Hickory Run, and Lehigh Gorge state parks; Montour Preserve; Wilkes-Barre and Scranton area offerings; and still more covered bridges (southern Columbia County, south of the Susquehanna River).

The drive

This drive explores the quiet highways and backroads of northern Columbia County to round up 11 covered bridges that date to the nineteenth century. East out of Forks, you will find the nation's only twin covered bridges—East and West Paden—at Twin Bridges County Park. Columbia County has the third richest concentration of covered bridges in Pennsylvania, with 20 of the classic structures spanning its waters.

Drive 16: Columbia County Covered Bridges Tour

Loop swings north from Interstate 80 at Bloomsburg

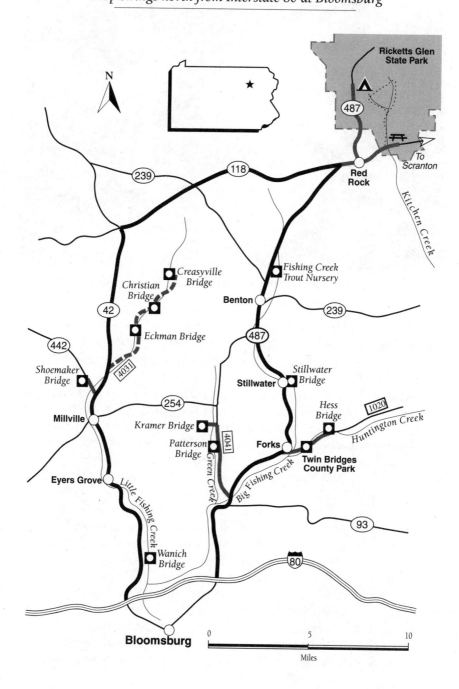

Mohawk Falls, Ricketts Glen State Park.

With only two covered bridges visible from the loop, this drive is about getting sidetracked and poking your nose around each bend in anticipation of what is ahead. So if wanderlust and curiosity are your guideposts, this is the drive for you.

Along with the bridges, 13,050-acre Ricketts Glen State Park is a shining attraction not to be denied. Its superb natural beauty and outdoor recreation won it approval for national park status in the 1930s, but a warring world shelved its opening. The area entered Pennsylvania's state park system in 1942. Its Glens Natural Area (a National Natural Landmark) encompasses the shady hollows of the Kitchen Creek drainage and showcases serial waterfalls (the tallest measuring 94 feet), old-growth trees, shale cliffs, a boulder tunnel, and a fine network of trails by which to admire it all.

To start this drive, take Exit 34 off I-80 near Bloomsburg and go north on PA 42. It begins as a wide highway through a full-service community at the exit, but quickly slips away into the rural countryside. Past the Veterans of Foreign Wars Hall, the highway parallels sycamore-shaded Little Fishing Creek upstream. Traffic begins light to moderate, but then quiets.

At 2.2 miles, you will reach the first bridge detour. Turn right on Covered Bridge Drive, passing between farmstead and cornfield to locate 1844-built **Wanich Covered Bridge** in 0.2 mile. Still in use, this one-lane, red-painted Burr-style bridge traverses Little Fishing Creek. A single window graces each of its walls, granting stream views. Here, low rock weirs span the breadth of Little Fishing Creek to shape tiny cascades. Near the covered bridge is road shoulder parking for one or two vehicles.

By instead remaining on PA 42 North at 2.2 miles, you will find woods again frame travel and alternately screen and reveal the creek. Where PA 42 itself crosses Little Fishing Creek (5.5 miles), the road narrows and grows more winding. In Eyers Grove, be sure to look right to see an old mill. In this narrow, rural valley, the occasional huge barn looms roadside, and teaser signs reading "cantaloupe," "peaches," and "sweet corn" whet anticipation for upcoming produce stands.

Stay on PA 42N to find basic services at the small country town of Millville. After an aisle of sugar maples ushers you back into the rural landscape, signs for antiques or cottage industries may call you aside.

The next bridge detour comes at 10.3 miles, at the junction with PA 442. To add this side trek, go west 0.9 mile on PA 442, turn left on Chestnut Lane and left again on Shoemaker Bridge Road to view the retired **Shoemaker Covered Bridge**. Built in 1881, it is painted classic red, has solid sides, and spans West Branch Run. Mud nests of swallows dot the rafters of this now quiet bridge.

All along the tour, you may notice small calling cards tacked to the interiors of the wooden bridges. These cards bear the names of visitors who

Wanich Covered Bridge, Columbia County.

belong to Covered Bridge Associations from neighboring states. Otherwise, the bridges are remarkably clean and free from vandalism and graffiti.

Opting for the main loop alone at 10.3 miles, you will pass through woods that open to fields and ridge views, coming to the next bridge summons at 11.5 miles. Here, a right turn on Sereno Road/State Route 4031 begins the longest detour—an 11.5-mile round-trip that will round up three covered bridges.

SR 4031 is alternately graveled or paved as it takes over the upstream pursuit of Little Fishing Creek. In 2.4 miles, arrive at **Sam Eckman Bridge**; it is on the left just off SR 4031. Built in 1876, the bridge is still active today. It is named for a local man who operated a farm, shingle mill, and birch oil factory. Goldenrod, daisy, and joe-pyeweed color the neighboring field and bank. This covered bridge links Greenwood and Pine townships. The steep, wooded hillside abutting SR 4031 resides in Greenwood; the rural hillside and beautiful barn just beyond the bridge are in Pine.

Resume travel, staying on Sereno Road/SR 4031 another 1.9 miles to locate the **Jud Christian Bridge** on a small graveled road to the right. At the turn, a farmstead and barn tightly hug SR 4031. Dairy cows nibble pasture grass near the bridge. Also built in 1876, this attractive bridge is in superb shape from its stone-and-mortar abutments to its rafters. A few knotholes in the bridge's sides allow for a peep-show look at Little Fishing Creek and its tight canopy of hemlock and birch.

Once more, continue upstream on SR 4031, crossing the creek on a contemporary bridge. In 0.6 mile, bear left on scenic but pot-holed Creasyville Hollow Road/Township Road 710, go 0.8 mile, and continue left at the fork on Township Road 683 to reach **Creasyville Covered Bridge** in 300 feet. It is a similar, solid-sided wooden bridge built in 1881. At one time, it was known as "Derr Bridge" for the Derr Sawmill that operated near here, but the present-day beauty of the forested drainage erases all memory of the bygone mill. When ready, backtrack the 5.75 miles to PA 42.

Without the bridges detour at 11.5 miles, the primary loop proceeds on PA 42N from the Sereno junction. For the next 18 miles, put aside the bridge chase, settle into your seats, and enjoy the passing as forest funnels travel along gently bending Lick Run. Rural enclaves dot travel before becoming an integral thread of the tour. You will find the terrain rolling, with Huckleberry Mountain looming north.

At 18.2 miles, turn east on PA 118 for the clockwise loop; a corner one-stop service center is at the junction. As PA 118 ascends into the Endless Mountains, aspens and white birch vary the look of the woods. Atop rises, overlook cornfields and win additional looks at the dark presence of Huckleberry Mountain. Stay the straightaway of PA 118.

As you near the junction with PA 487 (29.5 miles), Central Mountain replaces Huckleberry Mountain to the north. The loop swings south on

PA 487, but only 2.5 miles east on PA 118 lies the southern gateway to **Ricketts Glen State Park**. At Red Rock (0.8 mile east), PA 487 North leads to the upper park attractions, including Lake Jean and the campground, but people traveling with heavy trailers should avoid this steep climb into the park.

At the southern/lower park entrance, picnic and parking areas straddle PA 118; the deep hemlock shade of Kitchen Creek Glen creates a soothing backdrop. A 7.4-mile round-trip hike, with a 1,250-foot elevation change, follows Kitchen Creek north upstream into the heart of the Glens Natural Area, with its regal assembly of upper-canyon waterfalls. Although challenging, the hike fills each second with heart-quickening images of water, rock, and forest.

Reserved for hikers' eyes only are the glen's 20 back-to-back waterfalls. Enjoy close-up looks at both named and unnamed falls and cascades. On the zigzagging watercourse, it is difficult to tell where one falls ends and the next begins. For all who are physically fit, this is truly one spectacle to put on your lifetime "must see" list, but lace on your hiking boots for the uneven, wet, rocky trail.

On the hike north, you will arrive at the top of the first falls, 16-foot **Murray Reynolds Falls** at 1.4 miles. A rounded rock at the head of the falls forces the water to spout, while whorled bedrock adds interest to the falls cleft. You will then pass two more falls, enjoying base, side, and top views before reaching **Waters Meet** (the upstream confluence) at 1.8 miles. Now ready your cameras for the 3.8-mile waterfall loop that begins here and tours Glen Leigh and Ganoga Glen. The natural area's tallest falls, 94-foot **Ganoga Falls**, assumes a different face at every angle.

If you are not up to the main hike, a short walk downstream along Kitchen Creek reveals the last falls in the drainage line-up, 36-foot **Adams Falls**. Descend the footpath at the north end of the southern parking lot to overlook this picturesque gorge falls in 0.1 mile. Adams Falls spills snowy white through a recessed drop, just where the cliffs fold together forming a natural keyhole frame. By strolling atop the rocky vantage, explorers win a look at the swirling chute that escapes from the upper plunge pool, and view the many potholes filled by racing water.

For anyone able to resist the seductive call of Ricketts Glen State Park, an immediate turn south on PA 487 at 29.5 miles continues the Columbia County loop. Ahead lies twisting travel through forest, with the overhanging branches creating an arbor. In October, the hemlocks accentuate the autumn bonfire of the broadleaf species. Bypass a foundry, now following Big Fishing Creek downstream. Farms and wildflower fields open vistas.

At 35.6 miles (mileage excludes Ricketts Glen detour), reach the left-hand turn for the small **Fishing Creek Trout Nursery**. It sits alongside a golf course in 0.2 mile; here you will find fish pens, a weekend snack shack for two-legged visitors, and a concession for fish food. This stop is especially fun for youngsters. The packages of fish food are a good size and so are the awaiting rainbow, brook, brown, and palomino trout that race at the food pellets raining on the water. Remember to feed only the large fish, not the fingerlings, and use only the provided fish food.

When staying on PA 487S, the route skirts fields and pastures and passes through the tiny community of Benton. Prior to crossing a steel bridge over Big Fishing Creek at 40.5 miles, you can see a covered bridge off to the left. Ahead, in Stillwater, turn left (east) on Wesley Street to visit this bridge in 100 feet.

As you explore the retired **Stillwater Covered Bridge**, notice the arrow-pattern flooring and the arc trusses of its Burr design. On this long bridge, a single window opens to a view of the creek and the draping maples. An early settler built this bridge in 1849 at a cost of just over $1,100. Next door to the north stands a private, gray-sided chapel.

Southbound, PA 487 presents the long, shadowy presence of Huntington Mountain. Country settings are partitioned by woods, and Big Fishing Creek remains east of the highway. At Forks (43.5 miles) is the next spur, which leads to the loop's acclaimed twin covered bridges.

For a visit, turn left on SR 1020, crossing Big Fishing Creek to reach **Twin Bridges County Park**, with its impressive end-to-end placement of **East and West Paden Covered Bridges**. Find gravel parking at 0.4 mile, with additional parking on the right just after you traverse the modern bridge over Huntington Creek. Flush toilets and water are seasonally available.

This enchanting bridge pairing captures the imagination of artist and photographer and provides a soothing backdrop for a picnic lunch. If raindrops assault the paper plates, you can take your picnic indoors, beneath a bridge.

These red with white trim bridges are not identical in construction or in their present role of service. One spans 72 feet over land, with Queenpost design; and the other stretches 121 feet over water, with Burr styling; the gateways also differ. Both bridges, however, have long slat windows that stretch their full lengths, adding to their striking personas. Big sycamore, maple, basswood, hickory, and hemlock shade the creek flat, completing the site's tranquil yesteryear image.

Remain on SR 1020 another mile to view **Josiah Hess Covered Bridge**. You will discover it on the left on barricaded Covered Bridge Road, just before the intersection with Mountain Road. A walk of 50 strides leads to this 1875 bridge over Huntington Creek. Again, slat windows extend looks at the water. Bedrock slabs punctuate the clear stream, which parts untrampled green banks.

The primary loop, however, proceeds south on PA 487 from Forks to the next bridge detour on Rohrsburg Road/SR 4041 (46.1 miles). This side trip rounds up the final two bridges of the tour. Go 1.6 miles to find the first covered bridge, just to the left on Hartman Hollow Road. Park at a gravel turnout along SR 4041 a few feet beyond the bridge. This is **Patterson Covered Bridge**, which spans the deep, murky flow of Green Creek. Awning-covered windows allow for up and downstream views; willow and box elder are the trees of this drainage.

For the eleventh bridge, continue upstream on SR 4041 another mile, go left on Utt Road/T-456 for 0.4 mile, and turn left on Turkeypath Road/T-572, viewing the bridge on approach. **Kramer Covered Bridge** (1881) has an oak sentry and is a much shorter span over Mud Run, a feeder stream to Green Creek.

Without this final deviation at 46.1 miles, the drive follows PA 487 south along Big Fishing Creek to I-80, Exit 35 to complete the loop at 51.7 miles, ending one exit east of the tour's start. If desired, go 4 miles west on I-80 to return to Exit 34. Or, should you wish to find out about other area offerings or the southern county bridges, consider stopping at the Columbia-Montour Tourist Promotion Agency Visitor Center off Exit 35 at 121 Papermill Road.

17

Delaware Water Gap Scenic Drive

From Portland, Pennsylvania, to
Grey Towers (outside Milford)

General description: This 38.2-mile linear drive pursues the Pennsylvania shore of the unfettered Delaware River upstream through Delaware Water Gap National Recreation Area (NRA) to the charming old grace of Milford. The tour concludes at the country castle of Gifford Pinchot—the first chief of the U.S. Forest Service, twice Pennsylvania governor, and an early-day leader of the conservation movement.

Special attractions: Delaware Water Gap NRA; Grey Towers National Historic Landmark; The Columns museum; Delaware River access and views; formal vistas; shale palisades; spectacular waterfalls; autumn foliage and rhododendron blooms; April through June shad runs; picnicking, hiking, fishing, canoeing, tubing, swimming, winter sports, shopping, sightseeing.

Location: Pocono Mountains of northeast Pennsylvania, along the Delaware River between Interstates 84 and 80.

Drive route numbers: Pennsylvania Highway 611, River Road (State Route 2028), and U.S. Highways 209 and 6.

Travel season: Year-round.

Camping: Nearby private campgrounds serve this narrow corridor, along with the concession-operated Dingmans Campground, which lies within the NRA and has 50 water/electric sites, a separate tent area, showers, and dump station.

Services: Portland, Delaware Water Gap, and Milford provide traveler services along the route, with outlying Stroudsburg extending the offering.

Nearby points of interest: Bushkill Falls (a private recreation area), Shawnee Mountain Ski Area, Quiet Valley Living Historical Farm (Stroudsburg), Pocono Indian Museum (Bushkill), Water Gap Trolley tour (Delaware Water Gap), Appalachian National Scenic Trail, Promised Land State Park, Lake Wallenpaupack.

 The drive

This drive celebrates the natural splendor of the Delaware Wild and Scenic River. Much of the drive is centered in the popular, 70,000-acre Delaware Water Gap NRA that straddles the shores of Pennsylvania and New Jersey

Drive 17: Delaware Water Gap Scenic Drive
From Portland, Pennsylvania, to Grey Towers (outside Milford)

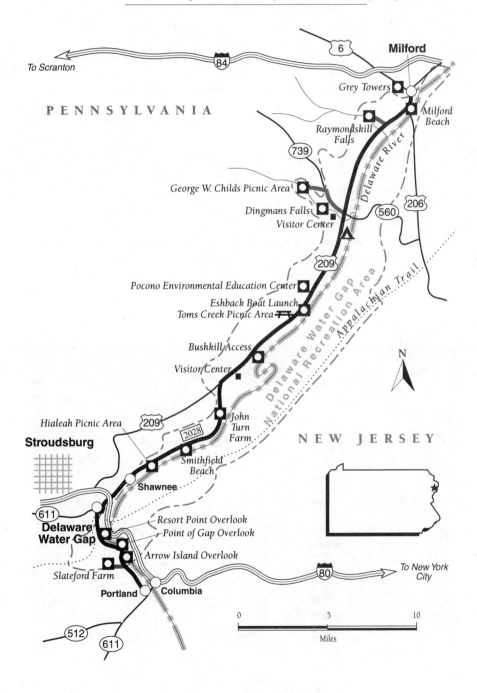

To Scranton

84

6

Milford

Grey Towers

P E N N S Y L V A N I A

Milford Beach

Raymondskill Falls

739

George W. Childs Picnic Area

Delaware River

Dingmans Falls Visitor Center

560

206

209

Pocono Environmental Education Center

Eshback Boat Launch
Toms Creek Picnic Area

Delaware Water Gap National Recreation Area

Appalachian Trail

Bushkill Access

Visitor Center

N

Hialeah Picnic Area

209

2028

John Turn Farm

N E W   J E R S E Y

Stroudsburg

Smithfield Beach

611

Delaware Water Gap

Shawnee

Resort Point Overlook
Point of Gap Overlook

Arrow Island Overlook

80

To New York City

Slateford Farm

Portland   **Columbia**

512

611

0			5			10

Miles

for a 40-mile stretch of the river. From the southern end of the park, view the S-shaped chasm of Delaware Water Gap, where the river cut a twisting path through 1,400-foot Kittatinny Ridge. Within the river watershed, discover steep wooded-and-rock slopes, bountiful rhododendron, dark hollows, tinsel-like ravines, and tumbling waterfalls.

Although the natural stage and recreation of the river canyon are outstanding, the corridor does suffer the problems of popularity. The NRA rests within a day's drive of nearly one-third of the country's total population and draws over 4 million visitors annually. Such numbers can set a hectic pace, but one well worth braving.

This northbound drive starts in Portland, Pennsylvania, but the nearest interstate exit is actually in New Jersey. From I-80 near Columbia, New Jersey, take Exit 4b if eastbound, Exit 4 if westbound for Portland, Pennsylvania, and cross the Columbia-Portland Bridge over the Delaware River. Once in Portland, go north on PA 611 through the quiet river town.

Portland is home to the fine handcrafted furnishings of Frederick Duckloe, and other specialty shops and eateries. From town, a **pedestrian bridge** invites visitors to hike out over the Delaware River for an unhurried look at the waterway and its impressive canyon. Delaware Water Gap looms north.

Rhododendron, Delaware Water Gap National Recreation Area.

Red eft, Delaware Water Gap National Recreation Area.

The contemporary pedestrian bridge occupies the former site of a covered bridge (1831–1955). Historically, 16 covered bridges spanned the Delaware River. The Portland bridge was the last of these charming structures to stand; in August 1955, it was claimed by flood, bringing an end to an era.

Outside of town, PA 611 is enfolded by woods of sassafras, birch, tulip, oak, silver maple, aspen, and sumac. Openings to the east permit river glimpses. At 2 miles, enter the NRA and come to the turnoff for **Slateford Farm.**

By going west on National Park Drive, you will reach a trailhead for **Arrow Island Trail** in 0.5 mile, the farm in 1 mile. Historic Slateford Farm dates back to the days when George Washington was president, and has a dual legacy as an agricultural site (1790–1868) and later as a slate quarry. Today, the farm is closed, except in winter, when the rustic farm roads shape a cross-country ski tour.

On PA 611 North in another 0.8 mile, you will come to **Arrow Island Overlook.** Its eastern view encompasses the free-flowing Delaware River, the southern extent of the Gap, and New Jersey's Mount Tammany. A glance west over your shoulder finds Pennsylvania's own towering Mount Minsi. Mounts Tammany and Minsi represent the two halves of Kittatinny Mountain driven apart by the river.

Less than 1 mile north on the left is **Point of Gap Overlook.** This cross-highway, cross-canyon view extols the Gap. It also serves up a bold look at the layered-rock cliff and tilted ledges that breach the leafy cloak of

Mount Tammany. At the base of the cliffs, a broad talus-and-scree slope tosses forth a white glare. Plaintive crows can be heard over the highway drone. In January and February, bald eagles may command the sky.

Ahead, a medieval-looking, toothy stone guardrail isolates PA 611 from the river. Across the bending, calm waterway in New Jersey, a sandy beach and Kittatinny Visitor Center add to views, while cascades, weeping outcrops, rhododendron, and wild grape embroider the west canyon wall.

Then, on the right at 4.9 miles, **Resort Point Overlook** completes this series of river vantages. It occupies the site of Kittatinny House, just one of several large resort hotels that once existed in Delaware Water Gap. Although I-80 is closely paired to the river here, the quiet passage of colorful canoes often dispels the intrusion. Licensed canoe liveries in the NRA provide rental/shuttle services.

Across PA 611 from Resort Point Overlook, a 0.25-mile foot trail ascends the west canyon slope, chasing the tumbling outlet of Lake Lenape to the **Appalachian Trail** (AT). But the AT can also be accessed by turning west off PA 611 on Mountain Road as you enter the hillside borough of Delaware Water Gap, 0.4 mile north—follow the steep residential street uphill, bearing left at the fork to reach the **AT Trailhead** in 0.2 mile.

For a short sampling of the white-blazed trail, follow Mount Minsi Fire Road uphill past ancient spread-arm oaks to reach the shore of lily-capped **Lake Lenape** in 0.1 mile. Here, some of the whitish pink blooms linger into September. Beyond the lake, you will ascend through forest. At 0.3 mile, watch for blazes to point you left onto foot trail; at 0.4 mile, claim a vista ledge. Despite the many young trees challenging the view, a jutting rock nose opens a window to the deep gouge of the Gap. The more ambitious hiker can follow the AT to Mount Minsi (2 miles); altogether, the national scenic trail lingers in the NRA for 25 miles.

If instead you remain on PA 611N, the drive descends through the attractive community of Delaware Water Gap, with its narrow streets squeezed all the more by roadside parking. Founded in the late 1700s, the town captivates with grand homes, historical inns, specialty shops, and eateries.

At the base of the hill (5.5 miles), cross over Cherry Creek and turn right at the light, leaving PA 611 via Broad Street/SR 2028. Then, remain on SR 2028 as it turns right at the **Pennsylvania Tourist Information Center** and becomes River Road. The center is a good place to stop, gain your bearings, and pick up brochures for side attractions. As US 209 carries most through-traffic out of Delaware Water Gap, River Road is left for sightseers.

Picturesque River Road then traverses the low, broad floodplain, with areas of fields and lowland woods. Upon crossing sparkling Brodhead Creek, you will discover a concession for canoes, rafts, tubes, and trail rides. Next, rhododendron-showered slopes address the route as it twists uphill to

Shawnee (8.3 miles), with its art galleries, Shawnee Playhouse, and still other canoe liveries. To stay on River Road, keep east toward the Delaware River, where a tunnel of deciduous trees and entangling grape funnels travel north.

At the NRA entrance sign at 9.2 miles is a rough gravel turnout, with a short, steep footpath descending to shore. If you choose to exit the vehicle and explore here, beware of poison ivy, nettles, and thorny rose in your eagerness to reach the river. Depue Island contributes to river views, and tiny sunfish, minnows, and bass dart through the clear water.

On the right in another 0.4 mile is rustic **Hialeah Picnic Area**, which stretches 0.5 mile along the river. Abrupt, makeshift trails also descend from its low plateau to the Delaware River. Beautiful old trees grace the well-spaced sites; spruce, maple, and beech are among the shade givers.

Where cornfields claim the floodplain, the drive affords open views of powerful Kittatinny Mountain. At 11.5 miles, you will come to the fee site of **Smithfield Beach**, with its separate canoe launch area, swimming area, changing house, and picnic tables. Turnouts along River Road allow you to let faster traffic pass or snap a photo. Midweek in fall, before the color bonanza, River Road is all but abandoned.

On the right at 14.1 miles are additional picnic tables at the site of the old **John Turn Farm**, started in 1815. Drawings and photos depict how the farm once looked. An 1875 smokehouse, a time-weary chimney and foundation, and old sugar maples are physical records of the past. Across the road sits an old lime kiln.

River Road now rolls and curves to skirt a snag-riddled and duck-weed-colored marsh; at the marsh's north end is the **NRA Headquarters**. The drive then temporarily departs the NRA, taking you past a golf course that is frequented by Canada geese. Upon meeting busy US 209, turn north to head back into the NRA, where you will soon pass **Bushkill Visitor Center** on the right. Both the headquarters and visitor center serve area travelers with print materials and information.

Next up, stay on US 209 North as Bushkill Falls Road heads west to its namesake attraction. In another couple of miles, **Bushkill Access** offers a canoe landing/launch on a sleepy river stretch; restrooms are available. Then, at 20.5 miles, a spur road heads left for primitive **Toms Creek Picnic Area**, a quiet, treed flat along an inviting stream, removed from the commotion of the river. Where US 209 passes between cultivated cornfield and grassy meadow, a fox may be seen as it slips between areas of concealment.

The next landmarks north are primitive **Eshback Boat Launch** and the west turn for **Pocono Environmental Education Center (PEEC)** at 24.4 miles. To visit this residential outdoor classroom and its public trail system, go west on Briscoe Mountain Road for 0.8 mile and bear right on Emery Road for 0.1 mile to reach the main building. Radiating out from the center are six color-coded foot trails that explore the Pocono Plateau and former honeymoon resort; they visit ponds, waterfalls, a fossil bed, mixed woods, and rocky ledges. Obtain a trail map at the center.

Without the PEEC detour, come to the Dingmans Falls turnoff at 29.1 miles. From **Dingmans Falls Visitor Center** (0.8 mile west off US 209), the popular 0.75-mile **Dingmans Falls Nature Trail** heads upstream into the hemlock mystery. Footbridges twice span Dingmans Creek for loop travel between the elegant 80-foot Silver Thread Falls on a side tributary and the 130-foot Dingmans Falls on the main creek. Upper and lower viewing decks present Dingmans Falls, an exciting multidirectional, multitiered white surge. When rain fed, billows of mist shroud the canyon; dry seasons present a quieter face.

Forgoing the Dingmans Falls turnoff, quickly reach PA 739, which leads west to **George W. Childs Picnic Area** and the three upper falls on Dingmans Creek. For a visit, go 1.1 miles west and turn left on Silver Lake Road to locate the first of the three Childs area accesses in 1.7 miles.

The 1.2-mile **Fulmer Falls Loop Trail** has five footbridges that span Dingmans Creek for loop travel and differing perspectives on the three falls: Fulmer, Factory, and Deer Leap. Fulmer Falls, the central falls, drops some 70 feet. The pyramid-shaped Factory Falls just upstream is about half as tall. Near Factory Falls, look for the stone wall ruins of an old woolen mill. The 15- to 18-foot Deer Leap Falls is at the lower end of the park, with bridges at its head and foot.

If you drove past both falls turnoffs, **Raymondskill Falls** at 34.3 miles puts forth one last bid for your attention. Turn west on SR 2009 and proceed 0.5 mile to locate a pair of parking areas on the left, each with trails descending to the falls. The upper parking area has a restroom, shelter, and information board. On the right (west) side of the shelter is a trail to the upper falls vantage; on the left side is one to the lower falls. Be careful when hiking between the sites as the terrain is steep, and the trail surface can be slippery.

Raymondskill Falls is a dramatic split-level falls fed by serial cascades. The upper falls spills at an angle, terraced and lacy, over layered rock. A large anvil-shaped ledge compresses the water at its head. From the upper falls plunge pool emerges the divided lower falls, which then spills into a remote cliff alcove. Beautiful forest crowns the scene.

From the Raymondskill Falls turnoff (34.3 miles), US 209N leads you out of the NRA, bypassing US 206 (the toll bridge to New Jersey). Near the Milford/Pike County information center, a road heads east to **Milford Beach** in 0.4 mile (follow signs). This developed, fee site sounds the last call to get wet; it has a launch and swimming area, as well as picnicking.

Factory Falls, Delaware Water Gap National Recreation Area.

By keeping to US 209N, you quickly enter Milford. This river community was founded in 1733 and captivates with a gentle yesteryear aura. Tourist shops, museums, eateries, inns, shade maples, and slate sidewalks invite visitors to park and stroll. In town, the chamber of commerce dispenses visitor information. Ask about **Upper Mill**, a nineteenth-century waterwheel-driven grist mill that is centerpiece to a collection of shops and a fine bakery.

Near the center of town, a detour east on Broad Street (US 209N/US 6E) for a half-dozen blocks finds the neoclassical building of **The Columns** (608 Broad Street), open Wednesday, Saturday, and Sunday 1 P.M. to 4 P.M., donation suggested. This museum boasts among its collection a candle from the Mayflower, Native American artifacts, and the authenticated, blood-soaked Lincoln flag. This is the banner that cradled the president's injured head after the shooting that fateful night at Ford's Theater in 1865. It came to Milford via a local performer who was there.

If instead you proceed straight at the corner with Broad Street, you now follow US 6 West for the tour's conclusion. Go 0.4 mile and at the outskirts of Milford, veer left at the sign for **Grey Towers** to conclude the tour at the country castle of Gifford Pinchot (38.2 miles), operated by the U.S. Forest Service.

The rock castle dressed in ivy and surrounded by stately trees and sweeping lawns quickly captivates. Tours (Friday through Monday, 10 A.M.

Grey Towers, Milford.

to 4 P.M.) explain the history of the castle, its teaching purpose, and the Pinchot family. Arbors, reflecting ponds, urns, statuary, a 1734 sundial, and cast iron benches blend into the enchanted setting. About the wooded grounds, you will find tunnel views toward Milford and the Delaware River, with Kittatinny Ridge beyond. The castle was designed by Richard Morris Hunt in 1885 and built for a total cost of $19,000.

While at Grey Towers, be sure to view the outdoor dining area, with its unusual "Finger Bowl," a raised pool around which the dinner guests sat and on which the wooden service dishes were floated back and forth. Garlands of wisteria twist skyward, fashioning a winsome overhead canopy.

While Grey Towers puts a regal stamp on the tour, the river corridor definitely welcomes an encore look. Return as you came or explore the Poconos.

18

West-central Pennsylvania Amish Country Tour

From Indiana to Plumville

General description: This nostalgic 36.7-mile lasso-shaped tour explores the verdant, rolling hills north of Indiana, passing covered bridges, churchyard cemeteries, the honest images of Amish life, and the quaint village shops of Smicksburg. The drive begins under the gentle watch of Jimmy Stewart and twice tags Plumville to complete its circuit.

Special attractions: Historic Indiana; Jimmy Stewart Statue and Museum; an old-order Amish settlement; the English-run shops of Smicksburg; nineteenth-century covered bridges; a winery; walking tours, fishing, winter sports.

Location: West-central Pennsylvania.

Drive route numbers: Pennsylvania Highways 286, 954, and 210.

Travel season: Year-round.

Camping: The nearest public campground to the drive is the Armstrong County–run Milton Loop Campground on Mahoning Creek Lake (2 miles north of Dayton off PA 839). It has 52 sites (some electric), modern restrooms with showers, and a dump station.

Services: Indiana is a full-service community, with Smicksburg and Plumville offering a variety of traveler amenities.

Nearby points of interest: Yellow Creek State Park, Blue Spruce County Park, Ghost Town Trail, historic Saltsburg and Johnstown, Punxsutawney Phil, Mahoning Creek and Crooked Creek lakes, Allegheny River, Conemaugh Gap, Pittsburgh, Laurel Highlands.

 The drive

This drive begins at the wholesome, Middle America, "Frank Capra"-esque heart of Indiana, Pennsylvania—the hometown of actor Jimmy Stewart. On the lawn of the Indiana County Courthouse, a bronze statue of the actor hails the start of the tour. To the caretaker's dismay, a familiar nightly prank of local teens is to put a beer can in the statue's hand, but even this prank has an innocence of a bygone time.

From the historic downtown district, the tour twists its way through the rolling countryside of pastures, Christmas tree farms, and classic white farmhouses. The images of the tour all reinforce the spell of yesteryear:

Drive 18: West-central Pennsylvania Amish Country Tour
From Indiana to Plumville

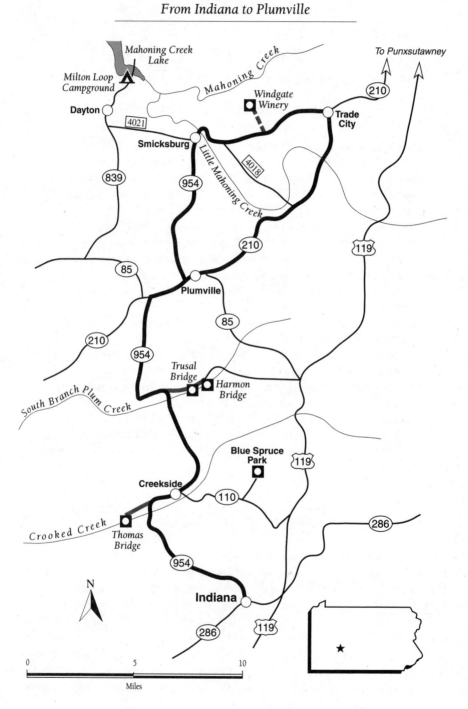

To Punxsutawney

Mahoning Creek Lake

Milton Loop Campground

Dayton

Windgate Winery

Trade City

210

Mahoning Creek

4021

Smicksburg

Little Mahoning Creek

839

954

4018

85

210

119

210

Plumville

85

954

Trusal Bridge

Harmon Bridge

South Branch Plum Creek

Blue Spruce Park

119

Creekside

110

286

Crooked Creek

Thomas Bridge

954

N

Indiana

286

119

0   5   10

Miles

lopsided covered bridges, woolly sheep nibbling grass, white-painted fences, time-faded gravestones, laundry flapping in the breeze, and the clip-clop of horse hooves and whir of buggy wheels. Country crafts and home-baked tastes complete the seduction.

Along the Amish Country Loop, which travels from Plumville to Smicksburg to Trade City, consider venturing off the main road. Perhaps you will see Amish children tending chores or be lured aside by hand-lettered signs for quilts or produce. Late summer into fall, watch for teams of workhorses as they bring in the harvest.

While on these excursions, be respectful of the Amish, their customs, and their lifestyle. Put away the camera and curb the tendency to stare. Also, remember that the Amish conduct no commerce on their Sabbath; on Sundays, bypass the doorsteps to their home enterprises. In Smicksburg and at other sites on the loop, the English-run shops are open daily; "the English" is how the Amish refer to non-Amish, English-speaking people.

Start in historic downtown Indiana, on Philadelphia Street (PA 286); a walking tour provides a closer look at the vibrant, old business district, with its quaint street lamps and brick sidewalks. Between eighth and ninth streets, you will find the **Indiana County Courthouse** and the **Jimmy Stewart Statue**, which was unveiled on the actor's 75th birthday. Across the street, a sundial marks the one-time store location of J. M. Stewart and Sons Hardware, which belonged to Jimmy Stewart's father.

On the 9th Street corner, the third floor of the Indiana Public Library holds the **James M. Stewart Museum.** Here, for a modest cost, motion picture fans can discover Hollywood and Stewart family memorabilia, view film clips, and see original movie posters. The museum is generally open Monday through Saturday 10 A.M. to 5 P.M., Sundays and holidays noon to 5 P.M. In winter, though, the museum is closed on Monday and Tuesday.

To begin the actual drive, zero your odometer at the corner of Philadelphia and ninth streets, and head north on ninth Street/PA 954 North. Beautiful, big single-family homes, some of Victorian architecture, and huge shade maples escort you from town. Reach a T-junction at 0.8 mile and turn left to remain on PA 954. This is the first of many turns this country highway will take, so be alert for junction signs.

Before long, pass Martin Road, which is indicated for **Blue Spruce Park** (it lies some 6 miles north of Indiana, near Ernest). This popular county park boasts quiet recreation on a 12-acre fish-stocked lake. The park has a rental concession for rowboats, pedalboats, and canoes and some 6 miles of trails that explore the outlying area and double as cross-country ski trails in winter. Ice skating and sledding are other popular pastimes when the snow mounts. During the winter holiday season, the park twinkles with the magic of the *It's a Wonderful Life* Festival of Lights.

Jimmy Stewart statue, Indiana.

As you remain on PA 954N, the two-lane paved road lacks shoulders or painted lines as it winds through the countryside of low, rounded, wooded hills. Although PA 954 skirts **White's Woods Nature Center,** it provides no access. Sassafras, cucumber magnolia, aspen, grape, tulip poplar, oak, maple, birch, and black cherry crowd the roster of this southern forest complex and put on a fine fall show. Country travel holds the potential for sightings of deer, raccoon, or skunk, or for hearing a hoot owl.

With the back-to-back crossings of a bridge over muddy Crooked Creek and a railroad track, you will come to a junction (5.4 miles). A left turn on State Route 4002 (indicated for Shelocta) adds a visit to a covered bridge in 1.6 miles; the scenic drive proceeds right.

Opting to look at the bridge, go 1.4 miles past cultivated fields and woods and veer left on a dirt road with low clearance as it passes under the railroad to visit **Thomas Covered Bridge.** The 1879 bridge has lattice supports and solid sides and is painted red with white trim. Today, it sits a bit cockeyed over Crooked Creek, and swallows have built a nest on a sign over the entrance.

At 85 feet long, Thomas Bridge is the longest of four remaining covered bridges in Indiana County. At one time, 50 of these structures spanned the county's waters. If your wanderlust takes you to Shelocta, you will be visiting the site of the earliest white settlement attempt in what is now Indiana County. In 1727, James Le Tort built his trading post there.

For the primary drive, though, continue north on PA 954, which now gains a dividing line but remains narrow. Go past Christmas tree farms and cornfields to enter the borough of Creekside. At 6.7 miles, meet PA 110, which heads east for a second approach to Blue Spruce County Park. An ice cream parlor near the junction may suggest a stop on hot summer days.

Keep to PA 954N. Somewhere along the twisting course, the road line again disappears, restoring the country lane appeal of the highway. At 9.9 miles, travel up and over a summit for sweeping rural vistas.

After the bridge crossing at South Branch Plum Creek comes the next covered bridges detour at 10.7 miles. Marking the corner is **Plumcreek Presbyterian,** with its white country chapel and churchyard cemetery. Several gravestones date to the 1850s, with those of the veterans specially marked. The honored dead fought in the War of 1812 or Civil War.

A detour to the right on Five Points Road/SR 4006 visits a pair of covered bridges over South Branch Plum Creek. Both are visible to the south (right) as you travel SR 4006. In 1 mile, Trusal Road leads to **Trusal Bridge,** a 35-foot span built in 1870. A half mile farther east is Donahue Road, with the 1910-built **Harmon Bridge,** named for a Civil War veteran. Both are now bypassed by their respective roads, allowing photographers to capture their images with side, front, and interior shots.

Historically, the barnlike appearance of the covered bridges made it easier to herd animals through them. Trusal (or Dice's) Covered Bridge and Harmon Covered Bridge, both show similar construction to Thomas Bridge. Vine-scaled Trusal Bridge sits along an S-bend of the creek with a woods backdrop. Harmon Bridge sits askew in an idyllic setting, with white fences, deep-grass pastures, sleek horses, and a barking farm dog.

If you forgo the bridges detour, follow PA 954N to the left at 10.7 miles. The stage for the drive unites leafy woods, Christmas tree-studded acres, and dairy, produce, sheep, and hog farms—a collage of quietude. Although turnouts are notably absent throughout the drive, the pace is relaxed.

At the T-junction at 15.8 miles, go right on the shared route of Pennsylvania Highways 954N, 85E, and 210N; the driving tour keeps to PA 954N all the way to Trade City. As the drive approaches the main part of Plumville (17 miles), turn left for PA 954N and a clockwise tour of the **Amish Country Loop.**

Terraced hills of alternating crops radiate outward from the tidy white farmhouses and classic Pennsylvania barns. On the pavement, you may notice the telltale scratches of buggy wheels. Amish buggies now share the road, so lower your speed.

Indiana County barn.

Amish buggy, Smicksburg.

The Amish homes are still lighted by kerosene and gas lamps, and each summer the families purchase huge blocks of ice to keep perishables fresh. Outside many homes are posted signs for "quilts," "pumpkins," "wagonwheels," "cabinets," and "harness repair." Boys in straw hats tend goats and sheep. Side roads beckon with detours deeper into the settlement.

Without digression, reach the borough of Smicksburg at 22.6 miles. It is an attractive, small community with its main street shrouded by sugar maples and lined by quaint shops. Just as you reach town, West Kittaning Street/SR 4021 (locally referred to as "Dayton Road"), heads west 4 miles to Dayton and more of the Amish settlement.

To get to know Smicksburg, it is best to park and stroll. The tiny **John G. Schmick Museum and Visitor Center** occupies the old post office and election hall; it is on the left as PA 954 passes through town. Inside are local artifacts, including old school records, domestic goods, and clay marbles and pipes. Smicksburg was founded in 1827 by Reverend John George Schmick. During the flood control project of 1938–1940, half of the town was swallowed by the newly raised water. Today, an ambitious plan calls for building a park and walking tour through what remains of the historic town plot. While at the museum, pick up brochures or view a video on Smicksburg shops. The museum is staffed Thursday through Monday noon to 4 P.M.

In the early 1960s, the old-order Amish moved to Smicksburg from New Wilmington. Some 230 Amish communities are scattered across the United States and Canada, but only seven are larger than the Smicksburg-Dayton settlement, which numbers more than 1,200. Each Amish settlement is divided into church districts, kept small because of the practice of home worship and the limitations of buggy travel.

The community in this area practices a stricter set of rules. Visitors will find the members of the old order cordial, but reclusive and protective. If they see your camera, they will whip the horses into a faster trot, draw shawls to their faces, and turn the children's heads away. So, grant them their privacy; do not allow your curiosity to become intrusive and disrespectful.

Shops in and around Smicksburg have a line-up of antiques, pottery, country collectibles, Amish hickory rockers, handpainted glass, handwoven linens, faceless dolls, quilts, and pillows. **Thee Village Sampler** in Smicksburg occupies an 1860s-built doctor's office and pharmacy. The charming shop complex tempts with the sweetness of fudge and honey and aromas of coffee and fresh-baked cinnamon rolls.

The many old houses now occupied by merchants enhance the shopping experience. Admire country decors with plaster walls, narrow stairs, beautiful banisters, and a maze of nooks and side rooms. A festival held the first weekend in October swells the Smicksburg crowds. Then music fills the air, and wind gusts release a winsome flurry of colored leaves.

To resume the drive, follow PA 954N toward Trade City, crossing the bridge over Little Mahoning Creek—a broad, clear waterway, shining up from a wooded bottomland. Ascend from the drainage and pass **Mahoning Cheese**, open Monday through Saturday. Just beyond it at 25.4 miles, a detour left on graveled Hemlock Acres Road leads to a natural complement— **Windgate Vineyard and Winery** (go 2 miles and turn right).

This family-operated winery offers tours and tastings; the warm aroma of wine permeates a visit. An eight-station self-guided tour also introduces the process, with windows and balconies overlooking the winemaking stages from grape to bottle. The award-winning wines are produced from French hybrid grapes grown in the immediate hills.

In the seventeenth century, William Penn fostered the first wineries in Pennsylvania, but the native grapes were undrinkable and European grapes failed to grow. Not until the nineteenth century did the Harmonists achieve success using a hybrid grape; their success ushered in the present wineries. Windgate Winery is open daily (except holidays) noon to 5 P.M.

Without this stop, proceed north on PA 954, exploring the rumpled terrain of wooded drainages and cultivated hilltops. Apples, crafts, bulk foods, and boots are the biddings of the road. At 28.3 miles, reach Trade City and follow PA 210 South.

Cottage industry signs, Indiana County.

Cross Little Mahoning Creek a second time. Autumn's color enhances the textured terrain. At 32.2 miles, McCormick Road/SR 4018 heads west, doubling back to Smicksburg; it bypasses **McCormick Castle** in 0.8 mile. This stone residence incorporates a turret-like structure that suggests the name. It was the 1800s home of John McCormick, inventor of the water turbine, and today is a private residence.

To complete the Amish Country Loop, keep to PA 210S at 32.2 miles. In about a mile, **Smicksburg Mercantile** makes for a fun family stop. Crowding its aisles are barrels, baskets, and bins loaded with bulk foods and old-fashioned candies. Hillbilly novelties may coax forth a laugh or an expenditure of coin. Old-fashioned lemonade or a hand-dipped cone may complete a visit.

Amish images then sign off the tour. Return to Plumville and PA 85 at 36.7 miles; the shops of Plumville sound one last call to purchase a hickory rocker or handwoven basket. Side roads still summon the curious.

19

Huntingdon County Heritage Trail

North-south figure-eight tour through Huntingdon

General description: This 118-mile figure-eight tour is part of the Path of Progress Heritage Trail, which celebrates the industrial and cultural contribution of the Alleghenies in the building of the nation. The tour can be shortened into its two loop components: the 53.8-mile North Loop or the 64.2-mile South Loop. Side excursions increase the distance.

Special attractions: Historic Huntingdon; Greenwood Furnace, Whipple Dam, and Trough Creek state parks; Alan Seeger Natural Area; Stone Valley Recreation Area; Raystown Lake; two commercial caverns; Trolley Museum and East Broad Top excursion train; rhododendron blooms; boating, fishing, parasailing, jet skiing, hiking, picnicking.

Location: South-central Pennsylvania.

Drive route numbers: U.S. Highways 22 and 522; Pennsylvania Highways 26, 45, 453, and 994.

Travel season: Year-round.

Camping: On the North Loop, Greenwood Furnace State Park (on Pennsylvania Highway 305 5 miles east of McAlevy's Fort) has 51 family sites with modern restrooms. On the South Loop, Raystown Lake (a U.S. Army Corps of Engineers project) has 170 modern campsites (some electric) at its Seven Points Recreation Area and 62 primitive sites at its Susquehannock Campground. For both, turn east on SR 3011 at Hesston and follow signs. Trough Creek State Park (on the east side of Raystown Lake off SR 3031) has 32 electric sites with rustic restrooms and rents out Trough Creek Lodge.

Services: Huntingdon offers full services; various traveler services are available at smaller communities on the tour.

Nearby points of interest: Mid State Trail, Railroad Memorial Museum (Altoona); The Pennsylvania State University and other offerings at State College; Pennsylvania Military Museum and Boal Mansion and Museum (Boalsburg); Broad Top Area Coal Miners Museum (Robertsdale); Canoe Creek and Warriors Path state parks.

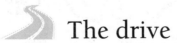 The drive

For the most part, this drive adheres to the official Heritage Trail for Huntingdon County, with a slight deviation at the southwestern part of the South Loop. This was done to provide a cleaner approach to the chosen

Drive 19: Huntingdon County Heritage Trail

North-south figure-eight tour through Huntingdon

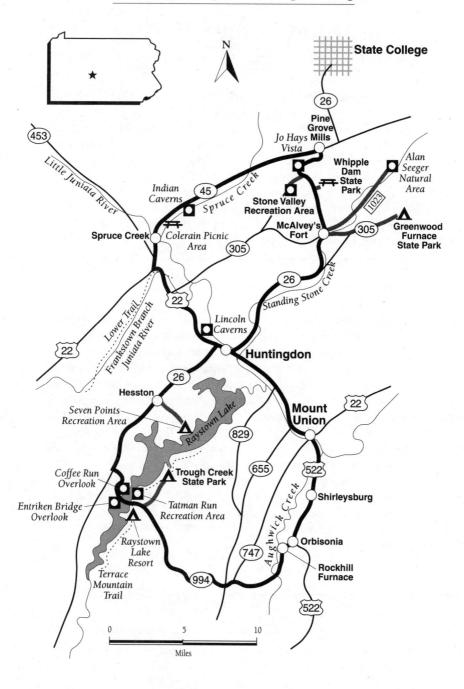

attractions, but otherwise it is a good idea to keep an unfolded copy of the Huntingdon County Heritage Guide beside you on the car seat. The brochure provides a quick consultation and introduces other sites and side features that may interest you. Copies are available from the Raystown Country Visitors Bureau.

At the eastern edge of the Allegheny Front, the drive rounds up a pleasant blend of images, with valley drainages, farmscapes, woods, and mountainous travel. On the North Loop, the history of the iron industry, fine nature parks, and the commercial caves shape discovery. Dominating the start of the South Loop is 28-mile-long Raystown Lake, with its full-scale recreation. Quiet hills, old-time trolleys, a steam engine, and a museum of antique cars wrap up the tour.

On PA 26, start the full figure-eight tour or **North Loop Drive** at the **Huntingdon County Courthouse** at Second and Penn streets in downtown Huntingdon. The nineteenth-century core of town has been recognized as a National Register Historic District. Plaques indicate noteworthy structures; pick up a walking tour brochure at the courthouse.

In 1767, Huntingdon was founded at what had been known as "Standing Stone," so called for a monolith erected by Native Americans at the Stone Creek and Juniata River confluence. The downtown district reflects the growth and development that took place during the height of the region's transportation era.

Follow PA 26 north out of town to parallel Standing Stone Creek upstream. Travel is between cornfields and wildflower-meadow slopes, with country homes and vine-covered barns. Pennsylvania history signs may add to your learning. Stone Creek Ridge looms to the east; later you will spy Warrior Ridge to the west as the route crisscrosses Standing Stone Creek.

At 12.1 miles, State Route 1019 offers a scenic 7.3-mile spur to Greenwood Furnace State Park, but postpone your visit until the charming village of McAlvey's Fort (16.3 miles). There, PA 305 East offers a 5-mile direct approach to the park. Opposite the town's 1842 general store is a monument relating the history of McAlvey's Fort as a defense post against the Indians in the late 1700s.

Greenwood Furnace State Park unfolds more of the region's past and suggests another self-guided walking tour. Cradled within the park's wooded slopes is a remnant of a nineteenth-century iron operation and company town—another National Register Historic District. Rustic information cupboards at the stops on the self-guided walk introduce the site, structure, or feature.

Be sure to peer in the cupboard at the ranger station to view a map depicting how the iron-making village appeared at its peak, with more than 100 structures. The map was drawn, as remembered, by a former resident and provides a strong sense of place. At the restored furnace stack, diagrams detail the blast operation that consumed 1 acre of trees per day.

The artifacts at the visitor center introduce the people and the day-to-day life at Greenwood Furnace (1834–1904). Teachers' records, an 1897 fabricated newspaper story (and follow-up retraction) about a disaster at the furnace, wage sheets, tools, and old photographs bring the village to life. Picnicking, the trails to Greenwood Tower and Rothrock State Forest, and a small lake further vie for time.

The primary Heritage Trail, however, proceeds north on PA 26 past PA 305E, coming to the next side-trip option in 0.3 mile. Here, **Alan Seeger Natural Area** entices you away from the route with its old-growth grove of pine, hemlock, and hardwoods and its captivating jungle of towering rhododendron that blooms in early July. Some of the trees are 500 years old. The natural area lies 6.2 miles off the route, along Standing Stone Creek. Reach it by following twisting SR 1023/Stone Creek Road. Watch for the initial right turn at 0.7 mile; afterward, let the creek and paved road be your guides. Rustic picnic pavilions and the 0.6-mile Alan Seeger Trail, which can be extended another 2 miles to Greenwood Tower, present the area.

If you forgo this trip as well, PA 26 continues north with blue, pink, yellow, and white wildflowers donning its shoulders. Cardinal flowers dot the drainage. Travel is rolling to the Whipple Dam Road at 20.2 miles. This road leads 1 mile to **Whipple Dam State Park**, with its 22-acre lake being

Greenwood Furnace, Greenwood Furnace State Park.

Greenwood Lake dam, Greenwood Furnace State Park.

the centerpiece to the day-use recreation. Swimming, quiet boating, and picnicking are pastimes of summer; in winter, lace on your ice skates or bring a Thermos bottle and sink your fishing line into the chilly depths. The manmade lake captures the water of Laurel Run, shows mats of lily pads, and has shoreline accents of rhododendron.

Past the park turnoff, look for the Heritage Trail to enter a woods passage. At the onset of autumn, the twining Virginia creeper that wraps up the tree trunks turns red. Where PA 26 hooks right at 21.7 miles, Charter Oak Road heads left 1.6 miles for **Stone Valley Recreation Area and Shaver's Creek Environmental Center**: a lake, a forest, and an interpretive center all open to the public and operated by The Pennsylvania State University. A 25-mile network of blazed trails explores the area; purchase maps at the park office or equipment rental.

By parking at the broad gravel turnout at the junction with Charter Oak Road and by carefully crossing PA 26, you will discover the **Monroe Furnace**. Unrestored, it still retains much of its integrity, although plants are starting to broaden the gaps in the stone and mortar. Bits of charcoal and red brick litter the site. Ironically, or perhaps appropriately, woods that were once consumed by the furnace are now swallowing its legacy. Watch out for poison ivy when exploring.

With the hairpin turn to the right at 21.7 miles, PA 26 climbs Tussey Mountain; expect a fairly steep pull to the top. Gum, maple, oak, beech, birch, and hemlock fashion the wooded aisle. In 2 miles, reach **Jo Hays Vista** for an overlook of the Spruce Creek and Nittany valleys, and State College. The multihued green and gold fields fashion an engaging valley quilt. Look for the Mid State Trail, which crosses PA 26 near the overlook. A winding descent follows.

In Pine Grove Mills, the Heritage Trail turns west (left) on PA 45, traversing Spruce Creek Valley at the western foot of Tussey Mountain. Fields and pastures open the terrain for broad views, and the low ridges to the west disappear in the blue haze. An extensive **Penn State Research Farm** now borders several miles of the tour. At dusk, the fireflies lift from the field to put on a dazzling light show. Grand, old stone houses, huge barns, and country chapels add to the rural storybook. You will glimpse Spruce Creek at 33.8 miles, as you pass the stone and white-shuttered Spruce Creek Church (1858).

At 37.3 miles, bear left to remain on PA 45W and enter the village of Franklinville with **Indian Caverns** on the left. (Individuals driving taller vehicles and who do not plan a caverns visit should instead follow the truck route at 37.3 miles to PA 453.) On the guided, mile-long underground tour, visitors view Indian Caverns' natural beauty and learn of Indian history.

The primary drive continues from Franklinville on PA 45W, pursuing Spruce Creek and pinching toward the base of Tussey Mountain. At 40.4 miles, **Colerain Picnic Area** welcomes with its shelters and individual picnic sites. At the village of Spruce Creek, you will reach the Little Juniata River confluence. Briefly follow the river before coming to a tunnel, clearance 8 feet 2 inches, and climbing out of the drainage to meet and follow south PA 453.

In just 0.7 mile, US 22 West takes the baton for a fast return to Huntingdon. In less than 1 mile, SR 4014 heads left 0.3 mile to the upper trailhead for **The Lower Trail**—a fine family rail trail for hiking or cycling that hugs 11 miles of the Frankstown Branch Juniata River.

Faster road speeds now blur the terrain of cultivated crops and treed ridges as you pass from rural to urban travel. On the left at 51.7 miles is **Lincoln Caverns**, which were discovered during the highway's construction in 1930. Guided tours, a gift shop, and picnic area may lure you away from the Heritage Trail.

At the outskirts of Huntingdon at 53.8 miles, meet PA 26 and go south for the **South Loop Drive**, north to conclude the North Loop Drive back in town. The South Loop passes through rural-residential areas. As it departs McConnellstown at 57.2 miles, you return to rolling farm country.

At 60.3 miles, a left turn on SR 3011 through Hesston leads 5.5 miles to **Raystown Lake**, **Seven Points Marina**, and the **Corps of Engineers**

recreation areas. Raystown Lake fills the thin canyon between Allegrippis Ridge (the west ridge) and Terrace Mountain to form a long watery playground. Boat launches, the marina, a beach, picnic areas, campgrounds, and trails urge you to abandon the drive and maybe even get wet. While at the marina, you can make arrangements for boat tours, boat and jet ski rentals, or a parasail. Eagles and shore birds likewise gravitate to the open water.

Without the marina detour, pursue PA 26 south for a straightforward rolling tour. Flash past barns, silos, fields, and woods. Perhaps a hawk on a wire will cause you to lean forward for a better look; deer may sometimes be spied in the field. Less-developed boat accesses lie east off the drive.

At the junction with PA 994 at 68.5 miles, turn left (east) for this edited version of the Heritage Trail. A pair of vistas precede Entriken Bridge, which spans Raystown Lake. On the left at 71.2 miles, **Coffee Run Overlook** extends a look at the mouth of Coffee Run and the ridge-framed reservoir. **Entriken Bridge Overlook**—the better of the two views—is on the right at 71.7 miles. It overlooks the bridge, with north and south views of the open waterway and impressive ridge canyon.

Soon after, pass the turnoffs for **Raystown Lake Resort**, which also books lake tours, and **Tatman Run Recreation Area**, which offers swimming and boating. Both areas have access to the **Terrace Mountain Trail**, which rolls across the lake's eastern ridge, slope, and shore for 18 miles.

Hardwood forest, Terrace Mountain Trail.

At 73.7 miles, a left turn on SR 3031 leads to **Trough Creek State Park**; find the headquarters and information in 1.6 miles. Here, too, the road forks. Go left for the campground, picnic areas, Rainbow Falls, Balanced Rock, and the Ice Mine; go right for Paradise Furnace (1830–1867), Trough Creek Lodge (the two-story stone mansion of the iron master, now open for travelers to rent), and the upper trailhead for the Terrace Mountain Trail. Without a boat launch, this park offers quiet, off-the-beaten-path lake recreation on the Trough Creek arm of the reservoir. Red rock cliffs, ledges, rhododendron, mixed forest, and tight hollows weave the tranquil backdrop.

Bypassing SR 3031, the Heritage Trail follows PA 994 east for a bouncing, roller coaster hill-and-dale journey. Woods and rural images settle you back in your seat. As the tour rolls up Rays Hill at 81.9 miles, **State Game Lands 121** nudges the route. On the descent, slow your speed for a few hairpin turns, tag the valley floor, and begin mounting Sideling Hill. At the junction with PA 655, or with PA 747 farther east, a turn north offers a quieter, shorter alternative return to Huntingdon. But for this tour, in each case, stay PA 994E to view more of the designated Heritage Trail. Small communities with services dot the route.

On summer weekends, congestion welcomes you to the pretty pastel-painted borough of Rockhill Furnace (95.5 miles). As PA 994 takes a right turn in town, look for the bookend attractions of the **Trolley Museum** and the **Orbisonia Train Station** for **East Broad Top**—a black-smoke-puffing steam excursion train. The narrow-gauge railroad is a National Registered Landmark. At the postcard-pretty station, visitors can purchase tickets for a 5-mile, one-hour train ride or buy a ticket for all day.

At the Trolley Museum, you can ride any of 2 dozen old-time streetcars. The trolley ride covers 1.2 miles, with cars running every 20 minutes. Tickets are good for all day. With different cars being rotated into service, you can ride several of the historic cars.

The Trolley Museum consists of a number of outbuildings, with a miscellany of streetcars about the grounds and in the repair shop. The museum exists largely due to its committed, energetic staff of volunteers; among this stable of knowledgeable help are many current, retired, and ex-railroaders. They do an amazing job with acquisition, authentic restorations, and storytelling. The paired attractions are open weekends Memorial Day through October between 11 A.M. and 4 P.M.

The Heritage Trail then resumes along PA 994E, quickly meeting US 522. For the loop, turn north on US 522 to pass through Rockhill's twin community of Orbisonia and afterward the rural countryside. East Broad Top may make an appearance on the narrow-gauge tracks that mirror the highway. Elsewhere, painted ads adorn the sides of barns.

At 99.2 miles, reach Shirleysburg, a frontier post during the French and Indian War. The drive then traverses a pass and crosses Aughwick Creek

East Broad Top steam excursion train, Orbisonia.

to the next rural valley. Along Aughwick Creek, the drive journeys past woods, pastures, a sawmill, and quarry. Later, the tour graduates to urban images, with food chains, traffic signals, and congestion at the tired, blue-collar community of Mount Union.

During its heyday, Mount Union was known as the "Silica Brick Capital of the World." Silica bricks could withstand extremely hot temperatures and were essential for steel furnace linings and coke ovens. When demand died, the community struggled and has yet to find its vitality.

Next up, meet US 22 at 106.8 miles and follow it west to conclude the figure-eight tour and South Loop Drive. Ahead, you will travel **Jack's Narrows**, a natural pass cut through Jack's Mountain by the Juniata River; the river flows below to the west. From a gravel turnout on the right, 1,000 stone steps climb to the top of Jack's Mountain, where the ganister rock used for silica bricks was quarried. Twice daily, the local labor force would pace off these stairs, passing to and from work.

Remain on US 22 for a fast track the entire way back to Huntingdon. There, meet PA 26 and follow it north to close the loop in the historical district at Second and Penn streets (118 miles). The **Swigart Antique Auto Museum** alone may draw you aside on this US 22 leg; it is open daily 9 A.M. to 5 P.M., Memorial Day through October.

20

Carlisle-Tuscarora
State Forest Auto Tour

From Carlisle to the forest loop west out of Alinda

General description: This relaxing, 76-mile backroads tour travels quiet highways and the gravel forest roads of Tuscarora State Forest, incorporating the forest's own 26-mile designated auto tour; brochures for the forest tour are available at the headquarters west of New Germantown. The forest roads are maintained for passenger vehicles, but expect some rough spots, narrowness, and dust.

Special attractions: Vistas; covered bridges; old mills; virgin forest; pioneer cemeteries; historic Carlisle; Big Spring and Fowler Hollow state parks; Hemlocks and Frank E. Masland natural areas; hiking, fishing, picnicking, antique shopping.

Location: South-central Pennsylvania.

Drive route numbers: Pennsylvania Highways 74, 274, 233, and 850; Forest Roads: Hemlock, Upper Buck Ridge, Union Hollow, Second Narrows, and Laurel Run.

Travel season: Spring through fall for full tour. Year-round for state highway sections.

Camping: Fowler Hollow State Park (off Upper Buck Ridge or Union Hollow roads) has 18 rustic campsites, with water, pit toilets, and a dump station.

Services: Carlisle has a complete line-up of traveler services; Loysville offers basic services.

Nearby points of interest: Cowans Gap, Colonel Denning, Little Buffalo, Kings Gap, Pine Grove Furnace, and Caledonia state parks; Gettysburg National Military Park; Harrisburg-Hershey area historical attractions and amusement parks; Penn National Race Course (Grantville); Indian Echo Caverns (Hummelstown).

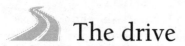 The drive

This drive through the Appalachian Mountain Region starts in the restored historical downtown district of Carlisle, with its fresh-scrubbed, red-brick look of yesteryear. The tour then swings north and west, managing to visit a handful of Perry County's 14 covered bridges and 25 old mills. Halfway into

Drive 20: Carlisle-Tuscarora State Forest Auto Tour
From Carlisle to the forest loop west out of Alinda

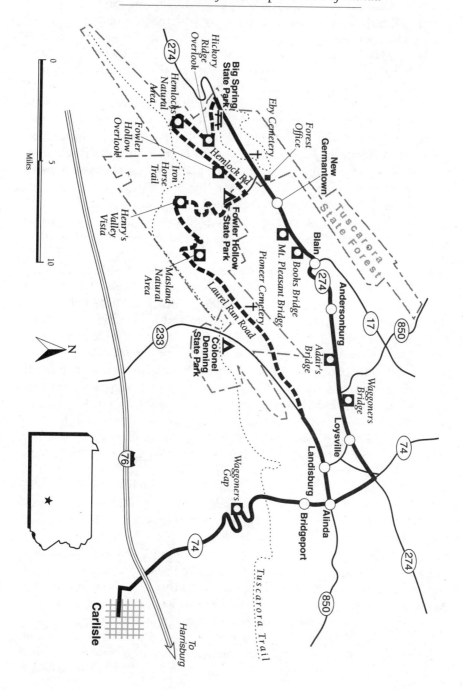

the drive, the Tuscarora State Forest Auto Tour plots your itinerary; its tour brochure points out a dozen noteworthy sites within the forest.

On the forest auto tour, you will revisit the logging railroad days and abandoned mill/tannery towns, and discover firsthand a remote ravine of old-growth trees, with hemlocks 300 to 500 years old. Sweeping forest-valley views, sparkling waterways, and laurel-clad rises complete the package. From the forest boundary, the drive then returns through rural south-central Pennsylvania to tie up the loop at Alinda.

In Carlisle, start at the **Old Courthouse**, at the southwest corner of the intersection of Hanover and High streets. It is worth parking and leaving the vehicle for a closer look at this 1846-built Georgian-style courthouse. One of the reddish sandstone entry columns bears a cannonball scar from the Civil War; on July 1, 1863, it was fired upon by Confederate troops on their way to Gettysburg.

At the northeast corner of the courthouse grounds, a directory and town map identify 42 historic sites that suggest a walking tour. It is said that George Washington worshiped at the First Presbyterian Church that dates to 1757 and sits on the opposite side of High Street. Along the walk, window displays at curio and antique shops may draw you inside.

If military history piques your interest, Carlisle is also home to the U.S. **Army War College**, where the Military History Institute holds thousands of war documents and military memorabilia, including items from General Omar Bradley. Famed athlete Jim Thorpe played football at the Indian School at Carlisle Barracks (now the U.S. Army War College).

Follow High Street/PA 74 North through the historic district past the attractive campus of Dickinson College. A flow of students passing between classes may delay travel, but you can read the Pennsylvania history marker for Forbes Road while you wait. At 0.4 mile, turn north on College Street and follow the signed route for PA 74N out of town. After crossing under Interstate 76, the tour becomes rural, traversing rolling farm country in the shadow of Blue Mountain.

By 6.3 miles, PA 74N begins to ascend the imposing barrier of Blue Mountain. Switchbacks allow for leisurely enjoyment of the southern forest of oak, tulip poplar, hickory, birch, maple, and sassafras. A few rock outcrops open the cathedral.

At 8.6 miles, reach **Waggoners Gap** (elevation 1,476 feet) for a southern view spanning the Cumberland Valley. The 180-degree vista pans across patchwork fields, hedgerows, silos, barns, and the drop-away flank of Blue Mountain. At the southern end of the valley rises a bookend ridge in Michaux State Forest. Vultures sometimes share or contribute to the view.

From the gap, you will then descend through the private trust lands of **Florence Jones Reineman Wildlife Sanctuary**. The forest breach of the road corridor extends views north. To the right on Polecat Road (10.9 miles) is

Old Courthouse, Carlisle.

an access to the blue-blazed **Tuscarora Trail**, a long-distance Appalachian Trail bypass and prized trail in its own right.

With an uphill roll, the drive tags the village of Lebo—a quiet speck on the map. Undulating travel through fields and woods follows. On the right in Bridgeport, view the **H. R. Wentzel and Sons Mill**. As you pass by, roll down your windows to hear the sounds of grinding and breathe the fresh grain.

Originally built by John Waggoner and taken over and operated by the Wentzel family for much of the last century, the creekside mill still produces and sells "Ivory" flour and cornmeal. The complex consists of the stone mill, outbuildings on stilts, grain elevators, and a small store.

At 14.7 miles, you will arrive at the village of Alinda and begin the tour's western loop. Remain on PA 74N for counterclockwise travel; PA 850 holds the loop's return. Tractors may share the road as the drive weaves through farmland and rolls over rises to meet PA 274 at 17.5 miles. Turn west on PA 274 to continue the loop. Tiny villages slow travel speeds, with country stores luring you aside with ice cream and cold sodas.

Just past Loysville, PA 274 dips to a drainage and the first covered bridge. Look for it on your right at 21.6 miles. There is a place to park at the gravel entrance to the bridge; avoid private property. The classic, red-painted **Waggoners Bridge** (open to pedestrians) sits on an abandoned segment of PA 274. It was built after the 1889 flood and spans Bixler Run.

Inside the bridge are uneven floorboards. Broadcast across the support beams are faded advertisements for "boots," "hats," and "clothier." From the west end of the bridge, overlook what remains of an old stone canal and upstream dam, clues to the nearby **Wagonner Mill**. This stone mill was built by Frederick Briner in the early 1800s to replace a 1762 mill that was built of logs. Waggoner, who later purchased the waterpowered mill, lends it his name.

Shermans Creek, flowing to the highway's south, structures the ensuing miles of travel. Side trips to this creek find the next four covered bridges. In the village of Cisna Run, a 0.4-mile detour south on State Route 3008 finds **Adair's Bridge**. Built in 1864 and rebuilt in 1919, it spans 150 feet across Shermans Creek; a neighboring dairy farm scents the air and adds a pastoral mood. If you park, be sure the road shoulder is stable.

If you remain westbound on PA 274, rural images follow, and the land rises in swells. Before long, the general store at Andersonburg causes heads to turn with its exterior collage of old-time advertisements. West of Blain comes the next bridge detour, at 34.6 miles, a left turn on SR 3003 leads to **Books Bridge** in 0.25 mile. This 1884 span shows signs of disuse, although an owl sometimes takes roost in its rafters. Forest frames the setting, with big sycamores along Shermans Creek.

Mellon estate in Westmoreland County, Pennsylvania (Drive 25).

Sugar Maple in Kettle Creek State Park (Drives 11 and 12).

Canoeing along the Clarion Wild and Scenic River (Drive 8).

A Great Blue Heron in Presque Isle State Park (Drive 1).

An Amish farmer at work in Lancaster County (Drives 18 and 29).

One of many well-kept dairy barns along U.S. 6 in Bradford County (Drive 5).

A bountiful squash harvest in Clinton County (Drive 13).

A hex barn in Berks County (Drive 21).

*On the edge in the
Shohola Gorge
Game Lands
(Drive 17).*

*East Broad Top
Railroad in
Huntingdon County
(Drive 19).*

Mountain laurel blooms in the Allegheny National Forest in late May to mid-July (Drives 3, 4, 5, 8, 9, and 26).

Bear Run in the Bear Run Preserve (Drive 25).

Washington's Headquarters at Valley Forge (Drive 30).

Artillery Park at Valley Forge (Drive 30).

Dairy, Perry County.

On PA 274, barely another mile rolls by before the next bridge detour at Mount Pleasant. The **Mt. Pleasant Bridge** lies 0.25 mile south on Mount Pleasant Road and spans 77 feet across Shermans Creek. Streamers of poison ivy and Virginia creeper adorn its red and white facade.

At 37.3 miles, the final covered bridge is found 0.1 mile south on Lower Buck Ridge Road as you enter New Germantown. The 1891 **New Germantown Bridge** is still active. The stone-and-mortar rails of its access piers (entry ramps) are part of its charm.

Without taking this series of bridge detours, you will come to the cedar-log office for the **Tuscarora State Forest District** at 38.4 miles (open weekdays 8 A.M. to 4 P.M.). Be sure to stop for a copy of the official auto tour brochure and Tuscarora State Forest map; the auto tour conducts the next 26 miles of travel.

Within the next mile, pass a Virginia pine seed orchard, spruce plantations, and the eastern trailhead for the **Iron Horse Trail**. This hiking trail travels 10 miles through the forest and along Conococheague Mountain, often following the grades of old logging railroads.

Eby Cemetery is just ahead on the right. Edged by a rustic rail fence and shaded by a multitrunk white pine, the cemetery houses stones dating back to at least 1855. Many of the dead were veterans. On this lightly traveled section of highway, squirrels cross the road in devil-may-care fashion.

At 43.1 miles, you may view the actual spring that gives **Big Spring State Park** its name and feeds Shermans Creek. A left turn into the park then finds nearly 100 picnic tables and five rustic picnic shelters, which suggest a leisurely stop and snack. The park's leafy woods hold little clue that the area was harvested in the 1800s to supply the needs of tanneries, charcoal furnaces, and barrel works.

For the drive alone, bypass the park entrance to turn left on rock-studded, dirt Hemlock Road in another 0.1 mile. In a matter of feet, a trailhead on the left serves both the Tunnel and Iron Horse trails. The 1-mile loop of the **Tunnel Trail** begins on the opposite side of the road from the trailhead and contours the wooded hillside to the gaping darkness of an 1890s unfinished attempt to burrow through Conococheague Mountain to Franklin County. Resistant flint and slow-coming pay brought about the project's demise.

Showings of laurel add to eastbound travel; go slow on this bumpy road. Travel along Hemlock Road is the roughest part of the auto tour, but added surface material should help ease the going. Taking the curve at 44.9 miles, you will reach **Hickory Ridge Overlook**, but be careful when pulling aside as visibility is restricted. The outpost offers an eastern vantage, looking across the valley traveled by PA 274 and framed by Conococheague Mountain. In autumn, golden hues dress the foreground ridges.

The auto tour then parallels the old-growth hollow of 120-acre **Hemlocks Natural Area**, before reaching the primary trailhead at 47.2 miles. A monument and seasonally stocked map box are at the trailhead; 3 miles of foot trail explore the wild character of this National Natural Landmark. Discover eastern hemlocks and white pines that shoot 100 feet skyward and boast diameters in excess of 4 feet. The foot-tall cascades of perky Patterson Run and bountiful mountain laurel of the Rim Trail enhance the acquaintance. As these ancient woods hold mystery and inspire reverence, tread softly.

Following Hemlock Road away from the trailhead, again pass a piece of the 220-mile-long Tuscarora Trail. Along the ridge, laurel becomes more abundant. Look for its bloom in late May and early June. As the road traces the natural decline of the ridge, the avenue grows narrow with a few more bumps. The gum and maple lend accents of autumn red; the birch, oak, and tulip poplar explore shades of yellow.

On the right at 50.2 miles is **Fowler Hollow Overlook**. Sandwiched below, between the ridge of travel and Amberson Ridge to the south, is Fowler Hollow. Behind Amberson Ridge is the First Narrows drainage and a distant Sherman Mountain. A few snags rise up at the edge of the view. Woodchucks and deer may be spied from the vehicle; the deeper woods seclude bear and bobcat.

Hiker bridge, Hemlocks Natural Area—Tuscarora State Forest.

The steady descent resumes, passing the **Alfarata Trail**, which leads 1 mile to Fowler Hollow; keep to the auto tour to reach the state park by road. At 52.3 miles, turn right on Upper Buck Ridge Road to find entry to **Fowler Hollow State Park** in 0.6 mile. The park has a picnic area, small campground, hiker and horse trails, and nearby cross-country skiing. A few attractive old stone fireplaces give the picnic area rustic charm. In the 1800s, a sawmill operated here.

If you skip the park visit, proceed east on paved Union Hollow Road toward Landisburg for a meandering ascent. At the crossroads at 54 miles, bear right on gravel Second Narrows Road to continue the tour. Just ahead, you will find the former site of the **Big Spring Civilian Conservation Corps Camp** (1933–1941) and present-day **Showaker Ranger Station**. A rustic corral is nearby but no longer usable for horses.

Beyond the ranger station, the roller coaster drive descends to Shaeffer Run, before turning left at 54.9 miles on Laurel Run Road for the ascent of Sherman Mountain. You will remain on Laurel Run Road for the remainder of the state forest sojourn.

Where the road next descends, watch for **Henry's Valley Vista** on the left. It overlooks the treed expanse of Frank E. Masland Natural Area and the Laurel Run headwaters. The vital community of Pandemonium once occupied this area, now forgotten but for a cemetery passed later on in the tour. It is difficult to believe that more than 100 families once resided in this now silent woods.

At 57.1 miles, the drive bears left to remain on Laurel Run Road. It now pursues the Laurel Run drainage on a meandering downstream course. In a couple of miles, cross North Branch Laurel Run to find a primitive access to **Frank E. Masland Natural Area**, named for an active conservationist, whose reach extended beyond the state.

At the natural area, a rich, earthy smell permeates the deep woods of old-growth and mature second-growth hemlocks. A surprise discovery may include a turtle ambling over a rock in the clear-flowing North Branch. In 1850, a sawmill operated at this site; among the few remaining clues is a rusting cable wrapped around a creekside birch. Over time, the growth of the birch has incorporated part of the cable into the wood.

The route next conquers Middle Ridge and passes more forest trails. Follow the signs for Landisburg, crossing the South Branch and later the main stem of Laurel Run. A full forest cathedral laces over the road, then is replaced by hemlocks as the road ascends.

At 64.7 miles, a spur veers left to **Pioneer Cemetery**; you may choose to walk rather than drive this 0.1 mile to the cemetery. This was the graveyard for the town of Pandemonium (1787–1912). The oldest legible headstone dates to 1855; time has likely erased or claimed older markers. If you wander among the tablets, you will likely discover the graves of many children and Civil War veterans.

The cemetery signals the last interpretive station on the Tuscarora State Forest Auto Tour; proceed east following signs toward Landisburg to wrap up the journey. You will rediscover Blue Mountain as you leave the state forest on paved road; ahead stretches more roller coaster travel. At 71.3 miles, meet and follow PA 233 north into Landisburg. There, take PA 850 east to end back at Alinda. Valley landscapes sign off the excursion.

21

Hex Highway–Hawk Mountain Tour

From Fogelsville through Lenhartsville to
Bethel swinging northeast to Hawk Mountain
and then back to Lenhartsville

General description: This 84-mile drive journeys past a remarkable line-up of picturesque stone and frame Pennsylvania bank barns adorned in hex signs—the colorful Pennsylvania Dutch folk art that brings good fortune. Rounding out the tour are rural images, historic churches, quiet villages, and a stop at one of North America's best hawk-watch outposts: Hawk Mountain Wildlife Sanctuary. Side spurs uncover more of the barn art; the longest side excursion travels 18.4 miles.

Special attractions: Colorful hex signs; covered bridges; The Rodale Experimental Farm; Hawk Mountain Wildlife Sanctuary; Roadside America (miniatures collection); hiking, birding, picnicking, shopping, Pennsylvania Dutch dining.

Location: Southeast Pennsylvania.

Drive route numbers: Old Route 22 (Hex Highway); Pennsylvania Highways 100, 501, 895, and 143; and Hawk Mountain Road.

Travel season: Year-round.

Camping: Private campgrounds out of Krumsville, Lenhartsville, Shartlesville, and off PA 895 serve travelers.

Services: Shartlesville, Hamburg, and Bethel have full services; basic services can be found at the smaller villages and at the Interstate 78 exits just off the drive.

Nearby points of interest: Crystal Cave (between Lenhartsville and Kutztown); Pennsylvania Dutch Folk Culture Society Heritage Center, Penn-Dutch Rail Excursion, and the Pennsylvania German Festival (Kutztown); WK&S Railroad (Kempton); Trexler Lehigh County Game Preserve (Schnecksville).

 The drive

Traveling mainly through northern Berks County, this cultural-theme drive explores the Pennsylvania Dutch country of southeast Pennsylvania between the Delaware and Susquehanna rivers. Where it migrates north, the tour rolls over and back up Blue Mountain to visit Hawk Mountain Wildlife

Drive 21: Hex Highway—Hawk Mountain Tour

From Fogelsville through Lenhartsville to Bethel swinging northeast to Hawk Mountain and then back to Lenhartsville

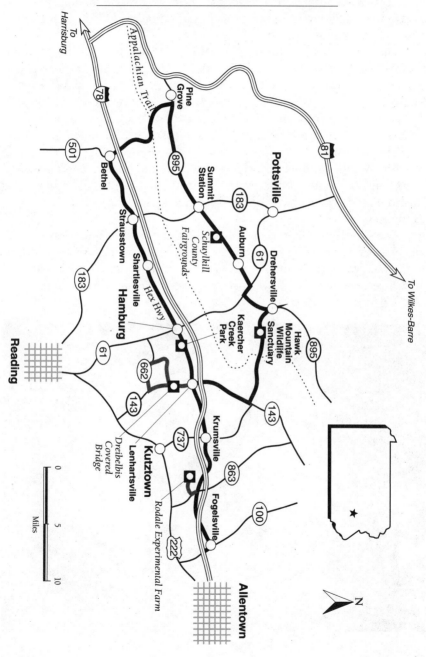

Sanctuary, which hosts an impressive fall hawk watch. Other sanctuary boasts include a "river of rocks," the legacy of a gravity-run railroad, mountain laurel and rhododendron blooms, vistas, and a fine hiking trail network that accesses the Appalachian National Scenic Trail. The sanctuary is wild enough to engage a grub-seeking black bear on occasion, and civil enough to have a small museum and gallery.

The adorned barns, which suggest this tour, belong to the "fancy" Pennsylvania Dutch versus the Amish and Mennonites, who are "plain" people. Barn art is a young form of expression. Prior to the 1830s, paint was too dear to be used on barns. After the 1830s, the folk art, which has its roots in medieval European symbolism, exploded in popularity, reaching its peak at the turn of the twentieth century. Efforts to sustain it are ongoing.

The adornments are referred to as "hex signs" because the early people were highly superstitious and the designs were intended to summon good fortune in life, home, and enterprise and to spell off evil. The hexes are painted directly on the barn, or hand-painted or screened onto plywood or metal discs.

The signs typically measure 4 feet or more in diameter. They display bold primary colors along with green, white, and black. Stars, rosettes, tulips, hearts, oak leaves, and birds are common emblems united in messages of hope, love, luck, fertility, plenty, and joy. Livestock are more recent depictions.

Hex symbol, Lenhartsville.

The number of any particular symbol, the point count of a star, the colors, borders, and combination of images jointly shape the message.

While admiring and photographing the barn art, be sure to park well to the side of the road and in plain sight, and do not trespass or block driveways or mailboxes. Although this description will attempt to point out hexes along the way, some will fade or be painted over and new ones may be added. Side roads swell the discovery; many Berks County travel materials also point out hex locations and should be sought out as additional sources.

To begin this drive, from Interstate 78 west of Allentown, take exit 14, go north on PA 100 to Fogelsville (0.3 mile), and turn left (west) on Main Street, which is Old Highway 22—the Hex Highway. Pass through the small business district, perhaps taking note of the Old Fogelsville Hotel (1798), and enter rolling farmland. Travel is relaxed and unhurried, with most of the area through-traffic taking I-78. Although the route parallels and crisscrosses under the interstate, woods and fields of tall corn mostly block the thoroughfare from view.

By looking north at 4.3 miles, you will view a red barn with a trio of hex signs; it sets the tone for the tour. In another 0.4 mile, a detour south via Pennsylvania Highway 863 leads to **The Rodale Experimental Farm**, an interesting learning ground for gardener, farmer, and naturalist. Go 0.3 mile south on PA 863 to a junction, bear straight on Siegfriedale Road, and follow it for 2.4 miles to the farm.

The farm is trying out new methods of organic gardening, natural pest control, rotation, and composting. It should come as no surprise that the name Rodale is associated with the project, given that J. I. Rodale started publishing *Organic Gardening* magazine back in 1942, when such ideas were scoffed at. Early May to mid-October, guided and self-guided tours of the farm are possible; workshops are also offered.

The farm has an interesting history—it had remained in the same family from the time William Penn issued the land grant in 1732 until 1972, when the farm was acquired for research. The stone barns, private stone dwellings, corncribs, and one-room schoolhouse (now a bookstore/visitor center) are all part of the legacy. On the first Saturday in August, the farm's annual GardenFest allows you to taste the results of the field. There are picnic tables and restrooms at the farm.

By foregoing this side trip and keeping to the Hex Highway at 4.7 miles, you will find a couple more of the decorated barns in the next mile. On the left at the intersection with New Smithville Road, a fully decorated barn overlooks the intersection; binoculars can help you admire the detail. Sheep feed in a nearby pasture.

Hand-lettered signs for homemade candies or fresh produce may start your mouths to water. The many soaring barns are a Pennsylvania trademark and beautiful in their own right. Where the route rises, view Blue

Hex barn, Lenhartsville.

Mountain to the north. At 8.7 miles, **Pinnacle Ridge Winery** brings the rhythmic beauty of a grape vineyard to the landscape.

Chiming church bells may announce the stone cathedrals that rise above the fields. Mt. Zion Lutheran Church precedes Krumsville, where PA 737 journeys south to Kutztown, the new home to the Pennsylvania Dutch Folk Culture Society and site of the Pennsylvania German Festival.

On Hex Highway, country stores, ice cream stands, and specialty shops will help you bide time between barns. At 10.3 miles, the highway crosses under I-78 for the last time, now staying south of the interstate. Mixed hardwoods often drape the travel corridor.

The drive then crosses Maiden Creek to enter Lenhartsville. Here, PA 143 South launches an 18.4-mile round-trip side tour that visits a dozen of the brightly decorated barns, a covered bridge, and an old mill, while circling close to Crystal Cave.

On this departure from the main tour, you will ascend away from Lenhartsville, following Maiden Creek upstream to view **Dreibelbis Station Covered Bridge** (1869) in 1.6 miles. This attractive Burr-style bridge is still in use and has eave-covered windows that stretch the length of its sides. The side tour then resumes south, winding deeper into farm country. In another 1.2 miles, at Strausser Road, glance over your right shoulder to see a barn with four big hex signs spanning its side. The signs show spiral and star images with scalloped and solid borders. You will get a second chance to view this barn on your return.

Continue south 0.8 mile along Maiden Creek, and turn right off PA 143 onto Virginville Road for a scenic loop. Terraced fields of alternating crops; barns with hex signs or faint shadows of past signs; fall-flocking swallows; and grazing dairy herds complement backroads travel. At 5.2 miles into the side trip, you will view a barn with hex signs of a hereford, horse, and traditional geometric symbols. More folk art follows.

At the T-junction with Windsor Castle Road (6.4 miles), go left for snaking travel past barns, stone farmhouses, and farm animals. Before reaching PA 662 at 8 miles, look for another cluster of the decorated barns; the side trip then heads south on PA 662. On the left at 10.9 miles is an old mill; at 12 miles, look left to see hexes that include eight-pointed stars, tulips, and a half a sunburst. In another 0.3 mile, you will meet PA 143. Turn north to bring the loop to a close at 14.8 miles (north of Virginville) and to return to Lenhartsville, 18.4 miles. Hexes still turn heads.

Forgoing the digression at 14.7 miles, you may choose instead to walk around the small community of Lenhartsville with its Pennsylvania Dutch touches, some left over from the days when it held the Folklife Museum. The Deitsch Eck Haus serves traditional Pennsylvania Dutch meals, and you may enjoy the folk art on the restaurant's walls while you savor the wholesome tastes.

For the primary drive, stay westbound on Old 22, ascending from town. The stone church of St. Paul's greets you as you enter Edenburg. Left at 18.9 miles is **Kaercher Creek (Berks County) Park**. At this large county park, Kaercher Creek Lake is the centerpiece to recreation. Boating, fishing, playing volleyball or horseshoes, and picnicking are pastimes. This family stop is also popular with Canada geese.

Farther west, the borough of Hamburg brings congestion. The town has an old brick business district and row houses that stretch south. Stay on Hex Highway (State Street), crossing the Schuylkill River at 20.3 miles to gradually edge back into the rural scheme. A tree farm, a showy crop of sunflowers, or chickens scratching around a corncrib vary windshield views.

Discover the next cluster of barns at 26.5 miles and then enter Shartlesville, another village that might suggest you park and walk around. Hex signs decorate the doorways of many businesses. Antique and second-hand shops call to the curious. Again, you may seek out traditional Pennsylvania Dutch hospitality and cooking. The food is hearty and often home-grown. Choose from a variety of meats and sausages, seasonal vegetables, pickles and preserves, homemade breads and butter, and fresh apple or traditional shoo-fly pie.

At the western outskirts of Shartlesville lies **Roadside America** (28.1 miles). You cannot miss it; a bombardment of billboards points the way. Central to the strip of shops is the acclaimed indoor miniature village. A modest fee is charged to tour this unique collection of hand-carved wooden miniatures that record America's past and progress. View miniature Native American villages, settlements, farms, caverns, coal mines, and more. Hours are 10 A.M. to 5 P.M. daily, with extended hours weekends and summer months.

The collection traces its beginnings to a young boy growing up around Reading, Pennsylvania, in the early 1900s. To five-year-old Laurence T. Gieringer, the distant Hiland Hotel atop Neversink Mountain seemed no bigger than a toy from his bedroom window. His fascination with this presumed "toy" brought about a misadventure in the woods when he attempted to hike to it, and later, a lifelong interest in carving exacting miniatures. The hobby grew for 60 years, resulting in the present collection.

Away from Roadside America, Hex Highway returns to rural calm and adorned barns, soon passing through Strausstown. At 32 miles, bear right. Where Hex Highway ends at Bethel (37.7 miles), follow PA 501 North.

PA 501 passes over I-78 and proceeds toward the steadfast presence of Blue Mountain. In 1 mile, a 1.5-mile detour right on Airport Road leads to a trout hatchery, where you pay to fish (open March to August). Soon after, you will pass the Fort Henry Pennsylvania heritage marker. Fort Henry (1756) was an important frontier fort in the French and Indian War. Next up comes a twisting ascent of forested Blue Mountain. At the summit is a trailhead for the **Appalachian Trail.** Hardwoods shade your descent; in autumn, enjoy an array of yellow, red, orange, and burgundy leaves.

Tagging the valley floor, you will cross Lower Swatara Creek to meet and follow PA 895 east at 45.5 miles. With roller coaster bends and curves, PA 895 pursues Lower Swatara Creek upstream. Overlook floodplain farms and riparian woods stretching south to Blue Mountain. The hex signs have not yet vanished. Before long, a covered bridge spans Lower Swatara Creek on the right. At farmhouses, eggs, chickens, and rabbits are for sale.

The dirt bike raceway of the **Flying Dutchman Race Track** at 48.7 miles hits a sour note in this otherwise rural anthem. Again, cross the creek and spy more hexes as a mix of forest and farms frames PA 895. To the left at 50 miles is a beautiful farmstead paired with a covered bridge, but unfortunately, the bridge has fallen victim to the spray paint can.

Remaining on PA 895, you will cross Lower Swatara Creek once more before entering the village of Summit Station, where Bear Creek takes over the tour. Stay PA 895E, traveling downstream past the **Schuylkill County Fairgrounds and Environmental Education Center (EEC).** The EEC has three trails, each less than 1 mile long. The road is narrow but lightly used, and there is nothing heavyhanded about this stretch; it is just relaxing, non-commercial, and moderately fast.

Pass through the borough of Auburn to cross back over the Schuylkill River. At 64.1 miles, PA 895E meets and follows PA 61 south for a brief, busy highway stretch. In 1.6 miles, turn left at a sign for Hawk Mountain, still following the route of PA 895E.

In another 1.5 miles, you will spy a trio of brightly painted hex signs on a weathered barn as you take a right turn off PA 895 onto Hawk Mountain Road/State Route 2018. Cross over a railroad and the Little Schuylkill River, and bear left at the fork to again ascend Blue Mountain.

On the right at 69.1 miles is the entry to **Hawk Mountain Wildlife Sanctuary.** Fees are collected at the visitor center or the gateway to the Lookout Trail. The visitor center is open 9 A.M. to 5 P.M. (except holidays), with extended hours in migration season. When sanctuary visitation peaks in October, a shuttle operates to ease traffic and parking congestion on the mountain; phone ahead for information.

This impressive 2,380-acre private nonprofit sanctuary was founded in 1934 to protect predatory birds' in migratory flight and is now a National Natural Landmark. Between mid-August and mid-December, an average of 20,000 eagles, ospreys, hawks, and falcons ride the winds south. The spectacle draws visitors from around the world. During spring migration, warblers also visit the mountain. Binoculars are available for rent.

The popular **Lookout Trail**, with its upper-end spurs, travels 1.75 miles round trip. The sanctuary's **River of Rocks Trail**, which explores an unusual periglacial boulder field, is a rugged 4-mile loop. Boots are recommended; heed posted rules.

All hikes begin at the information pavilion, where daily bird counts are posted. Follow the brick pathway indicated "to Lookouts and Sanctuary Trails." A foot trail replaces the walk as it enters the woods of black gum, oak, birch, maple, laurel, and sassafras.

Next, you will cross Hawk Mountain Road, pass through the trail gateway, and ascend to South Lookout (0.2 mile). At South Lookout, interpretive boards depict the various predatory birds in flight. The natural rock crest opens a view to the forested ridges, the River of Rocks directly below, and the serene rural valley beyond. To the east line up three prominent skyline features: Hemlock Heights, Owl's Head, and the Pinnacle.

As you follow the Lookout Trail along the ridge, you will find other hawk-watch outposts. Next up is the Appalachian Overlook—a rocky jumble with comparable views of the area skyline and migration path. Where log-reinforced and natural stone steps take the Lookout Trail into an area of hemlocks, you will find a T-junction (0.6 mile). To the left is a forked path leading straight ahead to The Slide (site of an 1890s gravity-run railroad)

South Lookout, Hawk Mountain Wildlife Sanctuary.

and left to Sunset Overlook (a western vantage reached via a short, difficult rock scramble). To the right, the Lookout Trail travels the Hall of the Mountain King to North Lookout (elevation 1,521 feet). This panoramic view sweeps Hawk Mountain, along which warm thermals build to carry the raptors south.

The red-blazed **River of Rocks Trail** (accessed from the Lookout Trail) lassos the periglacial boulder stream, with a rugged downhill and uphill hike. Rhododendron and laurel seasonally dress the sides of the path. At the outskirts of the boulder field, gurgling springs may draw notice. River of Rocks is a long, broad stream of glaring white boulders piled rock against rock and rock upon rock, defying plant growth. At the foot of the river is a cathedral woods of tulip poplar, maple, birch, and oak.

From the sanctuary turnoff, the main drive then descends along Hawk Mountain Road to depart Blue Mountain and travel the southeast farmlands at the mountain's base. On the left at 75.5 miles, a white barn sports brightly painted yellow, black, and white star hexes, with more barn art to follow.

Signs for quilts, pottery, and baskets or for coffee, cider, and baked goods suggest stopping. Overlooks are of Pine Creek. At 78.4 miles, a detour left on New Bethel Church Road finds a scenic stone church and another adorned barn. A cemetery mounts the hillside behind the church.

By staying on Hawk Mountain Road, you will pass the 1844 Albany Farm, with its faded geometric hex at the peak of the barn, and then meet and follow PA 143 south. Along the way, enjoy woods travel and stone dwellings before discovering an attractive hex sign on the right at 81.1 miles and more faded barn art at 83.7 miles. The final distance tracks Maiden Creek back to Lenhartsville to end at the Hex Highway, just shy of 84 miles.

22

Delaware River Scenic Drive

Interstate 95 to Easton

General description: This 55.8-mile one-way drive explores the natural beauty of the Pennsylvania shore along the Delaware Wild and Scenic River; revisits Christmas night 1776, when George Washington made his historic crossing of an icy Delaware River; and vividly recalls life and work on the Delaware River Canal (1831–1932). Due to the narrowness of the road, tight curves, and limited parking turnouts, this drive does not lend itself to travel by recreational vehicles or trailers.

Special attractions: Washington Crossing Historic Park; river/canal access and views; locks, aqueducts, and lockkeeper houses; the National Canal Museum; pedestrian bridge to the New Jersey shore; Nockamixon Cliffs Natural Area; rhododendron; autumn leaves; bird watching, fishing, hiking, canoeing, rafting, bicycling; barge and excursion train touring.

Location: Delaware River Canal National Heritage Corridor in southeast Pennsylvania; it lies along the Delaware River between Yardley and Easton.

Drive route numbers: Pennsylvania Highways 32 and 611.

Travel season: Year-round.

Camping: In Bucks County, Deer Wood Campground (part of Tohickon Valley County Park, 1.2 miles north of Point Pleasant) has 22 basic sites. Tinicum County Park (midway between Point Pleasant and Upper Black Eddy) has five primitive tent sites; no recreational vehicles, trailers, or pets.

Services: Find full services at Yardley, New Hope, and Easton, with a spattering of traveler services along the route.

Nearby points of interest: Historic Doylestown, Pennsbury Manor, Ringing Rocks Park, Lehigh River Canal, Bull Island New Jersey State Park.

 The drive

This drive starts at the easternmost Pennsylvania exit on Interstate 95 and follows the Delaware River and its associated canal north upstream through an engaging canyon of mature forest, cliffs, fields, residential areas of eighteenth- and nineteenth-century homes, and historic towns and villages. The tour concludes at Centre Square in Easton—a hub for events in early American history.

Drive 22: Delaware River Scenic Drive

Interstate 95 to Easton

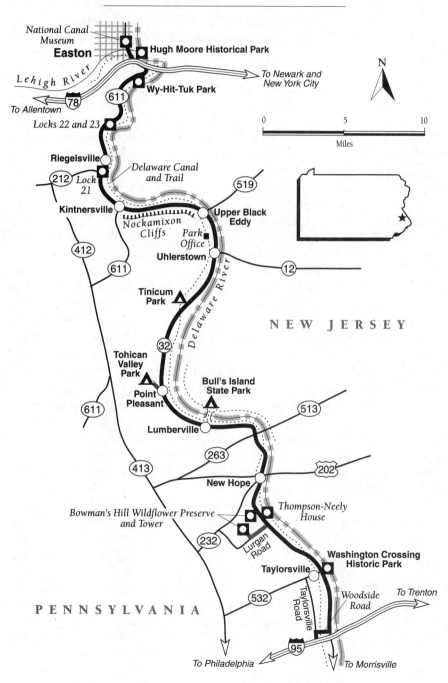

National Canal Museum

Easton

Hugh Moore Historical Park

Lehigh River

78

To Allentown

611

Wy-Hit-Tuk Park

To Newark and New York City

N

0   5   10
Miles

Locks 22 and 23

Riegelsville

Delaware Canal and Trail

212 Lock 21

519

Kintnersville

Nockamixon Cliffs

Upper Black Eddy

Park Office

412

611

Uhlerstown

12

Tinicum Park

Delaware River

NEW JERSEY

32

Tohican Valley Park

Bull's Island State Park

513

611

Point Pleasant

Lumberville

202

413

263

New Hope

Bowman's Hill Wildflower Preserve and Tower

Thompson-Neely House

232

Lurgan Road

Washington Crossing Historic Park

Taylorsville

Taylorsville Road

Woodside Road

To Trenton

532

PENNSYLVANIA

95

To Philadelphia

To Morrisville

The parallel-running Delaware Canal, a National Historic Landmark, stretches some 60 miles and represents the most intact canal system from the early to mid-nineteenth century, with many of its operational features still in place. Its towpath is a national heritage trail. While taking the river drive, you may enjoy frequent access to the canal corridor, its history, and recreation.

Mowed weekly, the canal towpath welcomes hiking, cycling, and nature study, as well as a slower paced appreciation of both river and canal. Towpath interpretive panels explain how the canal brought coal to fuel the industry along the Eastern Seaboard and piece together an intriguing tale about life on the canal. At New Hope and Easton, mule-pulled barges, now loaded with tourists instead of coal, recall the era. Inns and farms that sprang up along this vital river-canal transportation route still operate today.

To begin the driving tour, take the Yardley–New Hope Exit off Interstate 95 and go north on Taylorsville Road to the traffic light 0.1 mile north of the freeway. There, turn right on Woodside Road, go 0.3 mile, and turn left (north) on PA 32 to reach the actual river drive. The broad Delaware River is on your right; a picturesque residential area on your left.

The river is a familiar face throughout much of the tour, although sometimes shielded by forest or distanced by farms. Mature shade trees in both the settled and wild areas contribute greatly to the overall appeal of the drive. Maple, oak, tulip poplar, sycamore, and basswood overhang the twisting narrow road, with accents of wild grape, laurel, and rhododendron. Cross-river views present the wooded New Jersey shore. Canada goose, heron, kingfisher, and hawk share the river aisle; the list of sightings grows once you step away from the vehicle.

Travel speeds vary from 15 to 45 miles per hour, with necessary slowing where the road literally wraps around the corners of historic homes and old barns and where single-lane bridges pinch the traffic flow. With much of the area being private, turnouts are mostly limited to the public parks and businesses along the route. Notably absent are neon signs; instead, old-time business shields call visitors aside.

Proceed north past the intersection with PA 532 at Taylorsville to reach the **McConkey's Ferry Section** of **Washington Crossing Historic Park**, at 3.1 miles. At the PA 532 junction, you may have noticed a statue of "Washington Crossing the Delaware"; it is on the grounds of privately operated Washington Crossing Inn.

The park is open 9 A.M. to 5 P.M. Tuesday through Saturday, noon to 5 P.M. Sunday. Call before planning a holiday visit. The paid admission provides access to the visitor center's museum and film, the offered tours at McConkey's Ferry and Thompson-Neely House, Bowman's Hill Tower, and Bowman's Hill Wildflower Preserve. All park offerings are just off PA 32 and clearly signed.

The park museum has a few choice exhibits. View the commanding replica of Emanuel Leutze's famous painting, "Washington Crossing the Delaware," and discover a cannon given to the Continental Army by General Lafayette. It was fired in the Battle of Yorktown in 1781 and again in honor of Lafayette's return visit to the United States in 1824. In addition to battle artifacts are exhibits on early American life. Outside, view monuments commemorating the crossing.

The park faces the Delaware River, with an impressive row of ancient sycamores standing watch. Although most of the stone and stuccoed buildings at McConkey's Ferry postdate the American Revolution, the 1753 **McConkey's Ferry Inn** still stands.

This inn served as a Continental Army guardpost. It is also where George Washington and his aides took their Christmas Day meal before marching on General Howe and the unsuspecting Hessians at Trenton, New Jersey. The successful sneak attack in the Battle of Trenton bolstered the Continental Army and marked a turning point in the war, but on General Howe's desk sat an unopened informant's letter that could have changed history.

The interiors of McConkey's Ferry Inn and the park's other historic homes all reflect their respective periods. At the inn, you may read a copy of a letter dashed out in anger by George Washington when his officers failed to carry out a campaign; view an original 1759 map of eastern Pennsylvania; and see how the soldiers passed their boredom with corncob checkers and leather tankards. At the Mahlon Taylor House, you will step into the 1800s and the well-to-do lifestyle of a co-founder of Taylorsville.

In the area's boat shed sits a sturdy Durham boat, like the ones Washington commandeered for his bold and treacherous river crossing. In secret, with the use of these boats, George Washington transported 2,400 men and a complement of cannons and horses across the river. On the annual Christmas Day reenactment, the replica boat is manned and launched into the river. The New Jersey shore holds a companion park with a small visitor center and nature center; to the south, a road bridge links the two Delaware River parks.

North along PA 32 are several large picnic facilities (fee parking) and the remaining state park attractions. River views continue for the next 0.5 mile. At 5.2 miles, cross a single-lane bridge over the historic canal, the first of several one-lane bridges. The private homes that line the route complement the tour with gracious lawns, big shade trees, and their own history. You will pass many handsome, Federal-style homes constructed of fieldstone, stucco, or frame.

At 7.3 miles, turn left on Lurgan Road for a 2-mile detour to **Bowman's Hill** and its memorial stone tower built in 1930 (open daily April through

McConkey's Ferry Inn, Washington Crossing Historic Park.

October, weekends in November, and closed December through March). Atop this hill, sentries from the Continental Army monitored the activities of the British. Today, the 110-foot tower allows for a 14-mile survey of the Delaware River.

On a tower visit, you will ride an elevator and mount 23 steps, passing through a squeezed, spiral stone staircase to the view. The tower loft overlooks the Delaware River and canal, the Thompson-Neely House, the area woods, and a flagpole above the nation's first unknown soldier's grave. Shaping an arc around the flag are 13 polished stones, which represent the original 13 colonies, but to see this detail, you must hike the towpath south from Thompson-Neely House.

On PA 32 less than 1 mile north of the Lurgan Road turnoff are back-to-back turns for **Bowman's Hill Wildflower Preserve** (left) and the **Thompson-Neely House** (right). The preserve features 100 acres of native Pennsylvania flora explored by an interlocking network of trails. The Thompson-Neely House served as General Stirling's headquarters for the month preceding the Battle of Trenton. Animating the grounds of this eighteenth-century farm are sheep and other domestic animals.

As you resume northbound on PA 32, leaving Washington Crossing Historic Park, the canal separates the river from the road. Watch for the stacks of an old waterworks to the right. It is said that here, Washington secluded the Durham boats used in the crossing.

Although most of the river drive has been gently paced, all of that changes at 10 miles as you enter the borough of **New Hope**—a bustling, congested artist/tourist community laced with history and charm. Here, the quaint narrow streets of yesteryear's horse-and-buggy days are taxed by contemporary traffic. Stress heightens to hair-pulling madness until you locate a parking space; foot travel is faster. Off-season and midweek visits help to reduce stress.

The historic town holds a collection of trendy, chic, and country-classic shops, eateries, and galleries in its buildings that date to the 1700s. Old inns house overnighters; ivy scales the canal-side buildings. The Parry House Museum, mule-barge canal tours, horse-drawn buggy rides, an excursion train, and riverboat tour summon you from your vehicle. The visitor center at the corner of Main (PA 32) and Mechanic streets is a good place to begin a New Hope visit. Self-guided, guided, and ghost walk tours probe the corners of the old town.

The clip-clop of horse hooves, train whistles, and crossing bells weave a musical accompaniment to a stay. Suicidal squirrels bound across the roadway oblivious to the confusion. When walking about town, be sure to notice the ornate wrought iron designs in the fences. Elsewhere, white picket fences lend a simple signature.

New Hope traffic.

Near the center of town sits the **Parry House Museum**, shown by guided tour for a fee. This 1784-built home was owned and lived in by five generations of a Quaker family. Although occupied until 1958, the house is remarkably little altered. The furnished rooms represent life during five different eras: the Colonial, Federal, Empire, Victorian, and late Victorian periods.

The town name traces back to the Benjamin Parry family. When the family mills burned down in 1790, Benjamin Parry opted to stay and rebuild them. He renamed the business "New Hope Mills." Since the town's survival depended on the mills, the rebuilding also brought new hope to the townspeople and they adopted the name for their town. The mill had a second revival in 1949, when it re-opened as Bucks County Playhouse.

Through travelers on PA 32 face the longest mile before exiting New Hope; the progress is that of a snail with hiccoughs. But once past the snarl of cars, pedestrians, and horses, and the junction with U.S. Highway 202, you can again relax and take in the sights. A long straightaway of the historic canal serves up pleasing windshield views. Later, admire a fine display of natural woods and rhododendron, part of the **David R. Johnson Natural Area**. An impressive 1689 fieldstone farm complex may draw your attention right.

At 15 miles, again admire a close pairing of the canal and river, with cross-canyon views of New Jersey's wooded shore. Rhododendrons continue to dress the steep west canyon slope. Near Lock 12 at Lumberville, you will find a **pedestrian bridge** that spans the 0.25-mile breadth of the Delaware River to Bull Island New Jersey State Park. The bridge affords an easy leg stretch and lengthy river views.

Although the tour route bombards you with first-rate images, you must attend to your driving as the road passes startlingly close to trees, homes, stone walls, and barns. The village of Point Pleasant next marks off distance, with its small shops and an innertube and canoe rental. Here, a 1.1-mile detour north off PA 32 via Cafferty Hill Road leads to **Tohickon Valley Bucks County Park**, with its large picnic area and a campground just beyond.

From this park, hikers may access the 2.5-mile **Tohickon Valley Trail**, which tours the richly forested north canyon wall of Tohickon Creek to the High Rocks Area of Ralph Stover State Park. Find overviews and limited access to the snaking waters of Tohickon Creek, and top some exciting rock promontories.

To begin the trail from the day-use area of Tohickon Valley Park, hike the paved park road toward Doe Run Cabins, descending to a bend at 0.2 mile. There, you will step over a cable barrier on the right to ascend and skirt the campground plateau of Deer Wood Campground. Afterward, a

Delaware Canal mule barge ride, New Hope.

blazed trail wraps along the forested slope to the reddish cliffs and rocky vistas at High Rocks.

Beyond the county park turnoff, PA 32N continues to knit its quiet spell, harkening to a bygone era. Along the country highway, pass the 1852-built Point Pleasant Baptist Church. In fall, yellows, oranges, reds, and maroons lace over the road. Looks east feature the canal or both the canal and river.

Ragged shales protrude from the road cuts, but the impressive stone masonry, heavy wooden gates, cranks, and toothed gears of the locks inevitably draw eyes back to the canal. The channel itself may be dry, swampy, or hold canoeable waters.

Past Sand Castle Winery (23.5 miles), the route crosses the canal to hug the river once again. In another 0.5 mile, you will find **Stover Mill** on the right, the Isaac Stover House Bed and Breakfast on the left. The old water-powered grist and sawmill, which operated between 1823 and 1923, now holds the Tinicum Civic Association, with a rotating art exhibit from April through October. Millstones shape its walk, with old grain chutes and the heavy wooden floors viewed indoors.

Later, the restored, Federal-style **Erwin Stover House**, with its classic bank barn, welcomes travelers to **Tinicum Bucks County Park**. A few miles shy of the tour's midway point, the park welcomes you aside with its tree-shaded picnic areas, large open fields, disk golf, playgrounds, towpath access, and primitive camping. A boat launch opposite the park provides river access.

North on PA 32, open fields drift west, while a strangled riverine woods grows east. Road bridges now tie the New Jersey and Pennsylvania shores, keep to PA 32N. The river continues to travel along with you as the canal disappears west. Produce stands put a rural stamp on the tour.

To the left at 28.1 miles is the state park office, with another access to the canal towpath. An attractive residential area now claims the river drive. Another boat launch precedes the bridge to New Jersey Highway 519 in Upper Black Eddy (29.5 miles); stay PA 32N.

As the drive remains along the river, you will pass signs for Ringing Rocks Park and private campgrounds. The wide, glassy waterway reflects the eastern cliffs and woods. The towering western cliff no longer escapes notice. Stretching between Upper Black Eddy and Kintnersville are the 300-foot reddish cliffs of **Nockamixon Cliffs Natural Area**. Steep ravines part the rock walls providing habitat for rare vegetations; in places, a pale green lichen whitewashes the rock. A pair of turnouts below the cliffs allow for an out-of-car encounter.

In Kintnersville (34 miles), look for PA 32 to end and PA 611 to carry the tour north. Country furniture, pottery, and antiques call to collectors.

Lock, Delaware River Canal National Heritage Corridor.

The canal is once again just east of the road. Cross-canal looks are of riverside fields of grain, flowers, or pumpkins.

Ahead, Durham Furnace/Lock 21 has a few picnic tables and interpretive boards. At Riegelsville, a bridge spans the canal to reach a fishing access on the river. Also in town, discover canal-era inns and eateries still in operation and the regal stone demeanor of St. John Church.

PA 611 is generally wider than PA 32, but a stone wall pinches the roadway where it nudges to the canal and river. The corridor is largely settled. At 39.6 miles, reach Locks 22 and 23 at the **Theodore Roosevelt Recreation and Conservation Area**. This site holds some of the most impressive canal structures and offers picnic tables and a restroom. Here, one can better visualize the canal operation. At times, water cascades over the locks.

At 43.2 miles, pass **Wy-Hit-Tuk Northampton County Park**, with its tree-shaded lawns, tables, restrooms, five-site canoe camp, and footbridges spanning the canal to the towpath. No pets are allowed in the park. Muskrat and rabbit may be spied. *Wy-Hit-Tuk* is the Lenni Lenape term for the Delaware River.

The tour then shakes off its yesteryear image as it enters the outskirts of modern-day Easton. Cross under I-78 to find the interstate access at 44.5 miles—an alternative ending to the drive. To end at the chosen sites of Easton Centre Square and the National Canal Museum, remain on PA 611N.

After passing below a railroad track, you will find **Hugh Moore Historical Park** (site of the old Canal Museum) at 45.3 miles. The park still marks the northern terminus to the Delaware Canal, at the wooden gates of Lock 24. It also marks the start of the Lehigh Canal and its companion trail. Interpretive boards, picnic tables, and a chemical toilet are the lone remaining amenities. Gulls circle overhead.

The drive continues past the park on PA 611N to cross the Lehigh River and enter downtown Easton. Signs and banners point the way to the new canal museum and The Crayola Factory, which are both located at the southwest corner of **Centre Square** (the town's traffic circle at 55.8 miles).

A Civil War memorial fountain signals your arrival at the square. Plaques identify Easton's historical significance. Here, between 1756 and 1762, peace treaties with Native Americans were signed. Here, too, one of the first public readings of the Declaration of Independence took place.

The **National Canal Museum** is open Tuesday through Saturday 9:30 A.M. to 5 P.M., Sunday noon to 5 P.M. (call before a holiday visit). Paid admissions provide access to both the canal museum and its next-door neighbor, The Crayola Factory. The museum re-creates life and work on the canal through interactive exhibits, photo murals, artifacts, legend, and song and is a perfect sign off for the drive.

23

Pennsylvania Highways 18 and 231 Vista Tour

From Waynesburg to Avella

General description: This 40-mile drive draws a crooked line south to north across the rolling Allegheny Mountains in the remote southwest corner of Pennsylvania. From the drive's northern terminus at Avella, you have the option of adding a 5-mile extension to conclude the day on a wet note at Cross Creek Lake (heading east on Pennsylvania Highway 50) or immersed in the pioneer past at Meadowcroft (following signs west out of Avella).

Special attractions: Hilltop views; covered bridges; quiet-living Amish; old cemeteries; East Finley Park; Cross Creek Lake and Park; Meadowcroft Museum of Rural Life; fall foliage; relaxing, picnicking, fishing, boating.

Location: Extreme southwest corner of Pennsylvania.

Drive route numbers: Pennsylvania Highways 18, 231, and 50.

Travel season: Year-round; avoid when slippery conditions exist.

Camping: Ryerson Station State Park (24 miles west of Waynesburg off PA 21) has 50 family campsites (a few with electricity), rustic toilets, and a dump station; it offers lake recreation and trails.

Services: Waynesburg is a full-service community, with Claysville and Avella providing basic traveler services.

Nearby points of interest: Ryerson Station, Hillman, and Raccoon Creek state parks; the historic David Bradford House and LeMoyne House (Washington); Fort Necessity National Battlefield (U.S. Highway 40); Friendship Hill National Historic Site (New Geneva); Pittsburgh area attractions.

 The drive

Vistas are normally a rarity in Penn's woods, but this twisting drive over hill and through dale gathers up dozens of perspectives. This is a drive for settling back in your seat and surrendering to the tranquility. It travels a remote corner of the state, dotted by front-porch communities and scattered farms, some belonging to the quiet, hard-working Amish. Tourism does not have a stranglehold here; the pace is gentle, the images untarnished.

Names from the Revolutionary War permeate the region. Washington County, organized during the revolution, was named in honor of General

Drive 23: Pennsylvania Highways 18 and 231 Vista Tour

From Waynesburg to Avella

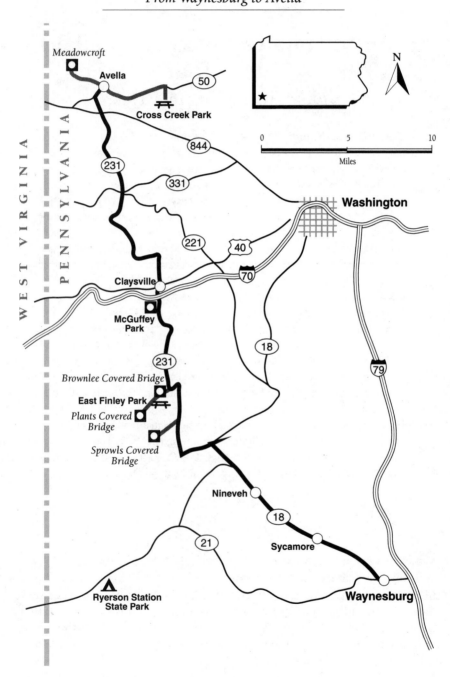

George Washington. Greene County to the south honors General Nathaniel Greene, Washington's favorite undergeneral and a key military strategist for the Continental Army. Waynesburg takes its name from "mad" Anthony Wayne, whose name is closely associated with the winter at Valley Forge.

At the time Washington County was formed, both Virginia and Pennsylvania staked a claim on this isolated corner. There was even a push to form a separate state—"Westsylvania." The territorial dispute was resolved in 1779, with Pennsylvania's priority upheld.

To begin the drive, from PA 21 at the western outskirts of Waynesburg, go north on PA 18. This thin, curving country road is quickly overhung by trees; a railroad track and Browns Creek are visible to the left. Maple, oak, hickory, cherry, locust, and walnut contribute to the leafy collage. Pass the occasional graceful old farmhouse or looming barn as you proceed upstream to the village of Sycamore (3.2 miles), named for the large trees growing streamside.

A field that explodes with goldenrod in the fall opens views to the left. Woodchucks graze along the road's grassy margins, while a heron may awkwardly lift into flight from a field drained by Browns Creek. Turnouts are rare, so when pulling aside or slowing, be careful. Even on this lightly traveled road, you must watch the rearview mirror.

At 8.2 miles, enter Nineveh, which was established in 1845 and is said to have produced superb wagons in its heyday. Today, U.S. flags fly from the porches and Hopkins Store proposes you stop for a soft drink or ice cream. The drive then crosses Browns Creek. Virginia creeper scales the sides of several old barns. Sagging fences, white chapels, and cemeteries with propped-up markers contribute to the peaceful spell.

At 11 miles, a side road to the left leads to **Ryerson Station State Park** in 13 miles. Keep to PA 18 as it rolls atop a rise for the first in a string of views. Overlook a drainage-cut canyon, with its steep pasture and wooded slopes. Perhaps a few woolly sheep will be spied; Greene County is the largest sheep-raising county in the state.

Meet PA 231 at 12 miles and follow it north, rounding a corncrib and passing into Washington County. Travel speeds fluctuate between 20 and 45 miles per hour on this weaving, rolling tour. While on PA 231, stay alert at road junctions because the highway makes several turns, some quick on the heels of others.

The dairy barns sport attractive emblems or name panels. Sometimes handkerchiefs of fog drift through the valley. Next up, big barns frame the intersection at East Finley (16.7 miles). The drive then proceeds straight on PA 231N, but a 1.5-mile detour left on State Route 3035 leads to **Sprowls Covered Bridge**. Over Rocky Run, this red, kingpost bridge has bookend windows and sits alone in a valley below a wooded slope.

Hopkins Store, Nineveh.

Washington and Greene counties cosponsor an annual autumn Covered Bridge Festival that includes a driving tour to several of the bridges, with scheduled events at the various locations. Craft and pioneer skill exhibitions, music, and food are paired with the bridge viewing. More than two dozen covered bridges dot the two-county area. Covered bridges had the practical purpose of protecting vital, hard-to-replace bridge supports; their barn-like appearance made it easier to herd livestock through them.

For the vista drive alone, follow PA 231 north from East Finley, going past Red General Store. Where PA 231 hooks right at 18.8 miles, you may follow the sign for East Finley Park to visit two more covered bridges and the quiet community park. For this 2.3-mile detour, on paved Templeton Run Road, go 0.2 mile and bear right to pass a guardian oak and maple and drive through **Brownlee Covered Bridge**. The kingpost-style bridge spans the Templeton Fork of Wheeling Creek and has a pleasant farm backdrop; the curvature of the road adds to its beauty.

Proceeding downstream, you will reach **East Finley Park** in another 0.4 mile. The Templeton Fork flows through this large, groomed valley park situated in a treed canyon; footbridges span the water to link the park areas. Among the amenities are a playground, picnic shelters, playing fields, concert stage, and pit toilets, but bring drinking water.

Oak, Washington County.

Washington County farmland.

Downstream 1.7 miles from the park is the second bridge, **Plants Covered Bridge**. To reach it, follow Templeton Run Road to a T-junction and go left. Plants Bridge, too, spans the Templeton Fork and is a traditional red covered bridge.

Without the bridges-and-park detour, PA 231 gains a tunnel effect, passing north through deep woods. The drive then wraps around the flank of a ridge to reach the crossroads with SR 3029 at 21.6 miles; west leads to Good Intent, east to Pleasant Grove. Again, keep to PA 231N, which climbs. Ridge saddles afford east-west views, with western views stretching to West Virginia. An Amish buggy may briefly share the highway.

Next comes the descent to Claysville. Prior to passing under Interstate 70, a 0.5-mile detour west on Beeham Ridge Road/SR 3019 leads to **McGuffey Community Park**. William Holmes McGuffey, author of the famous *McGuffey's Reader,* was born south of Claysville. The community park which bears his name occupies a grassy valley bottom bordered by wooded hills and has a children's playground for anyone restless in the backseat. Playing fields, sports courts, picnic shelters, and nonflush toilets are other offerings.

Choosing to forgo the quiet of McGuffey Park, proceed north under the interstate and into historic Claysville, meeting Main Street/US 40, the **National Road**, at 25.2 miles. The PA 231 tour briefly follows US 40 east into town before resuming north, but Main Street suggests a brief digression.

Attractive, old side-by-side homes and storefront businesses face the street; wreaths and ornamental flags adorn several doorways. Barns loom above the street scene, where Claysville grew up around them. A handful of the town's older brick homes were taverns on the National Road. Traditionally, taverns were traveler waysides that provided overnight accommodation, food, and drink. The National Road was built in 1818 at the persistent urging of Henry Clay, in whose honor Claysville was named. The town itself was founded in 1817 by John Purviance.

Where you first meet US 40, on the north side of National Road is the **Historic Purviance Cemetery.** It sits next to the brick United Methodist Church and opposite Sacred Heart Catholic Church. The stones date to the mid 1800s; several of the thin, carved tablets convey pieces of individual history. Among the graves is one for Robert Barr, a drummer boy in the Revolutionary War and veteran of the War of 1812. He was remembered for his heroism in whisking a woman and child away from enemy tribes to the safety of a blockhouse near Claysville. He was 101 years old when he died.

Several of the graves belong to Civil War veterans. During the Civil War, this corner of the state, which had been settled largely by individuals from Maryland and Virginia, had its share of southern sympathizers, yet the county played a key role in the Underground Railroad.

Historic Purviance Cemetery, Claysville.

After taking in the sights of Claysville, resume north on PA 231 (Wayne Street), climbing steeply away from US 40 and the town. Atop a rise, you will again gather farm and hillside views. Still the rolling countryside shows a marked vertical relief. On the left at 30.7 miles is Zion United Methodist Church with its churchyard cemetery. This was the first church west of the Allegheny Front. War memorials recognize veterans of the Revolutionary, Civil, and Spanish-American wars.

Creek crossings precede the intersection with PA 331. Here, PA 231N turns left, followed by a quick right. As the tour follows a tributary upstream, deer may be seen grazing in clearings or crossing the road; stay alert.

At 35 miles, round the old cemetery on Mount Hope Ridge; a beautiful old oak stands sentinel. Vistas again sweep terraced fields of corn and hay, folded ridges, and serial valleys. Corncribs, farm buildings, black mirror ponds, and scenic lone-standing trees punctuate the postcard pretty scenes. As you continue past Breezy Heights Tavern, watch junction signs because PA 231 again takes back-to-back turns.

Off Sugar Run Road in 3 miles, you will view the attractive Weatherbury Farm; plaques show it is a farm vacation member. The tour then dips one last time through woods to meet PA 50. Here, the first of several signs points the way to the Meadowcroft pioneer museum. To complete the drive, go east on PA 50 to Avella, ending at the core of town (39.6 miles). From town, nearly equidistant side trips west to Meadowcroft or east to Cross Creek Lake put a finishing touch on the tour.

Meadowcroft Museum of Rural Life lies less than 5 miles west of Avella alongside Cross Creek; follow the signs from town. Albert and Delvin Miller opened this museum in 1969 at the historic Miller family farm. The land was settled in 1795 by their great-great grandfather; a Virginia land grant transferred initial ownership. Today, the homestead is a nonprofit learning museum about nineteenth-century life and enterprise set amid historic buildings.

The facility has hands-on learning from grinding corn and spinning wool to throwing a prehistoric spear or atlatl. Hear the ring of iron at the blacksmith shop, smell the aroma of hearth-baked bread, or read the product labels at a 1900s general store.

Archaeological digs put habitation here before 16,000 B.C., among the earliest known in the United States. A covered bridge, museum exhibits, footpaths, gift shop, picnic tables, and heirloom garden are other Meadowcroft features. The facility is open by admission fee, Memorial Day through Labor Day. It operates Wednesday through Saturday noon to 5 P.M. and Sunday 1 P.M. to 6 P.M. A limited schedule is offered May, September, and October, with the museum open weekends noon to 5 P.M.

If instead you remain on PA 50E, depart Avella, pass through Cross Creek Valley for 5 miles, and turn south to reach **Cross Creek Lake and Park**. This park is open daylight hours, with the gate closing at 7 P.M. (5 P.M. during the winter season, which starts mid-October). While the central lake offers fishing and boating (10 horsepower maximum), swimming is prohibited. Thickly wooded rims frame the ragged-arm, 258-acre sparkling green lake; cattails crowd the shallows. A picnic area overlooks the lake, with a mile of trail stringing along shore and a fishing platform for visitors with disabilities.

24

National Road Heritage Park Tour

From Washington, Pennsylvania, to the Mason-Dixon Line

General description: This drive covers 64 miles of the 90-mile National Road Heritage Park in Pennsylvania and offers an unforgettable journey through the past. It follows the trace used by native peoples, American militias, stagecoaches, and the westward migration. A 35.4-mile round-trip side excursion leads to Friendship Hill, the home of Albert Gallatin—"Father of the National Road." As Secretary of the Treasury, Gallatin cleared the financial way to build this link between the commercial east and frontier west.

Special attractions: David Bradford and LeMoyne houses; Fort Necessity National Battlefield; Friendship Hill National Historic Site; historic tollhouses and taverns; monuments and mileposts; vistas; Youghiogheny Lake; history tracking, walking tours, hiking, picnicking, fishing, boating, dining, shopping.

Location: Southwest Pennsylvania.

Drive route numbers: U.S. Highway 40, variously known as the National Road, National Pike, Cumberland Road, or Old Pike.

Travel season: Year-round.

Camping: On the route, private campgrounds fulfill overnight needs. Just removed from US 40, Ohiopyle State Park (6 miles north of Farmington via PA 381) has a large family campground with 226 sites, restrooms with showers, dump station, and full line-up of recreation.

Services: Washington, Brownsville, and Uniontown offer full services, with various traveler amenities along the route.

Nearby points of interest: Pennsylvania Trolley Museum (Washington), Laurel Caverns, Ohiopyle State Park, Youghiogheny River whitewater rafting and rail trail, Frank Lloyd Wright's Fallingwater and Kentuck Knob, the Laurel Highlands Hiking Trail, Quebec Run Wild Area, vineyards, Pittsburgh area attractions.

 ## The drive

This drive follows an arc of history across the southwest corner of Pennsylvania. By 1818, the National Road spanned between Cumberland, Maryland, and Wheeling, Virginia. It was later extended to Illinois and now

Drive 24: National Road Heritage Park Tour

From Washington, Pennsylvania, to the Mason-Dixon Line

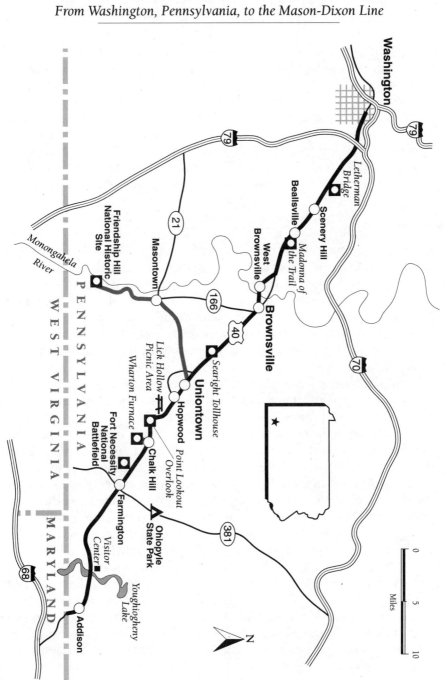

continues all the way to California. A transportation landmark, it was the first federally financed road in the country. The path it cut through this mountainous corner of Pennsylvania is still among the route's most beautiful and impressive stretches.

From start to finish on the National Road, sites and tales of historical consequence come rapid fire. Three presidents-elect traveled the National Road to the White House: Andrew Jackson, James Polk, and Zachary Taylor.

This drive begins in Washington, Pennsylvania, at the intersection of Main and Maiden streets. Locate the **David Bradford House** half a block north of the intersection at 175 South Main. Sandwiched in present-day downtown Washington, this 1788-built two-story stone house records events from the days of the Whiskey Rebellion. Candle lanterns of welcome glow through the small-paned windows. Guided tours are offered for a fee, Wednesday through Saturday 11 A.M. to 4 P.M.

A prominent, young attorney, David Bradford led farmers in the Whiskey Rebellion of 1794—a revolt against the nation's excise tax on distilled grain that financially burdened many in this region. Whiskey was the primary source for family cash, and the sizable tax fell squarely on the farmer. The tarring and feathering of tax collectors and mail theft to learn the names of informants were tactics used in the revolt. Story has it that David Bradford leaped from a rear window of this house to make his escape as President Washington's detachment of soldiers arrived to arrest him.

Today, the Federal-style house is authentically furnished in 1700s furniture, including a few original Bradford family pieces. The rich mahogany used in the house was brought from the Indies. On the tour, you will learn about daily life; pastimes and tools of the day; the stations of help, women, and children; taxes; and of course, David Bradford.

If you are in the mood for another house tour, it is a short walk to the **LeMoyne House**, at 49 East Maiden Street; find it just east of the Main Street intersection. This Greek Revival stone two-story with the twin doorways offers a look at life in the 1800s. This was the home of a progressive doctor and active abolitionist, who aided in the Underground Railroad. As the house remained in the LeMoyne family until 1943, many original pieces and portraits are on display. In 1943, the last remaining child, Madeleine LeMoyne Reed, gave the family home to the Washington County Historical Society.

While at the house, you may view early remedies of leeches, herbs, and powders; hear tales from the days of the Underground Railroad; and upstairs, tour a small military museum with artifacts from the French and Indian War through World War II. Among the collection are General Lafayette's lunchbox and a cane that belonged to General Ulysses S. Grant. Admission is charged, with the house open Tuesday through Friday 11 A.M. to 4 P.M., weekends noon to 4 P.M.

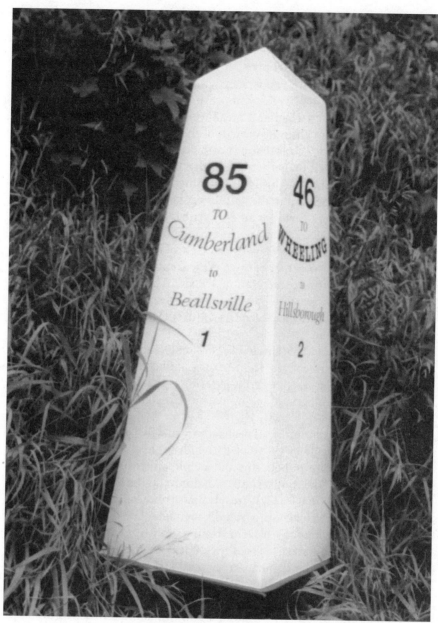

National Road Milepost.

When ready to start the drive, go east on Maiden Street/US 40, the National Road, going past Washington and Jefferson College, the dingy urban infrastructure, and some lovely old homes. The bustle of the road today affirms the success of the old pike.

At 4 miles, the roadway opens up with a north-south view of the countryside—a rural tapestry of grassy slopes and woods. Farm markets, pottery and antique shops, and a bed-and-breakfast serve travelers. Huge barns and homes that sprang up with the growth of the National Road frame travel.

At 7.7 miles, a 1.7-mile detour north via the west entrance to Crescent Road followed by a left on Letherman Bridge Road leads to **Letherman Covered Bridge**. This one-lane bridge spans tiny Pigeon Creek and has bookend windows that look out to the wildflower-shrub banks. After viewing, go southeast on Crescent Road for an easy return to US 40.

Country settings again grace the curving, historic route. As you reach Scenery Hill (9.9 miles), a southwestern view of rolling forest precedes your entry into town. At the center of town is the **Century Inn**. Open since 1794, it is the oldest tavern on the National Road. The attractively landscaped stone house that once catered to wagoners and stagecoach drivers now caters to contemporary travelers. On the south side of National Road are brick taverns of yesteryear.

Counting down the miles of the National Road are historic and replica white mileposts. These stone and fiberglass pillars are placed on the north side of the road. In attractive script lettering is the distance west to Wheeling and east to Cumberland, along with the distance to the next town in each direction.

Past the tidy community of Beallsville, you will view the Madonna of the Trail on the north side of US 40 at 15.1 miles. This statue of a determined mother with an infant in her arms and a child clutching at her skirt salutes pioneer mothers of the trail; a similar Madonna statue is found in each state traveled by the National Road. Pennsylvania's tribute is placed at the historic hunting ground of Nemacolin, a friendly member of the Delaware tribe, who helped the Ohio Company blaze a frontier trail from Cumberland to the Monongahela River—in part, what the National Road follows.

Although fast, the contemporary road still presents attractive windshield views of the steep, rolling Allegheny countryside and welcomes frequent stops. At 19.6 miles, follow Old Route 40 into West Brownsville, being greeted immediately by big stone buildings and later the red brick industrial section. Many of the brick walls are ivy-scaled or wear faded painted advertisements from the past.

Ahead, cross the bridge over the Monongahela River into the Commercial Historic District of Brownsville. At 22.8 miles, the tour crosses **Dunlaps Creek Bridge**, the first cast-iron bridge built in America. It was dedicated in 1839 and is still in use without weight restrictions.

National Road historic marker.

While in the Commercial Historic District, locate the descriptively named **Flatiron Building** (circa 1835), which now holds an interpretive center for the National Road. In its small museum, you will learn about the steel and coal industry along the Monongahela River and the history of the National Road and the people of Brownsville. Walking-tour materials for historic Brownsville and its many old churches are available. The steep, narrow streets of town are chock full of history, but are more easily negotiated on foot than by car.

In another 0.5 mile, a marked turn to the right leads to **Nemacolin (Bowman) Castle** (between Front and Brashear streets). Overlooking the river, this imposing brick structure (one-time trading post) is aptly named, with its many extensions, towers, and castle battlement crest. The Bowmans, too, were active in the Underground Railroad and frequently harbored escaping black slaves. Story has it that a tunnel beneath a hearth was used to hurry runners to the river below.

The old trees of the grounds are equally impressive: sycamore, maple, and gingko (a rare tree from southeast China). The interior may be viewed by guided tour for a fee, 11 A.M. to 5 P.M. weekends Easter through mid-October; Tuesday through Sunday in June, July, and August. Both the castle and Flatiron Building are on the National Register of Historic Places.

By keeping to Old Route 40, you will return to US 40 at 24.5 miles. En route, look left for a Pennsylvania history marker outside a beer distributor's building; from the doorway of this building (the old Brashear Tavern), Lafayette addressed the people of Brownsville on his triumph tour of America. Sometimes you find history in the strangest places.

Abandoned stone houses with vines pulling at the crumbling walls shape a first impression at Brier Hill. Keep to US 40, bypassing the Heritage Route Extensions that are pointed out along the way. Windshield images include more of the attractive Federal-style stone houses, cornfields, green hillsides, and perhaps a deer pausing to share a curious stare.

On the right at 30.5 miles, you will reach the **Searight Tollhouse Museum**, one of two original tollhouses along the route in Pennsylvania. In 1835, the National Road was turned over to the individual states it traversed, with state toll stations set up every 15 miles to collect fees for its upkeep.

Posted on the exterior of Searight Tollhouse are the historic fees. It cost 6¢ for every score of sheep or hogs driven along the road, 4¢ for a horse and rider. Sleds were 3¢, while wagons and carts were charged by the number and width of their wheels. The museum itself is open mid-May through mid-October, Tuesday through Saturday 10 A.M. to 4 P.M., Sunday 2 P.M. to 6 P.M.

The highway then builds to four lanes as it approaches the full-service community of Uniontown. At 34.6 miles, follow Business 40 through town to remain on the historical route. You may glimpse Mount Summit Inn atop Chestnut Ridge to the east; a large cemetery borders travel.

At the intersection of Business 40 and Pennsylvania Highway 21 South, you have a decision to make about adding the side trip to **Friendship Hill National Historic Site**, which measures just over 35 miles round trip. If your choice is "yes," follow PA 21S to win an audience with a hologram of the "Father of the National Road" and tour his estate above the Monongahela River.

You will stay on PA 21 heading southwest toward Masontown for 10.1 miles, and then go south on PA 166 another 7.6 miles to enter the National Historic Site (NHS) on the right. Much of the drive is relatively fast, although winding. The occasional barn, vultures roosting atop roadside snags, and the industrial Monongahela River are among the side-trip images.

On a bluff overlooking the Monongahela River sits the 1789 country manor of Albert Gallatin, a Swiss immigrant who played a key role in this nation's early adventure into democratic rule. He served as Secretary of the Treasury under Presidents Jefferson and Madison and secured funding for both the Louisiana Purchase (1803) and the Lewis and Clark Expedition (1804–1806). But in this corner of the world, perhaps his greatest accomplishment

Gallatin House, Friendship Hill National Historic Site.

was convincing President Madison and the National Road Committee to extend the "route to progress" through southwest Pennsylvania.

At the NHS (open daily except Christmas 8:30 A.M. to 5 P.M.), explore the mansion and grounds, learn about Gallatin, and rediscover the growth of our nation. The **Friendship Hill Trail System** (a 4-mile interpretive loop) holds national recreation trail distinction. It travels past the mansion, historic graves, an old-growth glen, waterfalls, floral hollows, and the Monongahela River.

If instead, you confine your travels to the National Road, pursue Business 40 through Uniontown. The drive will take you past a town square and Doughboy statue, with the Veterans of Foreign Wars Hall just beyond; the VFW Hall is the birthplace of General George C. Marshall. The Presbyterian church looms large. Engaging Victorian and antebellum homes lead away from the square; keep right to remain on Business 40.

Next up is the historic village of Hopwood established in 1794. The old brick and stone houses and taverns now hold everything from barber shops to fire stations. The town takes its name from John Hopwood, the aide-de-camp to General George Washington in the Revolutionary War. Later, the drive skirts a fancy home surrounded by a rock fence to begin the ascent of Chestnut Ridge and the Allegheny Front on four-lane divided highway. As engines whine and you draw skyward, a beautiful southern forest graces travel.

At 39.6 miles, **Lick Hollow Picnic Area** (eastbound access only) invites you into the tranquil midst of the tulip poplar, beech, cherry, locust, aspen, and wild grape of Forbes State Forest; it is open spring through fall. In June and July, you will be dazzled by dogwood and rhododendron blooms—in fall, by a multicolored umbrella. Footbridges over Lick Run stitch together adjoining picnic areas, some with rock fireplaces, while a mile-long trail climbs to Pine Knob.

If you remain on US 40, you will be tempted more than once to leave the vehicle and explore. The crescent turnout for **Point Lookout Scenic Overlook** serves up a superb view across Lick Hollow toward Uniontown— a scene especially pretty when splashed with autumn yellow. Next up, find Mount Summit Inn atop Chestnut Ridge and a pair of junctions—a detour north leads to **Jumonville** (part of Fort Necessity National Battlefield); south leads to **Laurel Caverns** (a private, fee attraction 5 miles away).

On US 40E, the route narrows to two lanes but keeps a passing lane. At 42.1 miles, a 1.8-mile detour south on Wharton Furnace Road, which departs US 40 at an angle, leads to **Wharton Furnace** (1839–1873), a quiet relic from the iron-production era. In Chalk Hill (43.6 miles), the private Farm Implement Museum or a winery may entice you aside. Here, too, Chalk Hill Road heads north for **Ohiopyle State Park** and **Kentuck Knob**.

Directing your eyes left, you will soon see **Stonehouse Tavern**, which is still a popular road stop noted for its fine food. Less than a mile to its east is **Braddock's Grave**, with a section of the historic military trace.

On the right, past **Mount Washington Tavern**, you will reach the turn for the main entrance to **Fort Necessity National Battlefield** (46.2 miles). The visitor center is open daily except Christmas 8:30 A.M. to 5 P.M. At the center, pay admission fees, view a slide show, and pick up brochures to learn how all of the park sites fit together in our nation's early tale.

You will journey back to a prewar fray and the opening battle of the French and Indian War. Picnic in cathedral forest, hike trails of history, cross the Great Meadows to the replica stockade of Fort Necessity (1754), and walk ahead in time to Mount Washington Tavern (1828) for a self-guided tour of a better-class stagecoach stop on the National Road.

Beyond the visitor center, the earthwork mound, trench, and circular fortress; open meadow; and sheltering woods vividly recapture the scene at the opening battle more than 200 years ago. Even the inexperienced eye can see how the nine-hour siege played out. With the French shielded by trees and showering gunfire and the British and colonial troops penned down in the stockade, Washington had no option but surrender. At the fort, interpretive panels and an audio recording further piece together the story.

Only a few months earlier, Washington's successful sneak attack on a detachment of French at Jumonville Glen (northwest of here) set in motion the events leading up to this battle and battles around the globe, pitting French against British. Although Washington had yet to acquire his military acumen, the lessons he learned early in 1754 would later help him lead a country.

About a mile past the main entrance to Fort Necessity National Battlefield, PA 381 heads north to **Fallingwater** and **Ohiopyle State Park**. National Road rolls east across the grain of Chestnut Ridge and Laurel Hill. Pastures and ponds claim the dips and woods, the rises. Each steep pitch and rise gives you a chance to reflect on the trials of wagon travel.

At 55.1 miles, you will begin to encounter the primitive boat recreation sites of Youghiogheny Lake, a large reservoir at the Pennsylvania-Maryland border. On the left at 57.2 miles is **Jockey Hollow Visitor Center**, open seasonally. An overlook platform, restrooms, and picnic tables are other offerings. Beyond the visitor center, cross the reservoir bridge for open-water views. As you depart the bridge, turn south for a developed marina or north for **Somerfield Recreation Area** and its activities at lake level. Steep forested slopes grade to a terraced earthen rim and open water.

US 40 then climbs from the lake canyon, past cornfields, woods, and Christmas tree farms. At 59.3 miles, bear right on State Route 3002 (Old Route 40) to enter Addison and view the second remaining tollhouse in Pennsylvania. The pleasant hamlet has a bed-and-breakfast and craft shops, with **Petersburg (Addison) Tollhouse** at its eastern outskirts. The stone-block tollhouse is receiving the finishing touches to be an interpretive center. When complete, it will depict the life of a tollkeeper and the experiences of early-day road travelers.

After the tollhouse, proceed east, returning to US 40. The National Road tops Winding Ridge Summit (elevation 2,601 feet) and then drops to the Mason-Dixon Line at 64 miles, where Maryland replaces Pennsylvania as your host if you continue on US 40.

25

Laurel Highlands Scenic Drive
From Fort Ligonier to the National Road

General description: This 42.5-mile drive follows the twists and turns of Pennsylvania Highway 381 as it journeys south through the attractive Laurel Highlands Region. Visits to public and private parks and preserves add to the tour's merit.

Special attractions: Fort Ligonier; Linn Run and Ohiopyle state parks; Powdermill and Bear Run nature reserves; Frank Lloyd Wright's Fallingwater; Youghiogheny River; seasonal accents of rhododendron, laurel, and autumn foliage; hiking, whitewater rafting, bicycling, fishing, picnicking.

Location: Southwest Pennsylvania.

Drive route numbers: U.S. Highway 30 and Pennsylvania Highway 381.

Travel season: Year-round.

Camping: Linn Run State Park (2 miles east of Rector) rents out ten rustic cabins and has a washhouse with showers. Ohiopyle State Park (at the borough of Ohiopyle) has 226 family campsites, modern restrooms, showers, and a dump station.

Services: Find full services at Ligonier and Ohiopyle, with various traveler services and conveniences along the route.

Nearby points of interest: Compass Inn Museum; Kentuck Knob; Fort Necessity National Battlefield; National Road Heritage Park; Laurel Highlands Hiking Trail; Laurel Mountain skiing; Laurel Caverns; Quebec Run Wild Area; Pittsburgh area attractions; and Kooser, Laurel Hill, and Laurel Ridge state parks.

 # The drive

This drive explores the celebrated Laurel Highlands Region. Although Pennsylvania has yet to establish a State Scenic Byways System, its legislature has recognized this route's "outstanding scenic, historic, natural, and archaeological characteristics and qualities" and the need to conserve them. Much of the highway has country road appeal or southern forest charm. Name-dropping is commonplace, but far from common with the likes of George Washington, Andrew Carnegie, the R. K. Mellon family, and Frank Lloyd Wright.

Drive 25: Laurel Highlands Scenic Drive
From Fort Ligonier to the National Road

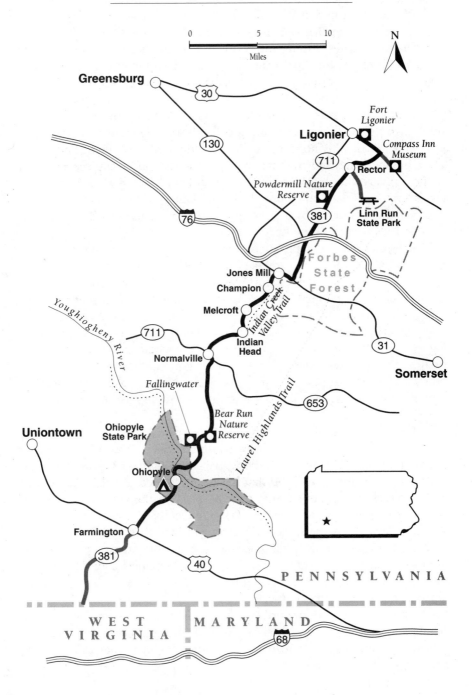

The drive begins at the junction of U.S. Highway 30 and PA 711 in Ligonier, site of **Fort Ligonier** (a nonprofit historical facility). A visit to the museum and the reconstructed fort starts your tour with a step back in time to the French and Indian War. This British fort (1758–1766) played a key role in the press for British/American control over the Ohio Valley. From here, the successful storming and taking of Fort Duquesne (Pittsburgh) was plotted and carried out. April through October, Fort Ligonier is open for the cost of admission: Monday through Saturday 10 A.M. to 4:30 P.M., Sunday noon to 4:30 P.M.

Although the reconstructed fort offers a first-rate tour, the museum is surely its rival, with an outstanding collection of eighteenth-century artifacts and portraits. Among the collection, discover a William Penn land grant, flintlock rifles and ornamental powder horns, and silver pieces awarded to the fort caretaker by William Penn, John Paul Jones, and George Washington. You may also come upon the bullet-damaged Ulery cabin door. This door was fired through by a father protecting his daughters during an Indian raid at the time of the Revolutionary War.

Reassembled and reproduced inside the museum are the parlors of Arthur St. Clair, the fort's caretaker, and Lord Ligonier, the British Commander in Chief for whom the fort was named. Although Ligonier directed the war, he never stepped foot on American soil. At the museum, a short film sets the scene for viewing the reconstructed fort just outside.

Archaeological clues have led to the detailed re-creation of this crude, log frontier fort—notice the chop marks on the wood, the joiner pegs, and small panes of untrue glass. The stockade, gun batteries, barracks, storehouses, and mess are all set up as they might have looked. Mannequins infuse life into the scene; plaques describe each room's use and explain fort life.

From Fort Ligonier, the drive heads east on US 30 for 1.9 miles to reach PA 381, which takes the tour south. However, you may choose to remain on US 30 East another mile to visit the **Compass Inn Museum**, an old stagecoach stop from 1799 that has been restored. It is furnished with period pieces and offers another looking glass to the past. The museum charges admission and is open May through October.

Doing without the stagecoach stop, you will turn south on PA 381, quickly skirting the R. K. Mellon estate—a beautiful, far-sweeping natural grounds, edged by split-rail fence. Elegant shade maples march the length of the picturesque fence and grounds, adding to the serene beauty of the curving, narrow country highway.

Although the lands are private, the windshield views are yours for the taking and thoroughly breathtaking. Wildlife at the estate have game preserve protection, which increases your chances for an animal sighting. The road suggests a slow speed.

Country setting, Westmoreland County.

At times, you may glimpse Loyalhanna Creek as it threads north through the valley. Bounding the valley to the west is Chestnut Ridge; to the east, Laurel Ridge. As horses graze the deep grass pastures, a colorful pheasant may burst from the fields. At 4 miles, view a lattice brick barn as the country tour continues to work its soothing spell.

At the Village of Rector, PA 381 crosses Linn Run, coming to a junction for **Linn Run State Park** (4.9 miles). This quiet, forested state park lies 2 miles east of the tour route and offers picnicking, trails, and trout fishing. For the drive alone, continue south, watching the signs for PA 381, which travels a crooked course.

Drive past woods, farms, big homes of unique architecture, and rustic, slot or zigzag rail fences. A sloping pasture at 7 miles extends eastern views to Laurel Highlands. Soon after, the route edges 2,200-acre **Powdermill Nature Reserve**, before reaching the main entrance at **Florence Lockhart Nimick Nature Center**, on the right at 8.7 miles.

A field station of The Carnegie Museum of Natural History, the center is open April through October, Wednesday through Saturday 9 A.M. to 4 P.M. and Sunday 1 P.M. to 5 P.M. The walking trails at the reserve are open daily during daylight hours, no collecting and no pets. The goal of the reserve is research and education.

While the nature center is small, it holds some surprising exhibits. The taxidermic displays that show various animal families in their natural habitats were originally exhibited at The Carnegie Museum at the turn of the twentieth century. To this day, they astound with remarkable detail and quality. Native American artifacts and a butterfly collection with extremely rare and endangered species also win notice.

Brochures for the nature trails are typically available in the map boxes at the sides of the information kiosk. Brochure descriptions aid in the identification of tree and plant species, and in the understanding of stream and woods habitats. The shortness of the trails welcomes slow strolling. In late summer, squirrels stir in the canopy, unleashing a rainstorm of acorns. The natural area brings together maple, oak, witch-hazel, gum, sassafras, dogwood, tulip poplar, and cucumber magnolia for a rich fall mosaic.

As the drive resumes south on PA 381, pass the southern extent of the reserve lands to travel more of the affluent countryside. Deer, raccoon, or skunk may be spied. At 11.1 miles, the drive crosses over Interstate 70/76 to follow the Indian Creek drainage downstream. Forbes State Forest and private holdings now frame travel. The state forest land is often young and thicket-like in appearance; a few turnouts access both named trails and woods roads, should you desire another walk.

Upon meeting Pennsylvania Highway 31, turn right (west) for Jones Mills, where the tour then resumes south in 0.6 mile and PA 711 shares the way. Travel is now faster, passing closer to Indian Creek. In the village of Melcroft, there is a charming greenway park along Champion Creek; find it just to the right on Melcroft Road (19.7 miles).

At 22.1 miles, a detour left across the bridge into the village of Indian Head leads to **Indian Creek Valley Hike and Bike Trail**. Look for this 5-mile rail trail as it heads north from C. W. Resh Memorial Park to Champion; there is a signed left turn as you enter the village for both the park and trailhead. This rail trail offers a quiet bike ride or hike and may one day link to the region's popular Youghiogheny River Rail Trail.

The drive keeps to PA 711/381 South and remains fast; rhododendrons dress its sides with pink floral pompoms in July. With a climb from the drainage, you will top a plateau for a rolling sojourn. At Normalville (25.5 miles), follow PA 381S as it turns left for solo travel.

Upon crossing the bridge over Mill Run Reservoir, you will return to rural landscapes with lovely old farmhouses, huge barns, dairy cows, cornfields, and woods. On the left at 32.3 miles is the Western Pennsylvania Conservancy's **Bear Run Nature Reserve**, which has an outstanding trail system and one of the best and densest showings of rhododendron in the state. The reserve trails explore the western slope of the Laurel Highlands. The site is threaded by the sparkling waters of Bear Run, a Pennsylvania Scenic Waterway.

A half mile downstream, **Fallingwater** overlooks the pristine run where it spills as a waterfall; find the turn on the right at 32.8 miles. Also owned and operated by the conservancy, this weekend retreat was built by Frank Lloyd Wright for the Kaufmann Family (well-known Pittsburgh retailers) and is open to the public via guided tour. Together, Bear Run and Fallingwater make up the Kaufmann Conservation—a treasured, generous gift from Edgar Kaufmann, Jr. to the conservancy and future generations.

Admission fees are charged and reservations are recommended at Fallingwater, for what many consider to be the most complete presentation of Wright's architecture: setting, structure, and furnishings. Tours are offered from 10 A.M. to 4 P.M. and each lasts about an hour. Fallingwater is open Tuesday through Sunday, April through November; weekends only December and March; and closed in January and February. A staggered fee is charged to encourage weekday visits; visitors also may opt for a less expensive, self-guided grounds tour.

The retreat blends Frank Lloyd Wright's signature architecture with nature. The exterior complements the natural woodland-run setting, while the interior brings the outdoors right into the room through open floor plans, windows, and natural lighting. Themes of movement and shape carry back and forth between the setting and house. On the tour, visitors gain a sense of how even the smallest detail was intentional to Wright's vision for

Fallingwater.

the home. The engineering seemingly defies concepts of gravity and physics. Priceless, original artwork and unique pieces of furniture further captivate onlookers.

The natural grounds win over guests as they won over the Kaufmanns. Enjoy deep woods, sparkling Bear Run and its waterfall, and an explosion of rhododendron blooms in early July. The changing seasons bring a changing beauty to the retreat. At the Pavilion, tours gather and visitor amenities are found.

From Fallingwater, the drive ascends from forest to farmland before descending to the Youghiogheny River, Ohiopyle, and **Ohiopyle State Park**. At 35.8 miles, King Road heads east to trailhead parking for the 70-mile **Laurel Highlands Hiking Trail**; this premier hiking trail has regularly spaced overnight shelters, vistas, and wonderful ridge travel.

At the PA 381 river bridge (36.1 miles), a turn west leads to Ferncliff Peninsula and the northbound Youghiogheny River Rail Trail. A 2-mile hiking loop explores **Ferncliff Peninsula**, a National Natural Landmark cupped in a horseshoe bend of the whitewater Youghiogheny River. Along the trail discover fossils, a falls overlook, and old-growth trees.

To walk the **Ferncliff Trail**, hike south on the closed fire lane to a kiosk and pass beneath the abandoned railroad bridge. Soon, a plaque for the National Natural Landmark signals the loop. As you proceed downstream, side paths break away to the roiling river. At 0.2 mile, tree fossils, both scaly and stringy, engage study; an interpretive sign helps with the identification.

Look down for more fossils as you stroll the river bedrock; black blazes indicate the way over the rock. At 0.4 mile, a rocky jut extends into the fury of Ohiopyle Falls for an unmatched front-row seat. Feel the energy, mist, and danger. Opposite the base of the falls, ascend right to enter the woods where rhododendron flourishes.

Along the peninsula rim, the spurs that branch left lead to river views; stay well back from the edge. Signed interior trails branch right. Old-growth hemlock, white pine, tulip poplar, hickory, oak, and maple generate a soothing backdrop. Where the trail descends at 1.25 miles, you may spy precarious rock overhangs and boxy boulders. The loop then travels a transitioning meadow-woods habitat to end back at the monument.

By following "Bike Trail" signs from peninsula parking, you tag the **Youghiogheny River Rail Trail** at its middle. This trail pairs up with a premier whitewater for the state and passes 27 miles between Confluence and Connellsville. You may rent bicycles at Ohiopyle, Connellsville, or Confluence.

On the rail trail, discover open and leaf-filtered Youghiogheny (Yough) River overlooks, tributary waterfalls, cliffs, rhododendron, and fall foliage. The river shows smooth straightaways, scenic bends, and churned pools

Youghiogheny River, Ohiopyle State Park.

with giant boulders. About half a mile north of peninsula parking, **High Bridge** draws spectators with its grand river view and chance to see fast-moving kayaks and rafts.

As the drive follows PA 381 south over the Yough, the first left leads to the visitor center, Middle Yough Take-out, and the southern leg of the Youghiogheny River Rail Trail. PA 381 then thrusts you into the bustle of tourist-driven Ohiopyle; summers and weekends, parking is prized. Souvenir shops, eateries, bicycle rentals, and four licensed rafting concessions generate the crowds. The Yough has exciting Class III and IV rapids, with Class I and II whitewater upstream toward Confluence.

In the center of town, marked turnouts on the right offer an alternative access to **Ohiopyle Falls**, a plummet stretching the river's width. In 1754, this wild churn forced George Washington to abandon his plans for using the Youghiogheny River to move troops and supplies in the capture of Fort Duquesne. A trio of platforms allow for different falls perspectives; heavy rains or drought can alter the disposition of the tumbling water.

Elsewhere in 19,046-acre Ohiopyle State Park, you may access foot trails that visit river and tributaries, picturesque waterfalls, and rocky promontories. At 36.3 miles, Sugarloaf Road heads east up Laurel Ridge to **Baughman Rock**. This natural rock incline extends an open overlook of the bending Yough; its wooded, 1,700-foot-deep canyon; The Flats; and the spectacular Laurel Highlands.

At 36.6 miles, Chalk Hill Road heads west to **Cucumber Falls**, the park campground, and **Kentuck Knob** (privately owned, this house designed by Frank Lloyd Wright is shown by guided tour; reservations and paid admission are required). Go 0.4 mile to reach the parking for Cucumber Falls; stairs descend at the old road bridge to the falls vantage. The attractive 50- to 70-foot droplet veil spills into a rocky bowl. The park's **Great Gorge Trail** passes along the west shore.

By ignoring these junctions and proceeding south on PA 381, you will leave the park in 2 miles. Out your window, the strong profiles of the tree trunks complement the leafy barrage. At 42.5 miles, reach US 40, the **National Road**, to end the tour. For an alternative ending, PA 381 does continue south another 9 miles to the West Virginia border for a quiet climax. To end at West Virginia, go west half a block on US 40 and turn south.

26

South Mountain Range Forest Tour

*From Interstate 81, Exit 11, loop south
through Michaux State Forest*

General description: This quiet, 56-mile loop explores the flank and ridge of South Mountain, overlapping, in part, with the 19-mile Michaux State Forest Self-guided Automobile Trail. As the automobile trail has an interpretive brochure paired to numbered posts along the final leg of the drive, you may wish to pick up a brochure prior to heading out on your excursion or while en route at the district office.

Special attractions: Pine Grove Furnace, Caledonia, and Mont Alto state parks; the Totem Pole Playhouse summer theater at Caledonia State Park; vistas; wildlife; laurel, rhododendron, and fall foliage; hiking, fishing, swimming, picnicking, quiet boating, and winter sports.

Location: South-central Pennsylvania.

Drive route numbers: Pennsylvania Highways 233 and 997, Ridge Road (a gravel forest road maintained for passenger vehicles).

Travel season: When free from snow; phone Michaux State Forest to learn about winter conditions on Ridge Road.

Camping: Pine Grove Furnace State Park (on PA 233, 8 miles south of I-81) has 74 rustic campsites, with drinking water, nonflush toilets, and dump station. The park's Ironmaster's Mansion now serves as an American Youth Hostel with dormitory accommodations. Caledonia State Park (at the intersection of U.S. Highway 30 and PA 233) has 185 developed, family campsites, with restrooms, showers, and dump station. It also rents out two cottages.

Services: Mont Alto has many services, with Carlisle (3 exits east of the tour's start on I-81) and Chambersburg (11 miles west of Caledonia State Park on US 30) offering full services.

Nearby points of interest: Kings Gap Environmental Education and Training Center; Gettysburg National Military Park; historic Carlisle, Waynesboro, and Chambersburg; Renfrew Museum and Park (Waynesboro); Appalachian National Scenic Trail; Harrisburg and York area attractions.

 # The drive

This drive travels a remote mountain region in the heart of where the Confederate Army made its northernmost push during the Civil War. At Caledonia State Park and in nearby towns, relive the blue-and-gray struggle. Mostly though, this drive features forest quiet and an escape from the pressures of traffic, city lights, and thoroughfares.

Natural offerings win out. Michaux State Forest shapes much of the tour; it was named for a famous French botanist, Andre Michaux, who explored this region late in the eighteenth century. On this drive, you will come to see what captivated him.

Start by taking Exit 11 from I-81, and follow PA 233 south through rolling, rural countryside. South Mountain looms beyond the immediate fields of corn. At 2.5 miles, drive past Pine Road/State Route 3006, which heads east 2.2 miles to **Kings Gap Environmental Education and Training Center**. The center has a fine network of nature trails; the paths explore along ridge, pond, and stream and journey through pine plantation and hardwood forest.

Southbound, PA 233 heads past a small cemetery, dairy herds, rural residences, and tree farms before woods become a part of and eventually dominate the scene. Evergreens blend with the maple, oak, tulip poplar, gum, and sassafras to complement the fall color array. As the road ascends, look for a sign at 5.2 miles that indicates where three babes were found in the woods in 1934. Soon after, you will enter Michaux State Forest.

At 6 miles is the loop junction. For clockwise travel, remain on PA 233S; the return will be via gravel Ridge Road to the west. A spruce plantation varies the woodland mosaic. Then, at 8 miles, you come to a T-junction at **Pine Grove Furnace State Park**.

Here, PA 233S turns right, providing access to the historic area, family campground, Fuller Lake, trails, and picnicking. Hunters Run Road heads left to the park's larger lake body, Laurel Lake, and its nearby trails. In the park's historical district, an American Youth Hostel and store cater to through-trail hikers on the Appalachian Trail.

A fine walking tour and brochure will guide you through the historic area, which has both standing structures and ruins from the charcoal-iron producing era. The area is recognized on the National Register of Historic Places. The furnace that lends the park its name began in 1764 and operated for more than 100 years, producing cast-iron products for home and military. The stone pyramid of the old furnace still stands. Among the other historical structures at the park are the Ironmaster's Mansion, a stable, stone grist mill, a company house and office, and an 1870s church.

Drive 26: South Mountain Range Forest Tour

From Interstate 81, Exit 11, loop south through Michaux State Forest

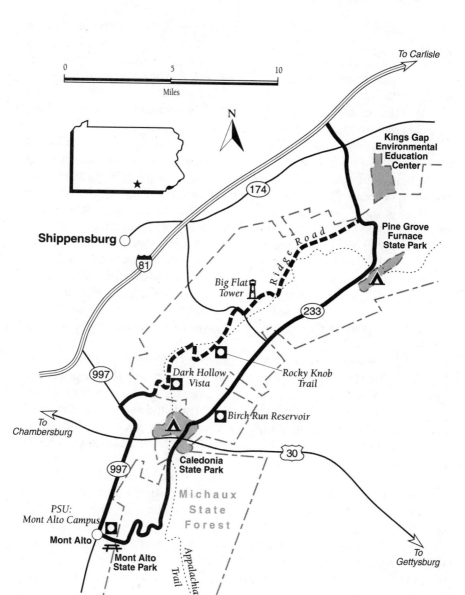

To Carlisle

Miles

N

Kings Gap
Environmental
Education
Center

Shippensburg

174

Pine Grove
Furnace
State Park

Ridge Road

Big Flat
Tower

233

997

Dark Hollow
Vista

Rocky Knob
Trail

To
Chambersburg

Birch Run Reservoir

30

997

Caledonia
State Park

*Michaux
State
Forest*

PSU:
Mont Alto Campus

Mont Alto

Mont Alto
State Park

*Appalachian
Trail*

To
Gettysburg

The park's Fuller Lake is actually a reclaimed iron ore pit that was filled by rising groundwater in the early 1900s. Laurel Lake supplied the water to power Laurel Forge, which further processed the cast iron made at Pine Grove Furnace into wrought iron for other uses. Today, both lakes offer recreation, with swimming beaches, fishing, and nearby picnicking. At 25-acre Laurel Lake, you will also find a boat and bicycle rental. Mill races and charcoal hearths are other records of the region's industrial past.

For more energetic visitors, the state park also boasts several fine, short hiking trails, besides the long-distance Appalachian Trail, and a popular bike trail that traces an old railroad grade. The 0.75-mile, steeply climbing **Pole Steeple Trail** is worthwhile, if you are in shape.

You will find its start off Railroad Road on the south shore of Laurel Lake. It tackles Piney Mountain to top its summit of lichen-etched quartzite outcroppings for a grand 180-degree overview of the park, South Mountain, and Michaux State Forest. Below, Laurel Lake appears like black satin with a corsage of water lilies. Because the final assault requires rock scrambling, this is not a good hike for young children or for the less daring or fit.

Unbroken, the drive simply pursues PA 233 south. Beyond the park's historic district stretches meandering travel, with scenic bends and over-hanging trees. In season, rhododendron and laurel add to the attractiveness of the corridor, and deer are commonly spied. Looking out the side windows, you may witness ant mounds of astonishing size, perhaps a foot-and-a-half high and twice as wide; these are colonies of the Allegheny mound-building ants.

As the drive continues, private inholdings intersperse the forest lands. Gum trees are the earliest to put on their fall mantle. A few turnouts and gated forest roads welcome you to pull over for a closer look or snap a picture. At 18.5 miles, pass the **Lippencote Trail**, and soon after, skirt Birch Run Reservoir. At this water supply for Chambersburg, shore fishing alone is allowed; heed posted notices. Changes in lighting and mood enhance forest travel.

More showings of rhododendron and a dark bower of hemlocks herald your arrival at **Caledonia State Park**. At 21.4 miles, a turn right leads to the park office, where information and trail brochures are available. Picnic facilities and **Whispering Pine Nature Trail** are also reached along this park road. Even if your time is limited, be sure to cross the threshold of Whispering Pine Nature Trail. While short (0.4 mile), the trail holds a jungle-like growth of rhododendron and some giant pines for an exciting lowland forest tour.

If your schedule allows for a longer outing and you do not mind a few soggy missteps, check out the 2.2-mile **Ramble Trail**. It travels in a shower of rhododendron, alternately overlooks a mill race and the East Branch

Conococheague Creek, and skirts a mill ruins to meander the floodplain of mature white pine and eastern hemlock. Big oaks and tulip poplar likewise draw eyes skyward.

For the park's history, you might consider walking the adjoining paths of **Thaddeus Stevens Historic Trail** (guidebook available) and **Charcoal Hearth Trail**. These trails travel the hillside east of PA 233 and north of US 30.

At the northeast corner of the PA 233-US 30 junction (0.1 mile south of the park office turnoff) sits **Caledonia Furnace**. This furnace was established by Thaddeus Stevens in 1837. Stevens was an advocate of public education and staunch abolitionist, and because of his beliefs on slavery, the furnace was targeted by Confederate General Jubal Early. In late June 1863 on the march to Gettysburg, Early ordered the furnace and ironworks destroyed. In the aftermath of the Battle of Gettysburg, which took place July 1–3, 1863, what is now the open lawn of the park served as a field hospital for the wounded.

At 21.5 miles, the drive then crosses US 30 to resume its forest ramble, but you may wish to make a short detour east on US 30 to the **Michaux State Forest District Office** (less than 1 mile). There, you may pick up a state forest map and auto trail brochure for the upcoming miles. At the T-junction at 25.8 miles, PA 233S turns right; a tiny lily pond is at the

Ridge Road, Michaux State Forest.

intersection. Pass through younger forest and plantations, as the route becomes more snaking with a hairpin turn. The drive then drops down the mountain into the shadow of bigger trees.

At 29 miles, the picnic areas of **Mont Alto State Park** face off along PA 233. To the right is a stylish picnic pavilion, with a spired-top cupola, green dome, wooden dance floor, and rimming boardwalk. West Branch Antietam Creek gurgles in the backdrop; north beyond the park spreads the rich, natural woodland of **Meeting of the Pines Natural Area.** Mont Alto State Park holds the distinction of being the first Pennsylvania State Forest Park; it opened in 1902.

South on the drive, you will pass the **Mont Alto Campus of The Pennsylvania State University.** On its grounds, many tree species have been identified for a short, arboretum-like tour. Opposite the campus, discover a Pennsylvania history marker on John Brown's raid. Ahead, enter the borough of Mont Alto, where basic services are available and the loop turns north on PA 997 at 30.1 miles.

The drive now passes through rolling farmland at the western foot of South Mountain. White cliffs pierce the leafy mountain flank. A large golf course and quiet residential areas bridge the gap to state forest land. Afterward, farm scenes alternate with the leafy cathedrals of the state forest. At

Picnic shelter, Mont Alto State Park.

Mountain laurel, Allegheny National Forest.

US 30 (35.1 miles), turn right followed by a left at the lighted intersection in one block to remain on PA 997.

In another 2 miles, turn right (east) on Ridge Road for the return leg of the loop. Ridge Road becomes gravel as it ascends into Michaux State Forest, and travel slows to 20 or 25 miles per hour, which is just right for window gawking. Rhododendron, laurel, hemlock, wild grape, and Virginia creeper vary the forest's signature look.

At 40.5 miles, the drive tops a ridge and in another 0.3 mile, you will come to a four-way junction. Here, a 0.4-mile detour right on Stillhouse Hollow Road leads to Dark Hollow Vista (site 6 on the Auto Trail). From the vista turnout, you take in a southeast panorama overlooking Dark Hollow, the nearby folded wooded ridges, and distant peaks of Maryland.

For the loop drive alone, you will proceed straight on Ridge Road at the 40.8-mile junction. Although Ridge Road is a primary forest artery, its junctions are not always well signed. Because of this, you may wish to keep handy a Michaux State Forest map. Turkeys, deer, hawks, grouse, and chipmunks are likely wildlife encounters. The Appalachian Trail has touch-and-go contact with Ridge Road.

On Big Pine Flat Ridge, the forest takes on a bushier look and has less stature. This is due to the thin, dry soil and the effects of weathering. Again, stay Ridge Road as it takes a big bend to the right at the forest-road intersection at 43.6 miles. At this intersection, the white blazes of the Appalachian Trail disappear into forest, and site 8 on the Auto Trail focuses your attention on the long-distance trail that extends from Georgia to Maine.

Upon coming to a triangle junction at 44.1 miles, follow Ridge Road left, soon passing **Flat Rock Plantation**, with its pines planted between 1917 and 1919. In a few places, rocks wear up through the road bed for bumpier travel. Site 10 on the Auto Trail identifies the 4.25-mile **Rocky Knob Trail**, which delivers vistas and has its own interpretive brochure and numbered stops.

Oaks and maples briefly replace the gum as the dominant roadside tree species, and washboarding creates a bouncier ride before the drive reaches the stop sign at 47.7 miles. Here, turn right on paved Arendtsville-Shippensburg Road, go 0.2 mile, and turn left to resume travel on gravel Ridge Road.

Past some communication towers, look left for a yellow gate (site 11 on the Auto Trail). By parking and hiking around the gate, you will reach **Big Flat Tower** (elevation 1,060 feet) in a few strides. This fire lookout stands 60 feet high and has nine flights of stairs that lift you above the treetops for far-sweeping Cumberland Valley–South Mountain views.

The crow's nest, still staffed during fire season, is closed to the public. Have no more than four people on the tower at any one time and no horseplay. The landing cages are open, and the upper landings narrow to just three boards. Also, at least one railing is in disrepair. So, be cautious and be diligent in the supervision of children if you allow them on the tower.

From the tower stop, Ridge Road slowly descends into taller, fuller forest and a parade of mountain laurel. You now follow signs toward Mount Holly Springs, proceeding straight at junctions. At 53.2 miles bear left, avoiding Michaux Road, to meet PA 233 at 56.1 miles, bringing the loop to an end.

27

Gettysburg National Military Park Auto Tour

Through Gettysburg National Military Park

General description: This 19.5-mile, lobed and circuitous drive follows the auto tour route through the national military park, retracing the chronology of the battlefield and tagging each of the 16 interpretive stops, but it omits the side tour to Barlow Knoll. The route twice backtracks on itself where spurs lead to the mini loops at Oak Ridge and East Cemetery Hill. The purchase of battlefield audio tapes or the hiring of a licensed battlefield guide can bring you a greater understanding of the battle and the people involved.

Special attractions: Monuments and statues; historical places and landmarks; original cannons; the National Cemetery; the Visitor Center and Gettysburg Museum of the Civil War; Electric Map; the Cyclorama; battlefield tower overlooks; hiking, bicycling, horseback riding, picnicking, shopping, historic walking tours.

Location: South-central Pennsylvania.

Drive route numbers: The drive follows nearly two dozen named streets through historic Gettysburg and Gettysburg National Military Park (NMP). Many NMP roads wear names associated with the battle. At junctions, look for the auto tour emblem: a white star on a divided field of blue and gray, with arrows to point the way. Some of the tour is on one-way road.

Travel season: Year-round, 6 A.M. to 10 P.M.

Camping: Private campgrounds in the Gettysburg area serve military park visitors.

Services: Gettysburg offers a full line of services.

Nearby points of interest: Eisenhower National Historic Site (adjacent to the military park); museums, historic structures, antique shops, rail tours, walking tours, and the National Tower (all in Gettysburg); Adams County scenic drives; Caledonia State Park; the attractions of Harrisburg and York.

 The drive

This drive travels the NMP, unfolding the events of July 1 through July 3, 1863—the bloodiest battle ever fought on American soil and a turning point in the Civil War. This would be General Lee's final press into the North. Two

Drive 27: Gettysburg National Military Park Auto Tour

Through Gettysburg National Military Park

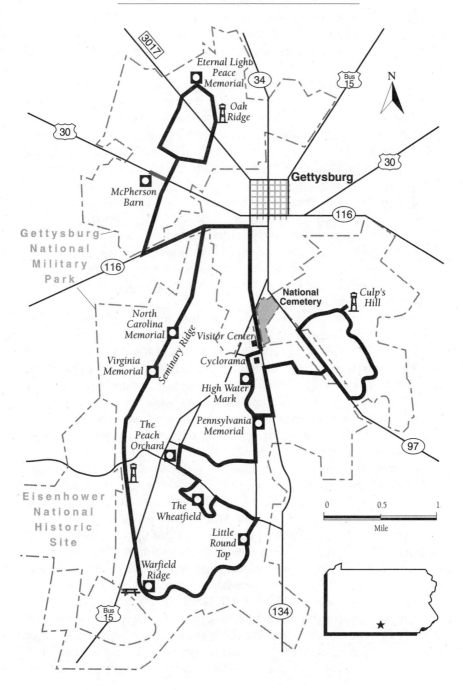

more years of hard-fought battles would follow, but Gettysburg signaled the "high water mark" for the Confederacy. After this battle, the momentum switched and events swung to the Union's favor.

Much of the modern landscape conveys the look of the land in 1863. You will find similar open and tilled fields, orchards, stone walls, pocket woods, farmhouses, and undeveloped ridges. In town, several stone and frame homes and gnarled, old trees bear the scars of battle.

Nearly a thousand monuments dot the park terrain and some 300 Civil War cannons line the solemn avenues. For the most part, the placement of the monuments and cannons helps relate the battle tale, showing key positions and commemorating losses. Several of the tributes were commissioned by surviving veterans. Confederate forces converged from the north and west, while General Meade made his stand to the south between the Confederate Army and Washington, D.C.

Within the park, there is no collecting and no climbing on monuments, cannons, or fences. Drivers must be alert for pedestrians and cyclists, and heed signs for one-way travel. Wide road shoulders, however, allow you to pull aside, walk among the monuments, and read the tributes and historical panels. There are only two places along the drive where picnicking is allowed: at the visitor center and at the picnic ground off South Confederate Avenue.

Begin the drive at the **Visitor Center/Museum** on Taneytown Road in south Gettysburg, accessed via U.S. Highway 15 (Business Route) or Pennsylvania Highway 134 as you enter town. A stop at the center (open daily except major holidays 8 A.M. to 5 P.M.) will help you gain your bearings. There, pick up a park brochure/map and consider buying a ticket to the Electric Map show, which will better help you visualize the battle as you follow the auto tour. You may also view the extraordinary Rosensteel Collection of Civil War artifacts, arrange for a tour guide, or purchase battlefield maps, books, tapes, and pamphlets at the gift shop.

When ready, drive north on Taneytown Road (which becomes Washington Street) and pursue the star emblem of the auto tour route to the opening battle of July 1, 1863. Many of the homes and businesses of Gettysburg stood witness to the Civil War; bronze plaques identify structures from the war era. History panels located throughout the town and walking tour brochures introduce the people and point out the garrets used by lookouts or for sharpshooter placements, narrow alleys of retreat, and the homes where Union soldiers were harbored or hospitalized.

In 0.8 mile, go west on West Middle Street/PA 116 for just over 1 mile and turn north on Reynolds Avenue to visit McPherson and Oak ridges, where the first rounds were fired. Pass between woods and open fields edged by monuments, coming to the first interpretive site at 2.5 miles. The battle began on July 1, near the barn seen from this site. Abutting the drive is

Lincoln bust, Gettysburg National Cemetery.

Reynolds Woods, which safekeeps the grave of Union General John Reynolds, who died here in the opening battle as the Confederate forces advanced on McPherson Ridge.

Cross U.S. Highway 30 at the lighted intersection (2.6 miles) and turn left on Buford Avenue to make a clockwise tour of Oak Ridge. Here, the Cavalry Division of Union Brigadier General John Buford stayed the Confederate advance. After crossing Mummasburg Road, the drive follows North Confederate Avenue to the **Eternal Light Peace Memorial** (site 2), atop Oak Hill.

On this site in 1938 (75 years after the conflict), more than 1,800 Civil War veterans who were by then in their 90s and 100s gathered for the dedication, to exchange memories and to extend handshakes. The memorial's gas-urn flame is held aloft by a white stone column and overlooks the now-quiet fields of Gettysburg. Back at the NMP museum, photographs and quotes of the gray and wrinkled veterans capture the emotion of the day.

From the memorial, the drive crosses back over Mummasburg Road, reaching the **Oak Ridge Observation Tower** (site 3 at 4 miles). The tower deck serves up a panoramic view of the battlefield—a landscape of modest undulations. To the east lies Barlow Knoll, where Confederate General Jubal Early collapsed the Union's front line. To its south stretch Culp's and Cemetery hills, where the Union troops regrouped.

Now, the drive follows Doubleday Avenue south between stone walls and monuments, passing a bed-and-breakfast; a few private holdings intersperse the park's fields and woods. Close this miniature loop at Reynolds Avenue and then backtrack south to PA 116.

Or, opt for a slight deviation. Where Reynolds Avenue crosses US 30, go west on US 30 for a block, south on Stone Avenue, and east on Meredith Avenue to pass additional war monuments. Meredith Avenue will then return you to Reynolds Avenue near site 1; there, turn right to get back to PA 116. The side excursion only slightly swells the distance, and it passes a noteworthy monument to John Burns, a 72-year-old citizen soldier who walked out onto the field of battle and joined the fray on the Union's side.

Once you return to PA 116, go east to West Confederate Avenue and turn south to continue the auto tour at 6 miles (mileage excludes deviation). You will now drive past historic homes, low stone walls, and woods, with cannons and monuments lining both sides of the auto route. This is **Seminary Ridge**, where the Confederate line was drawn. By 6.4 miles, travel becomes one-way, with through-traffic to the left and parking to the right. This drive is all about stopping, walking to the monuments, reading the inscriptions, and talking in whispers of respect.

A tranquil rural setting juxtaposed to silent cannons and loud-speaking monuments greets the eye. On July 3, 1863, this idyllic landscape witnessed two hours of ceaseless cannon fire, a confusion of heat and gray smoke, and the anguished cries of wounded men. Sites 4 and 5 on the auto tour present monuments to the North Carolina and Virginia regiments who fought here. These monuments bring together the faces and statistics of battle and look east over the field of "Pickett's Charge."

In a last, desperate, heroic effort to regain the Confederate advantage, Major General George E. Pickett led an advance of 12,000 men in a mile-long line of attack across the open field and into the hail of Union fire. Fully half of the men fell as casualties. General Robert E. Lee, who had witnessed the scene, rode into the turmoil to rally, console, and regather his beaten troops. Contemporary visitors can retrace Lee's path out into the field.

At the NMP, you may hear whistled battle tunes, see a tent encampment, or watch the drilling of a cavalry corps as Civil War–clad volunteers carry out reenactments. Southbound, the drive passes the Amphitheater, Pitzer Woods (auto tour site 6, at the north end of Warfield Ridge, where Confederate General James Longstreet took up position), and the memorials for Louisiana and Mississippi.

At Millerstown Road, **Adams County Scenic Valley Drive** heads west, while the NMP drive proceeds straight to a seven-story observation tower. The elevated post extends a full 360-degree panoramic view of Gettysburg, the battlefield, and adjacent **Eisenhower National Historic Site** (Eisenhower's retirement farm). The Eisenhower National Historic Site may be seen by

Cannon demonstration, Gettysburg National Military Park.

guided bus tour only; purchase tickets and board busses at the Gettysburg NMP visitor center. Panels on the observation deck provide an orientation and identify landmarks.

Trees shade the lane as the NMP drive continues south past a line-up of cannons; in the park, all but about ten of the cannons are authentic Civil War artillery. Pass the Arkansas Memorial and cross Emmitsburg Road to continue the tour on South Confederate Avenue. On the right at 9 miles is a wooded picnic area (open summers only), with a dozen parking spaces, 18 tables, and a restroom below.

Beyond the picnic area, travel is once again one-way only. On Warfield Ridge at 9.2 miles, reach site 7 and day two of the battle. From here, General Longstreet led assaults on the Union forces at Devils Den, the Wheatfield, the Peach Orchard, and the Round Tops—all landmarks that will be passed later on in the tour. This southern offense was intended to "roll up" and dislodge the Union Army. Lining the driving tour are Confederate States of America (CSA) monuments. The tour then arcs east into woods.

At 9.6 miles, an interpretive panel conveys the tragic tallies of battle: In three days, 7,708 men were killed and 26,856 were wounded, many of whom later died. For four months after the battle, doctors, nurses, and volunteers tended the injured men.

In 0.5 mile, the drive goes past the parking lot for Big Round Top, with its loop trail and battle history. Proceed ahead and cross Warren/Wright

Avenue to site 8, boulder-studded Little Round Top, where a last-minute defense was organized. When Union General Warren recognized that the taking of unprotected **Little Round Top** by Longstreet would give the Confederate Army a tactical edge, he slipped his men into position just in time to repel the Confederate advance. His savvy and action won him the title "Savior of Gettysburg."

While at Little Round Top, you may ascend a castlelike tower, view statues of General Warren and of Colonel Patrick O'Rorke of the New York Infantry, and discover the breastworks of stone that still exist. You might notice that the nose of Colonel Patrick O'Rorke is shiny; the sheen comes from visitors rubbing the statue's nose for luck. The odd part about the custom is that O'Rorke was killed here during his first combat command.

Resume north, descending from Little Round Top, only to turn left (west) on Wheatfield Road at 10.7 miles. You will pass between pole-and-rock fences to take the one-way tour left on Ayres Avenue, which meanders past woods and monuments to auto tour site 9 (11.5 miles). Here, at **The Wheatfield**, raged a 2.5-hour battle, with the upper hand changing six times. As monuments coax you from the vehicle, blue-sky days keep camera shutters clicking.

Back at Wheatfield Road, go west and soon after, turn north on Sickles Avenue to reach site 10 at 12.1 miles. On the rise to the southwest is a peach orchard just as there was in 1863; it recalls a Union hold that was overrun by Confederates. The tour then follows United States Avenue east past fences; private, historic houses; and site 11, **Plum Run**. This run lies along the pattern of retreat from the peach orchard to **Cemetery Ridge**, the Union line of defense in the great face-off.

Where the auto tour swings north on Hancock Avenue, more monuments usher the way to the **Pennsylvania Memorial** (site 12 at 13.5 miles). Nearby, look for the Minnesota Monument, which recognizes the 262 men from the First Minnesota. The First Minnesota suffered the highest regimental losses in modern times, with the squad having an 82 percent casualty rate.

The Pennsylvania Memorial is impressive in size and appearance, with its terraced steps, dome, statues, columns, and roster of 34,000 servicemen. Sometimes a flying artillery demonstration is staged in the area. The witnessing of just a single heart-stopping cannon blast and its accompanying gray smoke helps you appreciate the horror and confusion of war.

From the Pennsylvania Memorial, you may opt for a direct return to the visitor center and National Cemetery. For that, proceed north on Hancock Avenue and Taneytown Road, shortening the tour to 14.5 miles. Opting, however, for the full tour, turn right on Pleasanton Avenue.

Pleasanton Avenue will take you past a home that served as a Civil War hospital, before the auto tour turns left on Taneytown Road in 0.2 mile.

A rural setting next enfolds travel. In 0.5 mile, turn right on Hunt Avenue for a gentle, tree-shaded country tour to Baltimore Pike and the East Cemetery Hill side-loop junction (14.7 miles)—go right and then turn left on Slocum Avenue for the prescribed counterclockwise travel.

You will view scenic outcrops amid the hilly terrain and pass more monuments en route to **Spangler's Spring** (site 13), which quenched the thirst of both Union and Confederate soldiers. Auto tour emblems then point you to the right, uphill past still more monuments. At 16.3 miles, turn right to reach the five-story observation tower on Culp's Hill for a new battlefield perspective, surveying mainly forest. Plaques and monuments honor Major General George Greene and the valiant New York brigade that held their position.

The drive then descends to site 14 on East Cemetery Hill, where Confederate forces attained the crest before being pushed back. Where the drive again meets Baltimore Pike, turn left to close the loop at 17.3 miles. Then backtrack west-south-west via Hunt Avenue, Taneytown Road, and Pleasanton Avenue to the junction at the Pennsylvania Memorial (18.5 miles).

At the memorial junction, turn north to travel an impressive aisle of monuments to **The Copse** and **High Water Mark**, site 15, which marked the climax of the battle. The isolated cluster of trees on Cemetery Ridge (the Copse) was the landmark that Pickett ordered his men to charge, and the

Soldiers' National Monument, Gettysburg National Cemetery.

High Water Mark is where a handful of Confederate soldiers broke through the Union line only to be pushed back. A 0.4-mile self-guided walk helps you understand both place and event.

At 19.2 miles, the auto tour skirts the **Brian House** and **Cyclorama Center**. The Brian House recalls Abraham Brian, a free black man, farmer, and property owner, living here in 1863. As the battle approached, Abraham Brian fled and Union soldiers occupied his home and farm. On return, he found the farm was badly damaged and filed a claim against the government for $1,028; he received $15 in settlement. Other farmers received nothing.

The Cyclorama Center (with presentations 9 A.M. through 4:30 P.M.) features the enormous, 1884 oil painting "Pickett's Charge" by artist Paul Philippoteaux. The 356-foot-long canvas circles the room and comes to life through sound and light; tickets are required.

To complete the auto tour, follow the designated route as it arcs east around the Cyclorama Center to Taneytown Road and turn north. The **National Cemetery** signals an appropriate end to the tour at 19.5 miles. There, you will find the graves of the fallen Union soldiers arranged by state and in the shape of an arc about Soldiers' National Monument. This monument sits near where President Lincoln delivered his acclaimed "Gettysburg Address," November 19, 1863. Seated at the base of **Soldiers' National Monument** are the figures representing War, History, Peace, and Plenty, with Liberty towering 60 feet above their heads. Cannons and war monuments, squirrels and birds contribute to the somber, yet tranquil aspect of the hallowed graveyard.

28

Adams County Scenic Valley and Historic Conewago Tours

From the rotary in Gettysburg, the tours loop northwest and northeast through this rural county

General description: Two scenic loop drives explore outward from Gettysburg like mismatched butterfly wings; they may be toured together or separately. The western loop, the 35.5-mile Scenic Valley Tour brushes a chapter from Civil War history before exploring the county's prized apple and peach orchard country. The eastern loop, the 42-mile Historic Conewago Tour keeps its history theme from start to finish as it travels through farmland.

Special attractions: Historic Gettysburg; parts of Gettysburg National Military Park; Sachs Covered Bridge; historic churches and farmhouses; orchards, fruit stands, and farm markets; Apple Blossom and Harvest festivals; Victorian New Oxford and Early-American East Berlin; walking tours, antique shopping.

Location: South-central Pennsylvania.

Drive route numbers: The Scenic Valley Tour travels a series of town and country roads (named in text) before concluding via Pennsylvania Highways 234 and 34. The Historic Conewago Tour, likewise, travels a network of country roads (again see text) and for the most part, avoids numbered routes, except for short segments that bridge travel. Both drives are well signed with numbered junctions to correspond to the descriptions in their respective auto tour brochures.

Travel season: Year-round.

Camping: Private campgrounds in the greater Gettysburg area serve Adams County travelers.

Services: Gettysburg provides full service, with some traveler amenities available at communities along the routes.

Nearby points of interest: Gettysburg National Military Park and the adjacent Eisenhower National Historic Site; museums, antique shops, rail tours, walking tours, and National Tower (all in Gettysburg); Caledonia State Park; the attractions of Harrisburg and York.

Drive 28: Adams County Scenic Valley and Historic Conewago Tours

From the rotary in Gettysburg, the tours loop northwest and northeast through this rural county

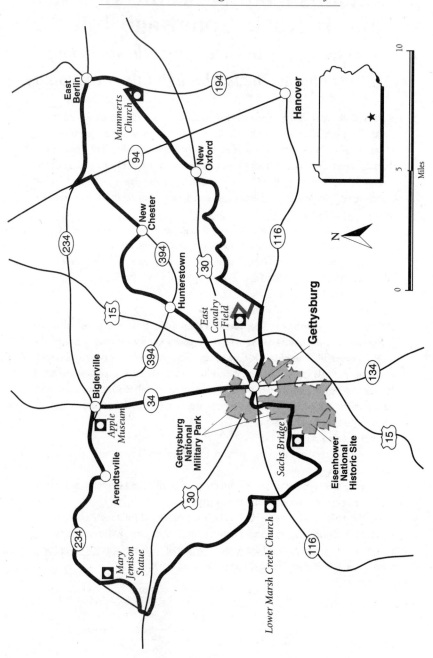

East Berlin

Mummerts Church

194

Hanover

94

New Oxford

New Chester

234

394

Hunterstown

30

116

East Cavalry Field

N

Miles

10

5

0

Gettysburg

15

394

Biglerville

34

Apple Museum

Gettysburg National Military Park

Sachs Bridge

134

15

Arendtsville

30

116

Eisenhower National Historic Site

234

Mary Jemison Statue

Lower Marsh Creek Church

116

 # The drives

These two drives laid out by the Gettysburg Travel Council showcase the quiet and history of Adams County and introduce the charm of rural backcountry travel. The sometimes deserted, winding roads welcome relaxation, while the countryside holds an abundance of changing images for pleasing windshield-sightseeing. The mingled scents of hay, just-turned soil, livestock, and apple blossoms; a bite into a crisp, tart apple taken right from the tree; or the static of crickets—all contribute to the country elixir.

Both drives trace quiet country roads, but ones that require attention. Be alert for blind intersections and keep to your lane while negotiating the curving, narrow roads. With few opportunities to pull aside safely, if you slow down for a better look, keep an eye on the rearview mirror.

Both drives start at the Lincoln Square rotary in Gettysburg. But first, go north one block on Carlisle Street to pick up the auto tour brochures at the Gettysburg Travel Council. Find its visitor center at 35 Carlisle Street, open 9 A.M. to 5 P.M. daily. It is housed in the Italianate railroad depot that was commandeered for a Federal Army hospital during the Battle of Gettysburg (July 1–3, 1863). At this train depot, President Lincoln arrived in November 1863, for the dedication of Soldiers National Cemetery, where he delivered the Gettysburg Address.

Adams County countryside.

For the **Scenic Valley Tour**, head west on U.S. Highway 30 (Chambersburg Street) and in 0.3 mile, proceed straight on Springs Avenue past the Meade School, a large red brick building masked in maples, occupying the intersection triangle. At the corner is a statue honoring the Pennsylvania Emergency Infantry, whose military advance prior to the Battle of Gettysburg stalled the Confederate push by one day.

A tree-lined street with stately old homes ushers the tour forward. On the right at 0.7 mile, view the beautiful grounds and brick buildings of the **Lutheran Seminary**, founded 1826. The seminary was used by sentries of both armies during the Battle of Gettysburg.

Just beyond the seminary, the tour turns left on West Confederate Avenue, entering **Gettysburg National Military Park** (NMP), where it briefly shares the way with the NMP auto tour. Cannons, plaques, monuments, statues, and history panels grace this stretch along Seminary Ridge—the Confederate battle line. Vistas pan east across a rural scene—an image of how the land looked in 1863.

At 2.9 miles depart the NMP, turning right on Millerstown Road, soon passing along the fences and fields of **Eisenhower National Historic Site**— President Eisenhower's retirement farm. The Eisenhower National Historic Site may be seen by guided bus tour only; purchase tickets and board busses at the Gettysburg NMP visitor center on Taneytown Road.

Where the drive crosses Marsh Creek (4.2 miles), look left (downstream) to view pretty, red-painted **Sachs Covered Bridge**. As you depart

Cows, Eisenhower National Historic Site.

the concrete bridge of the auto tour, you will discover a history panel on the celebrated Sachs Bridge. For a closer look, take the first left on Scott Road.

On the National Register of Historic Places, this Ithiel Town–style lattice covered bridge, built in 1852, spans 91 feet across the murky-green water of Marsh Creek. Washed downstream 100 yards in the flood of June 1996, the historic bridge was recovered, restored, and re-dedicated June 1997. In the days leading up to the Battle of Gettysburg, Sachs Bridge was used in the movement of Civil War troops. Later, it was the location of a Confederate base camp and field hospital and carried the southern retreat of General Lee's troops.

As you continue west on the auto tour, Millerstown Road becomes Pumping Station Road. Traverse a mild terrain of farms and low treed ridges, with hay bales, windmills, rustic fences, and attractive old farmsteads. At 5.7 miles, turn right (north) onto Camp Gettysburg Road and continue working your way north and northwest for the next 10.3 miles via Knoxlyn, Knoxlyn-Orrtanna, Orrtanna, Scott School, and Bingaman roads. Auto tour signs with numbered junctions guide the way. Have your auto tour brochure handy for times of doubt; the brochure also warns of tricky turns and busy intersections.

The rural signature of the tour continues, with kestrels on the telephone wires and corn, hay, and fallow fields. Horses with shining coats wade the deep pasture grasses; in autumn, look for flocking birds. Where the tour crosses PA 116, view the stone **Lower Marsh Creek Presbyterian Church** (1790) that served as a Civil War hospital. Shutters protect the decorated glass windows.

As the route rolls and meanders, woods of oak, hickory, birch, elm, and hemlock vary the tapestry. By 10.8 miles, the drive tops a hill to enter orchard country. Adams County grows apples, peaches, cherries, grapes, apricots, plums, nectarines, and quinces. The climate, gentle hills, and well-drained soils, all contribute to the cornucopia. Look for blossoms in early May, ripened peaches mid-August into September.

Late September into October, the branches of apple trees hang heavy with fruit, and stacked crates sit ready to be filled. Elsewhere, tractors pull apple-filled carts to warehouses and stands. Across the undulating, hilly terrain, you may view both new and mature orchards. The life span of an apple tree is about 35 years; new trees do not produce fruit until their sixth year, but the result is worth the wait.

Where the tour takes a right turn at junction 12, view the Knouse Foods Cooperative Building, another symbol of the orchard country. Adams County is the leading fruit producing and processing county in Pennsylvania. Past a railroad track, the drive travels a straightaway with mountains rising in the distance.

Apple stand, Adams County.

At 16 miles, go left on Old Route 30 following **Cashtown Pass**, where General Lee's troops marched to Gettysburg and a wagon train of Confederate wounded passed on the retreat south. Cashtown Pass divides orchards in the shadow of rounded hills. Sumac and goldenrod grow wild along the road shoulders. Cross US 30 and proceed 100 yards on PA 234 only to take a quick right on Church Road, ascending a wooded aisle; the kaleidoscope of autumn even coaxes locals to the backroads.

At 19.5 miles, reach the first apple stand, where you can purchase apples by the peck or half bushel to satisfy your tastebuds. Woods again set the stage as Church Road descends. On the right at 20.4 miles are the 1816-built **St. Ignatius Loyola Church** and **Statue of Mary Jemison**. In 1753, a small band of French and Shawnee raided the Jemison household and that of a neighbor, abducting and later murdering the families, all but young Mary and a small boy. Mary grew up among the Shawnee and eventually became a respected leader. She was known as the "White Squaw." If your travels should lead you to Letchworth State Park in New York State, you will learn even more about this independent woman.

Next on the drive, you will overlook Buchanan Valley, which takes its name from President James Buchanan, before reaching and resuming travel east on PA 234 (21 miles). Produce stands, orchard communities, and woods frame travel. Where the auto tour tops Piney Mountain (elevation 1,350 feet), enjoy a panorama of orchards and fields before descending to cross and follow Conewago Creek, which courses clear and swirls around boulders and past gravel bars.

In places, rich, deep shadows accent the bending route. Christmas tree farms bring variety, while poison ivy drapes the sides of beautiful old barns. At 26.8 miles, the drive passes **South Mountain Fairgrounds**, which hosts the Apple Harvest Fest the first two weekends in October and the Apple Blossom Festival the first full weekend in May.

Now, follow signs for the auto tour and PA 234 east through Arendtsville to return to the textured landscape; ease from orchard country back into farmland. At the junction with PA 394 (30.5 miles), a 0.1-mile detour right leads to the **Apple Museum**, housed in a restored 1857 bank barn. It is open April through October, Saturdays and holidays 10 A.M. to 5 P.M. and Sundays noon to 5 P.M.; the museum is shown by guided tour for a fee. Among the collection, view sheepskin deeds, early-day orchard tools, and a honeybee display.

The auto tour then follows PA 234 east into Biglerville to meet and follow PA 34 south. Traffic is now moderate. At 33.7 miles, bypass the historical marker for **Russell Tavern**, where George Washington took lodging in October 1794 while suppressing the Whiskey Rebellion. A 0.3-mile detour right on Goldenville Road will allow you to view the now private, stone Federal-style tavern. It sits near the intersection of Goldenville and Russell Tavern roads.

Forgoing the detour, you will reenter Gettysburg National Military Park and return to historic Gettysburg. Drive south past the Gettysburg Travel Council to return to the rotary at 35.5 miles, thus ending the Scenic Valley Tour.

For the **Historic Conewago Tour**, go east on US 30 (York Street) past the **David Wills House**, where President Lincoln spent the night and polished the Gettysburg Address before delivering the speech at the dedication ceremony for the National Cemetery. In 0.2 mile, the tour bears right on Hanover Street, easing out of town and crossing Rock Creek.

Soon you will pass **Benner's Hill**, part of **Gettysburg National Military Park**, with its plaques and cannons. The site recognizes the Army of North Virginia, which participated in the cannonade of July 2, 1863. Remain eastbound on Hanover Street and Road, passing fieldstone farmhouses, acres of crops, and milling livestock and passing under US 15.

At 3.7 miles, turn left on Low Dutch Road. In just over 0.5 mile, you may opt for a 3-mile round-trip detour to **East Cavalry Field**, where the Union cavalry finally proved itself against the superior Confederate horse soldiers who were commanded by Major General J.E.B. Stuart. For the Historic Conewago Tour alone, proceed north and at 6.6 miles, turn east on Salem Church Road.

You may spy farm cats slinking through fields or deer browsing, as the route weaves past barns and fence lines and as heady country smells waft on the breeze. Before long, the zigzagging route heads left on Kilpatrick Road and right on Centennial Road. Barking farm dogs, pigeons strutting along the peak of a barn, or line-drying diapers on the front porch of a Mennonite farmhouse add bold strokes to the country portrait. As the tour turns left on Cedar Ridge Road, Pennsylvania bank barns capture notice.

At junction 9 (10.6 miles), turn right on Fleshman Mill Road closely rounding a milkhouse and dairy barn; the white-painted barn stands in dramatic contrast to the verdant, green setting. Where the auto tour route enters a bend past the junction with Kohler School Road, look for a Mennonite country market. It sells bulk goods plainly packaged and labeled, with everything from baking staples to licorice and hard candy.

Beyond the market, cross the South Branch Conewago Creek and turn left on Kohler Mill Road. At 12.4 miles, the drive skirts a horse pasture and track where harness racers are put through their training.

Next, enter **New Oxford** and turn right on Lincolnway West (US 30). Attractive stone, brick, and frame Victorian and Colonial homes and numerous antique shops front the tour. Brick sidewalks and shade trees add to the charm of the town streets. At 13.4 miles is the picturesque circle for which New Oxford is known; go three quarters of the way around and follow Carlisle Street north.

In 0.4 mile, Berlin Road carries the tour right. More bank barns contribute to the Adams County tour—trademarks of the Pennsylvania landscape. At 15.4 miles, look for back-to-back turns: left on PA 94, right on Pine Run Road. Afterward, rolling travel resumes across the rumpled farm landscape.

While negotiating a bend at 19 miles, be alert for the tour's hidden right turn onto Mummerts Church Road. A tooth-topped stone wall edges the cemetery of **Mummerts Church of the Brethren Meeting House.** Next, go north on PA 194, passing a farm market and brick lattice barn. Farm tractors may briefly share the road, slowing travel.

The tour next heads west on PA 234 into historic East Berlin, with its bed-and-breakfast establishments and basic services, but a short detour east as far as the Beaver Creek crossing finds **Sweigarts Mill,** a 1794-built stone mill on the National Register of Historic Places. **East Berlin,** founded 1764, has received both Pennsylvania Historic Site and National Historic District recognition, with 52 of the original structures depicted on an 1856 map still in place. A walking tour will best introduce the town, with its various architectures and a few homes originally constructed of logs.

Cross Conewago Creek upon departing town and return to the rural countryside. At 26.8 miles, the tour briefly follows PA 94 south before turning right on PA 394 in Hampton. Glancing east, you will discover the low,

Downtown East Berlin.

dark profile of Pigeon Hills. Roadside tables of squash and pumpkin beckon in autumn. Almost anytime, roly-poly woodchucks may be seen ambling between grass and cover. On the left at 30.3 miles, a black iron fence surrounds the pre–Civil War cemetery of **St. Johns Church**.

In New Chester, the auto tour turns right on Oxford Road and crosses Conewago Creek. Here, **Sharrer's Grist Mill** is being restored and the original millrace may be spied. Studebaker Lane next takes the tour left on a smaller backroad, until Red Bridge Road takes the tour south to Hunterstown. To the distant west, view South Mountain.

At 36.2 miles is **Great Conewago Presbyterian Church,** a 1787 stone church with white shutters—one of the two oldest churches in the county. Its cemetery holds markers for Revolutionary War and Civil War veterans. Among the old stone tablets are some colored orange with lichen. If you visit the churchyard cemetery, notice the different stones and carving styles used in the 1700s and 1800s.

Shortly after the church, turn right on PA 394 West, followed by a left on Hunterstown Road, for a rolling sojourn between farms and woods. Return to US 30 at 41.1 miles and follow it west to the rotary in Lincoln Square (42 miles). The shops and history of Gettysburg await.

29

Lancaster Valley Amish Country Tour
From Morgantown to Lancaster

General description: This 73.5-mile drive traces a serpentine path through the Lancaster Amish Country, avoiding for the most part the highly promoted tourist routes. It offers glimpses of Amish life and despite following the path less traveled, still offers opportunities to shop. Side trips to Landis Valley Museum and Ephrata Cloister offer looks at daily life centered around two distinct religious cultures. The narrow streets of the eighteenth-century villages and towns on this tour make parts of the drive unsuitable for recreational vehicles.

Special attractions: Amish country images; Ephrata Cloister; Landis Valley Museum; historic Lititz and Lancaster; James Buchanan's Wheatland; Mascot Roller Mills and the Ressler Family House; walking tours, museums, shopping, Pennsylvania Dutch dining, and Amish buggy and hot-air balloon rides.

Location: Southeast Pennsylvania.

Drive route numbers: Pennsylvania Highways 23, 897, 340, 772, and 441; U.S. Highway 30.

Travel season: Year-round.

Camping: Private campgrounds serve the Lancaster Amish Country traveler. A public campground, French Creek State Park (off PA 345, 10 miles northeast of Morgantown) has 201 modern family campsites and also rents cabins. Its facilities include flush toilets, showers, and dump station.

Services: Morgantown, Intercourse, Leola, and Lancaster are full-service communities; many traveler amenities and services are available at other stops along the route.

Nearby points of interest: Hopewell Furnace National Historic Site, French Creek State Park, Nolde Forest Environmental Education Center, historic Columbia, the lower Susquehanna River/Lake Aldred, historic Rock Ford and the North Museum of Natural History and Science (Lancaster), Robert Fulton Birthplace (Quarryville), Railroad Museum of Pennsylvania and historic Strasburg Railroad (Strasburg), Hershey Museum and Gardens, Harrisburg and Philadelphia attractions.

Drive 29: Lancaster Valley Amish Country Tour

From Morgantown to Lancaster

 # The drive

This drive starts in Morgantown and snakes its way south and west across the verdant Lancaster Valley, passing through Amish villages and historic towns before ending at Lancaster. The Lancaster County Amish settlement is the oldest in the United States. Their presence and various sites along the tour emphasize the significance of one of this country's founding tenets—"freedom of religion."

On this drive, you will share the road with the clip-clop of horse hooves and whir of buggy wheels. Views span an engaging farm tapestry of classic white farmhouses, massive Pennsylvania bank barns, silos, livestock, and corncribs. Farm stands, roadside tables, and wheelbarrows loaded with seasonal produce put forth tasty invitations to interrupt the drive.

While the quiet, centuries-old lifestyle of the Amish and Mennonite peoples intrigue, do not allow your curiosity to become intrusive. Avoid staring and put your cameras aside when the "plain people" pass. As the Amish conduct no commerce on their Sabbath, forgo calling on their home trades on Sunday.

At the junction of PA 23 and PA 10 North (the Penna Turnpike access) in Morgantown, go west on PA 23 (Main Street) through the small community to enter the rolling farm country. Traffic is generally moderate. On the right at 1.4 miles is the **Amish-Mennonite Information Center**, with brochures, information, and maps. On its grounds, find a picnic table with a fine countryside view.

Hand-lettered signs for wood crafts, quilts, and baked goods may entice you onto the side roads, where some of the best discoveries can be made. The possibilities include seeing a work team bring in a corn crop, children in straw hats and aprons playing outside their one-room schoolhouse, a farmer pedaling a scooter between fields, or a barefoot Amish toddler daydreaming beside a fence. The primary tour proceeds forward through the pretty village of Churchtown, only to return to country landscapes that stretch north and south. Tranquil images and rural smells bombard senses.

The tidy farm community of Goodville next marks off distance. At 7.7 miles, turn south on PA 897 for quieter travel, passing a Pennsylvania Dutch restaurant. Watch junction signs to remain on PA 897 South. Beyond the Cedar Grove Presbyterian Church and graveyard, the drive ascends from farm country into a mixed hardwood forest with mountain laurel.

Where the route next descends, drive past a Mennonite Church, Mount Airy Cemetery, and peach and apple orchards. As the tour drifts back into open farm country, you will pass a blacksmith shop—a vital addition to the rustic agricultural community. Still follow the weaving route of PA 897S.

At 16.9 miles, turn left on PA 340, one of the more highly promoted and commercial Amish tour routes, and in another 0.5 mile, turn right to continue south on PA 897. Ahead stretches more of the unhurried, zigzagging travel past scenes of farm life, which help unravel the mystique of the plain people. During harvest season, the families are particularly busy in fields and gardens.

At 21 miles, bypass **Salisbury Township Park**, where picnic tables are available. The park abuts the tour all the way south to US 30, another of the popular tourism routes. Turn right on US 30 to enter Gap and reach the next travel leg, PA 772 West. As you pass through Gap, you may notice **Auntie Anne's Hand-rolled Soft Pretzel Training Center**—pretzels are a sure-fire sign that you are in Pennsylvania Dutch Country.

Track PA 772 west, again sharing the road with buggies, bicycles, and scooters; drive carefully. In places, the pavement may show the telltale scratches of buggy wheels. Across the folded terrain, beltways of corn alternate with other crops. Beautiful old fieldstone and frame farmhouses contribute to the postcard images. A few of the barns have open slats for drying tobacco.

At 27.5 miles, enter **Intercourse** (the unofficial capital of Pennsylvania Dutch Country) to again tag PA 340. Between the villages of Intercourse and Bird-in-Hand (west on PA 340), shoppers find a myriad of outlets selling

Pennsylvania Highway 897, Lancaster County.

Amish goods and original Pennsylvania Dutch food, as well as tours, museums, and accommodations.

For this drive, continue west, following the country highway of PA 772, passing more family-run cottage enterprises. Some cater to the Amish alone, with harness repairs, buggy sales, and boots. At the Saturday garage sales, it is not uncommon to see a cluster of parked black buggies; the frugal, industrious Amish frown on waste and make good use of the bargains.

At 31.1 miles, the drive crosses the broad, pollen-coated waters of Mill Creek just below a small dam. To the left are the **Mascot Roller Mills** and **Ressler Family House**. Along Mill Creek to the right is **Mascot Community Park**, with picnic tables and a small memorial bird sanctuary where egret and blue heron may be spied. May through October, the roller mill and Ressler house are shown by guided tour: Monday through Saturday 9 A.M. to 4 P.M.

This stone mill was built in 1760 and served the Amish agricultural community until 1977; it is preserved intact and fully operable and serves as a living record of the flour milling industry. It began with millstones and water wheels and then modernized to water-powered turbines and chilled iron rolls. The Ressler family acquired the mill in 1864 and through their generosity, the mill and their family home of 12 decades have been opened to the public. The home is untouched, with original pieces all in place, conveying the wholesomeness of country life and one family's history.

Amish farm, Lancaster County.

At 33.6 miles, you will cross over PA 23 at Leola, following signs for PA 772W. Keep to PA 772 until its junction with PA 272, where you have the option of adding a side trip to Ephrata Cloister in 4.3 miles (go north on PA 272 and then right on Main Street in Ephrata) or to Landis Valley Museum in 4.6 miles (go south on PA 272 and then right on Kissell Hill Road). The primary drive remains on PA 772.

At **Ephrata Cloister,** visitors enter the medieval-style village of an austere, eighteenth-century religious communal society. Ten of the original buildings are restored and interpreted to introduce the disciplined lifestyle of the society. The Cloister was founded in 1732 by separatists from the Dunkard Church and is now a National Historic Landmark. It is open Monday through Saturday 9 A.M. to 5 P.M. and Sunday noon to 5 P.M.; admission is charged.

At its height, the Cloister consisted of 300 members. The white-robed, celibate brothers and sisters left behind a legacy of art, music, poetry, decorated calligraphy, and publishing. Married householders contributed to the community and practiced the rigid faith of purification. During the American Revolution, wounded soldiers from the Battle of Brandywine were cared for by Cloister members. After the 1768 death of Cloister founder, Conrad Biessel, however, the society began to drift from its stern purpose and essentially vanished after 1814.

At the Cloister, you will view a slide program, take a guided building tour, and then walk the tranquil grounds for a self-guided tour of the community. The small, harsh sleep cells and low doorways of humility help introduce the life and the people.

Landis Valley Museum, on the other hand, is an agricultural hamlet of historic stone and frame buildings that introduces the lifestyles and traditions of the Pennsylvania Dutch or Pennsylvania Germans. "Dutch" is an Americanization of "Deutsch," which means German, and "Pennsylvania Dutch" is an all-encompassing term for the peoples of germanic origin who settled in this region in the eighteenth century. By the 1790s, they made up 40 percent of the population of southeast Pennsylvania.

Occupying a rural setting, this living history museum is open Tuesday through Saturday 9 A.M. to 5 P.M. and Sunday noon to 5 P.M.; an admission is charged. May through October, visitors may tour all of the buildings, talk with on-site interpreters, and view a full schedule of ongoing craft demonstrations where artists use traditional materials and techniques. November through April, a one-hour escorted tour fills in the history before you roam the village streets. Historic breeds of livestock and heirloom gardens further capture the time frame.

Nostrils flare at the intermingled aromas of straw, earth, livestock, and slow-burning wood. At the walking tour stops, you will learn how the

Meetinghouse, Ephrata Cloister (National Historic Landmark).

Pennsylvania Dutch viewed luxury and responsibility and what was considered an individual's role within the family and the community. The germanic heritage was carried on in the language, traditions, art, and architecture. Although farming was the mainstay for much of the community, the Pennsylvania Dutch also labored at clock making, leatherworking, tinsmithing, shopkeeping, and weaving.

George and Henry Landis, founders of the museum, came from a Pennsylvania Dutch ancestry and saw the need to preserve the culture's qualities. Their collection of Pennsylvania Dutch articles from the 1700s and 1800s numbered well over 75,000 objects when the Commonwealth acquired the museum in 1953, and the collection has since grown.

For the valley drive alone, proceed west on PA 772 from its junction with PA 272, heading toward Lititz. Beyond the busy intersection, rural images and meandering travel return, but now with moderate traffic. Rothsville presents a pleasant sidewalk community with Federal-style homes and a classic church. By 43 miles, enter Lititz with its many eighteenth-century homes and structures.

Lititz, founded in 1756, was once a closed community, centered around the teachings of the Moravian Church. Rigid rules governing personal, business, and societal behavior discouraged outside contact. Lititz derives its name from the town of Lidice in Bohemia, Czechoslovakia, where the

Moravian Church got its start 300 years earlier. **Moravian Church Square** still occupies the heart of the community, but the town gates are now wide open and tourists welcomed.

At the eastern edge of Moravian Church Square is the Sisters' House, which later became Linden Hall, the second oldest girls' residence school in the United States. The old Moravian Church of 1763 is now the parsonage. From December 1777 to August 1778, the Single Brethren's House (1759) served as a hospital for the Continental Army. A quarter of the hospitalized men died; you will find their graves at the east end of Lititz.

Opposite Church Avenue, find the stone and white-shuttered building of **Lititz Museum** and the adjoining **Johannes Mueller House** (1792). Memorial Day through October, the museum is open Monday through Saturday 10 A.M. to 4 P.M. There, you may arrange a tour of the Mueller House—the only Moravian home open for viewing. The Mueller House was originally owned by a local tanner, and it provides a glimpse back at life within the closed community. In the museum, one room is devoted to General John Sutter of California Gold Rush fame; he lived out his final years in Lititz.

The town itself is highly walkable, and the narrow streets suggest you park and do just that. Country wreaths adorn many doors, while simple plaques identify the year a structure was built. Throughout the historic village, discover stone, frame, log, and brick buildings dating to the 1700s. Many now house professional offices, service industries, and attractive shops.

Favorite stops for tourists include the **Sturgis Pretzel Bakery** and **Wilbur Chocolate**. On the National Register of Historic Places, the Sturgis Pretzel Bakery was the first such bakery in the New World, established in 1861. For a century, Wilbur Chocolate has produced fine handmade chocolates; its Candy Americana Museum features a collection of antique candy-making tools and molds, advertisements, tins, and packages.

If you journey up Water Street, check out the **Heritage Map Museum**. Its original maps date to the fifteenth century and for an admission charge, may be viewed. Many are indeed art. Besides recording the physical features of the world, the cartography chronicles how our thinking of the world has changed over time.

From Lititz, the drive resumes west on PA 772, returning to a canvas of broad fields, silos, barns, dairy cows, and alcoves of trees. Next, pass through the narrow streets of Manheim, with its tidy, side-by-side older homes closely fronting the street. The town was founded in 1762, with glass-blowing an important early industry. Still follow signs for PA 772 West.

At 50 miles, you may glimpse a covered bridge 0.1 mile east on West Sunhill Road; it spans Chickies Creek. The valley drive itself continues to track PA 772 southwest to Mount Joy (55.4 miles); in Mount Joy, again watch for junction signs to remain on PA 772. In another 5 miles, this highway ends at PA 441; turn left on PA 441 South to continue the drive. Straight ahead is Marietta, a river town with a historic canal and elegant old homes. A more hurried pace and increased traffic often accompanies the remaining journey to Lancaster.

Heads up, as PA 23 East takes the baton in less than 1 mile; at the corner sprawls a huge, ornate estate. Where the tour becomes more suburban, you may still spy a tobacco barn. The growing communities virtually wrap around the farmhouses and barns of old. Antiques and collectibles, produce stands, and specialty shops dot travel.

Beautiful, old shade trees and sprawling, groomed lawns grace travel where civilization becomes firmly implanted. In Rohrerstown, admire a lineup of grand Victorian and Federal-style homes. Keep to PA 23E as an incredible aisle of elegant living precedes **President James Buchanan's Wheatland** (72.4 miles). This brick, two-and-a-half story, Federal-style country estate of the fifteenth president barely stands out in its present-day neighborhood. From April through November, the estate may be toured daily (except Thanksgiving) 10 A.M. to 4 P.M. for a fee.

Amid the artifacts in the Visitor Center/Carriagehouse are original letters, a note from Jefferson Davis to Buchanan, and gifts from the first Japanese delegation to the United States. Here, too, view an introductory video before being welcomed on the guided tour by docents in period dress.

On the tour, you will learn about James Buchanan, his ambitions and personal philosophy, and about the lifestyle in the mid-nineteenth century. You are also introduced to Harriet Lane, the niece who served as first lady for the bachelor president. Wheatland was a source of tranquility and contentment for Buchanan, whose troubled term in office came on the precipice of Civil War.

From Wheatland, follow PA 23E to the center of historic Lancaster; eventually the street becomes one-way. At the intersection with North Mulberry, a heritage marker indicates where liberal-thinker Thaddeus Stevens is buried at **Shreiner's Cemetery**. The drive then comes to its end at the junction with US 222 (Prince Street).

If time allows, you might consider taking a guided or self-guided walking tour of the Lancaster Historic District, with its memorials, churches, courtyards, alleyways, hitching posts, and more than 50 stops. You will find information at the Visitor Center at 100 South Queen Street. It is open Monday through Friday 8:30 A.M. to 4:50 P.M., Saturday 9 A.M. to 4 P.M., and Sunday 10 A.M. to 3 P.M. On the walk, you may want to visit **Steinman Park**, with its fountain, 20-foot-high waterwall, and bronze statue of a park gentleman reading a newspaper; the **Heritage Center Museum; Fulton Opera House;** and **Central Market**—site of the oldest, continuously used farmers' market in the country, open Tuesday, Friday, and Saturday.

History abounds in the city. On September 27, 1777, Lancaster became the capital of the United States for a day, when the exiled Continental Congress held session here after the British overtook Philadelphia. Lancaster was the capital of Pennsylvania, 1777–1778. As you walk her streets, you will bump into the names of signers of the Declaration of Independence, generals, and presidents.

30

Encampment Auto Tour
Valley Forge National Historic Park

General description: This 10.1-mile auto tour introduces the terrain and conditions of the Continental Army's winter encampment at Valley Forge, the hardships endured, and the triumph of character that eventually won out.

Special attractions: Washington's Headquarters; General Varnum's Quarters; the reconstructed encampment huts; National Memorial Arch; statues and reenactments; Washington Memorial Chapel; museum collections; hiking, bicycling, horseback riding, and picnicking (in designated areas only).

Location: Southeast Pennsylvania.

Drive route numbers: Outer Line Drive, Pennsylvania Highways 252 (Valley Creek Road) and 23, and Inner Line Drive. Drivers should avoid finding themselves on the Pennsylvania highway segments during the morning and evening rush hours, when the commuter traffic swells the flow.

Travel season: Year-round, with auto tour open 6 A.M. to 10 P.M.

Camping: Private campgrounds serve Valley Forge travelers; contact the Valley Forge Convention and Visitors Bureau for names and locations.

Services: King of Prussia and much of the western extent of greater Philadelphia provide a full line-up of services.

Nearby points of interest: Independence Hall, the Liberty Bell, and other historic sites, museums, and attractions; art, garden, and entertainment offerings; Fairmount Park/Wissahickon Creek Gorge (all in Philadelphia); Mill Grove/John James Audubon's first American home (Audubon); historic Waynesborough (Paoli); Daniel Boone Homestead (Birdsboro); Brandywine Battlefield Park (Chadds Ford); Hopewell Furnace National Historic Site; Schuylkill Trail (bikeway to link Philadelphia and Valley Forge).

 The drive

This drive through the 3,600-acre national historic park takes you past historical structures and sites and contemporary monuments to relate the six-month tale of the Continental Army's winter encampment at Valley Forge, 1777–1778. On December 19, 1777, some 12,000 bedraggled, dispirited, half-naked troops arrived at Valley Forge and set about building primitive huts to stave off the bite of winter.

Drive 30: Encampment Auto Tour
Valley Forge National Historic Park

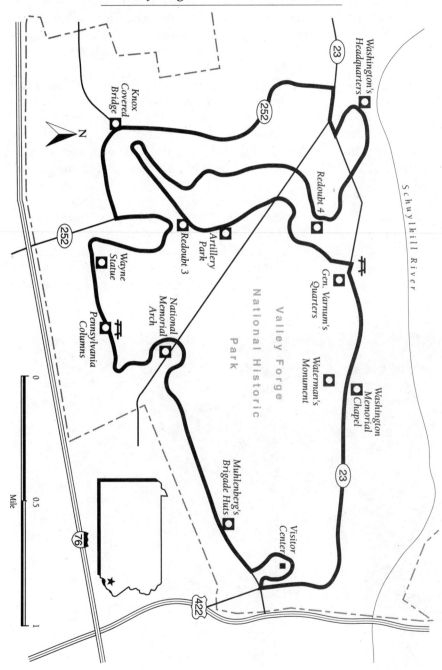

Food shortages; a lack of even basic supplies; rampant sickness, disease, and death; and a series of British victories that culminated in the taking of Philadelphia, all had shaken the army's foundation. Nonetheless, General George Washington guided his troops through the crisis. He carried out the immediate task of monitoring British movements and left the camp June 19, 1778, with a well-drilled professional army that would successfully meet the British at Monmouth, New Jersey.

For the drive, watch for the blue-and-white auto tour emblem that depicts a soldier and hut; there are ten interpretive stops, with other points of interest in between. On-site interpreters at the buildings and seasonal productions and demonstrations help flesh out the events at the winter encampment. Although short in mileage, the tour is long on history, so plan on spending a good deal of time outside of the vehicle, exploring the grounds and reading history panels.

Reach Valley Forge National Historic Park by taking Exit 24 off the Pennsylvania Turnpike (Interstate 76/276). The park **visitor center**, located at the junction of PA 23 and North Gulph Road, signals the start of the tour (site 1). It is open daily (except Christmas) from 9 A.M. to 5 P.M. There, you may acquire a park map for the auto tour, learn of any scheduled site presentations and what buildings are open, view an 18-minute film, and tour

Encampment Auto Tour road, Valley Forge National Historic Park.

the museum collection. An outstanding feature in the collection is the marquee (a camp tent) actually used by General Washington.

Along the tour route, picnicking is only allowed in the designated sites at Wayne's Woods and Varnum's picnic areas. On the north bank of the Schuylkill River, Betzwood Picnic Area also invites the opening of a basket lunch.

Start the clockwise drive at the visitor center with one-way travel on Outer Line Drive. It journeys west along the southern extent of the park and has a speed limit of 25 miles per hour. The park is a natural island in the civilized sea of greater Philadelphia. General Washington specifically selected Valley Forge for the winter camp because of its location 18 miles from the city of Philadelphia; it was close enough for his men to monitor British troop movements there, yet far enough to be safe from British surprise attacks and supply raids.

At 0.5 mile, a parking area on the left welcomes you to site 2, with attractions on either side of the road. View the reconstructed redoubts (earthworks) and cannons to the south; the reconstructed huts of Brigadier General Muhlenberg's Brigade to the north. The broad grassy southern slope attracts browsing deer in the morning hours. Beautiful full-crowned maples and oaks lend spreading shadows to the grassy expanse that sweeps away to woods.

Although the log huts were built to specifications, they showed some differences in character due to materials and the backgrounds of the builders. In a letter to Benjamin Franklin, Thomas Paine compared the camp's hut-building activity to that of a beaver colony, with the steady toting of logs and mud and the teams of men plastering the huts together. Twelve soldiers were housed in each of the cramped, leaky quarters; today starlings dwell in the fireplace chimneys. From this location, the Muhlenberg Brigade anchored the army's outer line of defense. Sometimes costumed interpreters enliven the site.

As the auto tour continues west, an exercise/bike path passes alongside for an alternative means for seeing the historic sites and monuments. Within a mile, cross North Gulph Road to reach parking for **National Memorial Arch** (site 3). It was dedicated in 1917 and commemorates the "patience and fidelity" of the soldiers who endured the winter at Valley Forge. The memorial arch occupies a commanding location atop a knoll that overlooks the rolling terrain.

The tour then continues past additional monuments erected by individual states to their servicemen. All 13 original colonies were represented at Valley Forge, although three did not have state-named brigades. At 1.9 miles, pass through **Pennsylvania Columns**—eagle-topped twin gateway columns with the images of officers. Dogwoods grow in the vicinity. Just beyond is **Wayne's Woods Picnic Area**, its tables shaded by oaks and tulip poplars.

Site 4, the **Wayne Statue** next calls travelers aside; there is 30-minute parking here. The bronze equestrian statue features Wayne atop his mount and looking toward his home in Chester County. The statue sits where Brigadier General Anthony Wayne's first and second Pennsylvania Brigades were camped. During the winter encampment, Wayne led an important foraging expedition into New Jersey; its success and the acquired new rations uplifted troop morale.

Beyond a memorial to the unnamed soldier, one-way travel ends as you meet PA 252 and turn right for the auto tour; the posted speed is now 35 miles per hour. The drive skirts **Valley Forge Farm**; its buildings (closed to the public) served as officers' quarters. Then at 3.5 miles, the drive bypasses attractive **Knox Covered Bridge**, keeping to PA 252 as it parallels Valley Creek downstream. Woodland replaces the open field as your host for the auto tour. On the left in 0.3 mile is a parking lot with a trail leading back to the covered bridge.

Park, cross the footbridge spanning Valley Creek, and hike the wide, cinder path upstream to the restored, white-painted 1865 bridge. Another path ascends Mount Misery, while a third travels downstream. Willow and sycamore lean over the creek; beech, elm, box elder, and gum climb the

Knox Covered Bridge, Valley Forge National Historic Park.

slope of Mount Misery. Beware of poison ivy and also be alert to the possibility of poisonous snakes, which dwell in the park but are reclusive.

Knox Bridge shows a Burr-truss styling, with awning-covered windows that stretch the length of each side. If you enter the bridge, do not dawdle because the bridge sits at a dangerous intersection and vehicles have a quick approach and only a narrow lane of passage. During the Revolution, two forges occupied Valley Creek downstream from the bridge's trailhead parking. The lower of the two forges gave Valley Forge its name.

The auto tour proceeds downstream, winding along the creek and shaded by trees to meet PA 23 at 4.6 miles. Turn right on PA 23, only to follow it up with a left turn off PA 23. This part of the tour wraps around the **Dewees' House** to visit **Washington's Headquarters** (site 5), with its entourage of historic structures and replica guard huts. A walking tour introduces the "historic zone" grounds; the two-story stone headquarters is open for viewing for a modest charge.

Washington set up his command central at the Isaac Potts House, paying a rent of 100 Pennsylvania Pounds. The rooms are furnished to re-create the scene of command. View the staff officers' workroom, General Washington's office and bedroom, and an aide's room. The nearby Dewees' House, home of a Pennsylvania Militia colonel, was used by the Baker General of the Continental Army and was raided for its stores by the British three months prior to General Washington's arrival. The Dewees' House too is open to the public, but on a limited schedule.

From the headquarters area, follow the Encampment Auto Tour as it crosses back over PA 23, returning to one-way travel along Inner Line Drive. At 5.6 miles reach **Redoubt 4** (site 6). From this earthwork, troops protected the camp from northern approaches.

Ahead, cross North Gulph Road to ascend the wooded rise of Mount Joy. A noisy gathering of crows may indicate the presence of an owl in a grove of older tulip poplars. Now, pursue a twisting course accented by blooms of laurel and rhododendron, June into July. At 7.3 miles, reach the parking area for **Redoubt 3** (site 7), with its array of cannons. This post secured the southern end of the inner line of defense. A platform overlooks the human-made molehills intended to stop cannonballs; interpretive panels explain the construction of these barriers.

Next up is **Artillery Park** (site 8), where the camp's cannons were centrally kept, maintained, and the gun crews drilled. The game plan was that at the first sign of attack, the cannons could be rushed to the site of engagement. It is fortunate that the artillery was never called upon because winter mud and failing horses may have thwarted the plan.

A string of cannons face out over the field in memory of the park; National Memorial Arch is visible in the distance. Beyond Artillery Park, two-way travel returns. Pass more encampments and the **Site of the Marquee**, where the military campaign tent of General George Washington was erected on his arrival at Valley Forge, December 19, 1777.

With the 7.9-mile crossing of North Gulph Road, again find one-way travel to PA 23. Deer are abundant within the national historic park; some are tagged and radio-collared. At the PA 23 intersection is parking for site 9: **General Varnum's Quarters** (open on selected summer days) and the **von Steuben Statue**, which depicts the Prussian commander as he arrived at camp with a letter of introduction from Benjamin Franklin.

General Varnum occupied a single room within the Stephen family fieldstone farmhouse. It served as his living quarters, brigade office, and site for conducting court martial hearings. The family's farmland served as the Grand Parade, where General von Steuben trained and drilled the Continental soldiers into a first-class fighting force. The statue of von Steuben overlooks the open field of the **Grand Parade**.

Now, continue right on PA 23 to wrap up the auto tour. East of **Varnum's Picnic Area** are a pair of adjacent private attractions making up site 10: the beautiful, Gothic **Washington Memorial Chapel** and the **Valley Forge Historical Society Museum**.

Patriot's Tower, the belltower of the memorial chapel, holds the Washington National Carillon; recitals follow Sunday service. Along the tower base is an impressive roll call of names—the Patriots Wall of Honor. A chapel walking tour introduces other features of the grounds.

Washington's Headquarters, Valley Forge National Historic Park.

Knox artillery, Valley Forge National Historic Park.

The Valley Forge Historical Society Museum boasts a prized collection of more than 4,000 authentic pieces arranged to represent Washington, the military equipment, Colonial history, and Valley Forge. Among the items, view the Commander in Chief's flag, Martha Washington's letter box, Brigadier General Muhlenberg's pistols, and General Washington's telescope, sundial, and spur. The museum is open Monday through Saturday 9:30 A.M. to 4 P.M. and Sunday 1 P.M. to 4:30 P.M.; an admission is charged.

Across the street from the chapel rises a 50-foot granite obelisk marking the only identified grave within the park, but honoring all of the soldiers who perished at Valley Forge. **Waterman's Monument** receives its name from fallen soldier Lieutenant John Waterman of Rhode Island, who died April 23, 1778, and is buried here.

For the drive, proceed east on PA 23, quickly passing the right-hand turn to the **Nature Center**, which is open three days a week for selected hours. In another mile, the tour ends back at the visitor center.

Appendix
Sources for more information

For more information on lands, hours, and events, please contact the following agencies or organizations.

Drive 1

Erie Area Convention and Visitors
  Bureau
1006 State Street
Erie, PA 16501
(814) 454-7191

Erie County Historical Society
417 State Street
Erie, PA 16501
(814) 454-1813 (Tuesday through
  Saturday)

Erie Maritime Museum
U.S. brig *Niagara*
150 East Front Street
Erie, PA 16507
(814) 452-2744

Presque Isle State Park
P.O. Box 8510
Erie, PA 16505
(814) 833-7424

Drive 2

Crawford County Convention and
  Visitors Bureau
242-1/2 Chestnut Street
Meadville, PA 16335
1-800-332-2338

Drake Well Museum
R.D. 3
Titusville, PA 16354
(814) 827-2797

Erie National Wildlife Refuge
11296 Wood Duck Lane
Guys Mills, PA 16327
(814) 789-3585

Oil Creek State Park
R.R. 1, Box 207
Oil City, PA 16301
(814) 676-5915

Oil Creek and Titusville Railroad
P.O. Box 68
Oil City, PA 16301
(814) 676-1733

Drive 3

Allegheny National Forest
P.O. Box 847
222 Liberty Street
Warren, PA 16365
(814) 723-5150

Bradford Ranger District
Star Route 1, Box 88
Bradford, PA 16701
(814) 362-4613

Chapman State Park
R.R. 2, Box 1610
Clarendon, PA 16313
(814) 723-0250

Simpler Times Museum
(814) 484-3483

Travel Northern Alleghenies
Northern Alleghenies Vacation Region
P.O. Box 804
315 Second Avenue
Warren, PA 16365
(814) 726-1222 or 1-800-624-7802

Drive 4

Allegheny National Forest
P.O. Box 847
222 Liberty Street
Warren, PA 16365
(814) 723-5150

Bradford Ranger District
Star Route 1, Box 88
Bradford, PA 16701
(814) 362-4613

Kinzua-Wolf Run Marina
P.O. Box 825
Warren, PA 16365
(814) 726-1650

Travel Northern Alleghenies
Northern Alleghenies Vacation Region
P.O. Box 804
315 Second Avenue
Warren, PA 16365
(814) 726-1222 or 1-800-624-7802

U.S. Army Corps of Engineers
Kinzua Dam
P.O. Box 983
Warren, PA 16365
(814) 726-0661
Fishing hotline: (814) 726-0164

Drive 5

Allegheny National Forest
P.O. Box 847
222 Liberty Street
Warren, PA 16365
(814) 723-5150

Bureau of State Parks
Department of Conservation and Natural
  Resources
P.O. Box 8551
Harrisburg, PA 17105-8551
1-800-63-PARKS

Endless Mountains Visitors Bureau
R.R. 6, Box 132A
Tunkhannock, PA 18657
(717) 836-5431 or 1-800-769-8999

French Azilum, Inc.
R.R. 2, Box 266
Towanda, PA 18848
(717) 265-3376

Pennsylvania Lumber Museum
P.O. Box 239
Galeton, PA 16922
(814) 435-2652

Wellsboro Chamber of Commerce Visitor
  Center/Tioga County Tourist
  Promotion Agency
114 Main Street
Wellsboro, PA 16901
(717) 724-0635 or (717) 724-1926

Drive 6

Dorflinger Glass Museum/Dorflinger-
  Suydam Wildlife Sanctuary/Wild-
  flower Music Festival
Long Ridge Road
P.O. Box 356
White Mills, PA 18473
(717) 253-1185

Upper Delaware Scenic and Recreational
  River
R.R. 2, Box 2428
Beach Lake, PA 18405-9737
(717) 685-4871

Wayne County Chamber of Commerce/
Visitors Center
303 Commercial Street
Honesdale, PA 18431
(717) 253-1960; 1-800-433-9008

Wayne County Historical Society
P.O. Box 446
810 Main Street
Honesdale, PA 18431
(717) 253-3240

Drive 7

Goddard State Park
684 Lake Wilhelm Road
Sandy Lake, PA 16145
(412) 253-4833

Jennings Environmental Education
Center
R.R. 1, Box 281
Slippery Rock, PA 16057
(412) 794-6011

McKeever Environmental Learning
Center
55 McKeever Lane
Sandy Lake, PA 16145
(412) 376-7585

Mercer County Convention and Visitors
Bureau
835 Perry Highway
Mercer, PA 16137
1-800-637-2370

Moraine State Park
225 Pleasant Valley Road
Portersville, PA 16051
(412) 368-8811

Drive 8

Allegheny National Forest
P.O. Box 847
222 Liberty Street
Warren, PA 16365
(814) 723-5150

Ridgway Ranger District
R.D. 1, Box 28A
Ridgway, PA 15853
(814) 776-6172

Travel Northern Alleghenies
Northern Alleghenies Vacation Region
P.O. Box 804
315 Second Avenue
Warren, PA 16365
(814) 726-1222 or 1-800-624-7802

U.S. Army Corps of Engineers Tionesta
Lake
1 Lakeshore Drive
Tionesta, PA 16353
(814) 755-3512

Drive 9

Allegheny National Forest
P.O. Box 847
222 Liberty Street
Warren, PA 16365
(814) 723-5150

Cook Forest State Park
P.O. Box 120
Cooksburg, PA 16217-0120
(814) 744-8407

Knox, Kane, Kinzua Railroad
Box 422
Marienville, PA 16239
(814) 927-6621

Marienville Ranger District
Star Route 6, Box 130
Marienville, PA 16239
(814) 927-6628

Travel Northern Alleghenies
Northern Alleghenies Vacation Region
P.O. Box 804
315 Second Avenue
Warren, PA 16365
(814) 726-1222 or 1-800-624-7802

Drive 10

Elk County Recreation and Tourist
   Council
P.O. Box 35
Ridgway, PA 15853
(814) 772-5502

Elk County Visitors Bureau
P.O. Box 838
Saint Marys, PA 15857
(814) 834-3723

Elk State Forest
P.O. Box 327
Emporium, PA 15834
(814) 486-3353

Drive 11

Big Woods Country Tourist Promotion
   Agency
Courthouse Annex
51 Susquehanna Avenue
Lock Haven, PA 17745
(717) 893-4037

Cameron County Tourist Promotion
P.O. Box 118
Driftwood, PA 15832
(814) 546-2665

Elk State Forest
P.O. Box 327
Emporium, PA 15834
(814) 486-3353 or (814) 483-3354

Sinnemahoning State Park
R.R. 1, Box 172
Austin, PA 16720
(814) 647-8401

Sproul State Forest
HCR 62, Box 90
Renovo, PA 17764
(717) 923-1450

State Parks Region 1 Office
R.R. 4, Box 212
Emporium, PA 15834
(814) 486-3365

Drive 12

Clinton County Tourist Promotion
   Agency
Courthouse Annex
Lock Haven, PA 17745-2319
(717) 748-5782

Kettle Creek State Park
HCR 62, Box 96
Renovo, PA 17764
(717) 923-6004

Ole Bull State Park
HCR 62, Box 9
Cross Fork, PA 17729-9701
(814) 435-5000

Sproul State Forest
HCR 62, Box 90
Renovo, PA 17764
(717) 923-1450

Susquehannock State Forest
P.O. Box 673
Coudersport, PA 16915
(814) 274-8474

Drive 13

Cherry Springs State Park
c/o Lyman Run State Park
R.D. 1, Box 136
Galeton, PA 16922
(814) 435-5010

Clinton County Tourist Promotion
 Agency
Courthouse Annex
Lock Haven, PA 17745-2319
(717) 748-5782

Potter County Recreation Inc.
P.O. Box 245
Coudersport, PA 16915
(814) 435-2394

Sproul State Forest
HCR 62, Box 90
Renovo, PA 17764
(717) 923-1450

Susquehannock State Forest
P.O. Box 673
Coudersport, PA 16915
(814) 274-8474

Tiadaghton State Forest
423 East Central Avenue
South Williamsport, PA 17701
(717) 327-3450

Drive 14

Little Pine State Park
HC 63, Box 100
Waterville, PA 17776-9705
(717) 753-6000

Lycoming County Tourist Promotion
 Agency
848 West Fourth Street
Williamsport, PA 17701
(717) 321-1200

Tiadaghton State Forest
423 East Central Avenue
South Williamsport, PA 17701
(717) 327-3450

Tioga State Forest
P.O. Box 94, Route 287 South
Wellsboro, PA 16901
(717) 724-2868

Drive 15

Endless Mountains Visitor Bureau
712 SR 6E
Tunkhannock, PA 18657
1-800-769-8999

Sullivan County Chamber of Commerce
Sullivan County Courthouse
P.O. Box 269
Laporte, PA 18626
(717) 946-4160

Tiadaghton State Forest
423 East Central Avenue
South Williamsport, PA 17701
(717) 327-3450

Worlds End State Park
P.O. Box 62
Forksville, PA 18616
(717) 924-3287

Wyoming State Forest
Arbutus Park Road, Box 439
Bloomsburg, PA 17815
(717) 387-4255

Drive 16

Columbia-Montour Tourist Promotion
 Agency
121 Papermill Road
Bloomsburg, PA 17815
(717) 784-8279 or 1-800-VISIT 10

Ricketts Glen State Park
R.R. 2, Box 130
Benton, PA 17814-8900
(717) 477-5675

Drive 17

The Columns
Pike County Historical Society
608 Broad Street
Milford, PA 18337
(717) 296-8126

Delaware Water Gap National Recreation
Area
Bushkill, PA 18324
(717) 588-2418

Grey Towers National Historic Landmark
P.O. Box 188
Milford, PA 18337
(717) 296-9360

Pocono Mountains Vacation Bureau
Box 5, 1004 Main Street
Stroudsburg, PA 18360
1-800-POCONOS or (717) 424-6050

Drive 18

Indiana County Parks
Blue Spruce Park Road
Indiana, PA 15701
(412) 463-8636

Indiana County Tourist Bureau
1019 Philadelphia Street
Indiana, PA 15701
(724) 463-7505

James M. Stewart Museum
P.O. Box 1
Indiana, PA 15701
(412) 349-6112 or 1-800-83-JIMMY

Smicksburg Heritage Society
P.O. Box 89
Smicksburg, PA 16256
(814) 257-8653 (afternoons, Friday
through Monday)

Drive 19

Greenwood Furnace State Park
R.R. 2, Box 118
Huntingdon, PA 16652
(814) 667-1800

Raystown Country Visitors Bureau
241 Mifflin Street
Huntingdon, PA 16652
(814) 643-3577 or 1-800-269-4684

Raystown Lake
U.S. Army Corps of Engineers
R.D. 1, Box 222
Hesston, PA 16647
(814) 658-3405

Trough Creek State Park
R.R. 1, Box 211
James Creek, PA 16657
(814) 658-3847

Drive 20

Big Spring and Fowlers Hollow State
Parks
c/o Colonel Denning State Park
1599 Doubling Gap Road
Newville, PA 17241
(717) 776-5272

Carlisle Economic Development Center
114 North Hanover Street
Carlisle, PA 17013
(717) 245-2648

Perry County Tourist and Recreation
Bureau
Box 447
New Bloomfield, PA 17068
(717) 582-2131

Tuscarora State Forest
R.D. 1, Box 42-A
Blain, PA 17006
(717) 536-3191

Drive 21

Hawk Mountain Wildlife Sanctuary
1700 Hawk Mountain Road
Kempton, PA 19529
(610) 756-6961

Reading-Berks County Visitor Bureau
P.O. Box 6677
Reading, PA 19610
(610) 375-4085 or 1-800-443-6610

The Rodale Institute Experimental Farm
611 Siegfriedale Road
Kutztown, PA 19530
(610) 683-1400

Drive 22

Bucks County Department of Parks and
  Recreation
Core Creek Park
901 E. Bridgetown Pike
Langhorne, PA 19047
(215) 757-0571 or (215) 348-6114

Delaware Canal State Park
Box 615A, R.R. 1
Upper Black Eddy, PA 18972
(610) 982-5560

Easton Area Chamber of Commerce
P.O. Box 637
157 South 4th Street
Easton, PA 18042
(610) 253-4211

New Hope Chamber of Commerce
P.O. Box 633
New Hope, PA 18938-0633
(215) 862-5880

Parry Mansion Museum
P.O. Box 41
45 South Main Street
New Hope, PA 18938
(215) 862-5652 or (215) 862-5460

Washington Crossing Historic Park
P.O. Box 103
Washington Crossing, PA 18977
(215) 493-4076

Drive 23

Greater Waynesburg Area Chamber of
  Commerce
26 West High Street, Suite 101
Waynesburg, PA 15370
(412) 627-5926

Meadowcroft Museum of Rural Life
401 Meadowcroft Road
Avella, PA 15312
(412) 587-3412

Washington-Greene Counties Tourism
  Promotion
59 North Main Street
Washington, PA 15301
(412) 222-8130

Drive 24

Bradford House Historical Association
175 South Main Street
P.O. Box 537
Washington, PA 15301
(412) 222-3604

Central Fayette Chamber of Commerce
11 Pittsburgh Street
Uniontown, PA 15401
(412) 437-4571

Fort Necessity National Battlefield/
Friendship Hill National Historic Site
Superintendent
1 Washington Way
R.D. 2, Box 528
Farmington, PA 15437
(412) 329-5512

LeMoyne House
49 East Maiden Street
Washington, PA 15301
(412) 225-6740

National Road Heritage Park of
  Pennsylvania
3543 National Pike
Farmington, PA 15437
(412) 329-1560

Youghiogheny Lake, Resource Manager
R.D. 1, Box 17
Confluence, PA 15424
(814) 395-3242

Drive 25

Bear Run Nature Reserve
Western Pennsylvania Conservancy
(412) 288-2777 or (412) 329-8501

Fallingwater
Western Pennsylvania Conservancy
P.O. Box R
Mill Run, PA 15464
(412) 329-8501

Fort Ligonier
216 South Market Street
Ligonier, PA 15658
(412) 238-9701

The Laurel Highlands Travel and Tourism
120 East Main Street
Ligonier, PA 15658
1-800-333-5661

Ohiopyle State Park
P.O. Box 105
Ohiopyle, PA 15470
(412) 329-8591

Powdermill Nature Reserve
The Carnegie Museum of Natural History
HC 64, Box 453
Rector, PA 15677
(412) 593-2221

Drive 26

Caledonia State Park
Mont Alto State Park
40 Rocky Mountain Road
Fayetteville, PA 17222
(717) 352-2161

Cumberland Valley Visitors' Council
1235 Lincoln Way East
Chambersburg, PA 17201
(717) 261-1200

Gettysburg Travel Council
35 Carlisle Street
Gettysburg, PA 17325
(717) 334-6274

Michaux State Forest
Forest District 1
10099 Lincoln Way East
Fayetteville, PA 17222
(717) 352-2211

Pine Grove Furnace State Park
1100 Pine Grove Road
Gardners, PA 17324
(717) 486-7174
American Youth Hostel Manager:
(717) 486-7575

Drive 27

Gettysburg National Military Park
97 Taneytown Road
Gettysburg, PA 17325
(717) 334-1124

Gettysburg Travel Council
35 Carlisle Street
Gettysburg, PA 17325
(717) 334-6274

Drive 28

Adams County Fruit Growers Association
P.O. Box 515
Biglerville, PA 17307
(717) 677-7444

Gettysburg National Military Park
97 Taneytown Road
Gettysburg, PA 17325
(717) 334-1124

Gettysburg Travel Council
35 Carlisle Street
Gettysburg, PA 17325
(717) 334-6274

The National Apple Museum
154 West Hanover Street
Biglerville, PA 17307
(717) 677-4556

Drive 29

Amish-Mennonite Information Center
151 North Red School Road
Morgantown, PA 19543
(610) 286-9870

Ephrata Cloister
632 West Main Street
Ephrata, PA 17522
(717) 733-6600

James Buchanan's Wheatland
1120 Marietta Avenue
Lancaster, PA 17603
(717) 392-8721

Lancaster Visitor Center and Historic
  Walking Tour
100 South Queen Street
Lancaster, PA 17603
(717) 392-1776

Landis Valley Museum
2451 Kissel Hill Road
Lancaster, PA 17601
(717) 569-0401

Lititz Historical Foundation and Museum
137-145 East Main Street
Lititz, PA 17543
(717) 627-4636

Pennsylvania Dutch Convention and
  Visitors Bureau
501 Greenfield Road
Lancaster, PA 17601
(717) 299-8901 or 1-800-PA DUTCH

Drive 30

Valley Forge Convention and Visitors
  Bureau
600 West Germantown Pike
Plymouth Meeting, PA 19462
(610) 834-1550

Valley Forge National Historic Park
P.O. Box 953
Valley Forge, PA 19481
(610) 783-1077

Suggested Reading

Bonta, Marcia. *More Outbound Journeys in Pennsylvania*. University Park, PA: Penn State University Press, 1995.

———. *Outbound Journeys in Pennsylvania*. University Park, PA: Penn State University Press, 1991.

Dillion, Chuck. Guide to *The Susquehannock Trail System, Second Edition*. Wellsboro, PA: Pine Creek Press, Publisher, 1994.

Donehoo, George. *Indian Villages and Place Names of Pennsylvania*. Lewisburg, PA: Wennawoods Publishing, 1997.

Hoffman, Carolyn. *Fifty Hikes in Eastern Pennsylvania, Second Edition*. Woodstock, VT: Backcountry Publication, 1989.

Hostetler, John A. *Amish Society, Fourth Edition*. Baltimore, MD: Johns Hopkins University Press, 1993.

Kent, Barry C. *Discovering Pennsylvania's Archeological Heritage*. Harrisburg, PA: Pennsylvania Historical and Museum Commission, 1994.

Martin, Jere. *Pennsylvania Almanac*. Mechanicsburg, PA: Stackpole Books, 1997.

Merrit, Joseph E. *Guide to the Mammals of Pennsylvania*. Pittsburgh, PA: University of Pittsburgh Press, 1987.

Miller, E. Willard, ed. *A Geography of Pennsylvania*. University Park, PA: Penn State University Press, 1995.

Ostertag, Rhonda and George. *Hiking Pennsylvania*. Helena, MT: Falcon Publishing, 1998.

Ostrander, Stephen J. *Great Natural Areas in Eastern Pennsylvania*. Mechanicsburg, PA: Stackpole Books, 1996.

———. Pennsylvania *Hiking Trails, Eleventh Edition*. Cogan Station, PA: Keystone Trails Association, 1993.

Peterson, Roger Tory. *A Field Guide to the Birds: A Completely New Guide to All the Birds of Eastern and Central North America*. Boston, MA: Houghton Mifflin Co., 1998.

Smith, Helene and George Swetnam. *A Guide to Historic Western Pennsylvania*. Pittsburgh, PA: University of Pittsburgh Press, 1991.

Symonds, George W.D. *The Shrub Identification Book*. New York, NY: William Morrow and Company, 1963.

Thwaites, Tom. *Fifty Hikes in Central Pennsylvania, Second Edition*. Woodstock, VT: Backcountry Publications, 1985.

———. *Fifty Hikes in Western Pennsylvania, Second Edition*. Woodstock, VT: Backcountry Publications, 1993.

Van Diver, Bradford B. *Roadside Geology of Pennsylvania*. Missoula, MT: Mountain Press Publishing Company, 1990.

Venning, Frank D. *A Guide to Field Identification: Wildflowers of North America*. New York, NY: Golden Press, 1984.

Zacher, Susan M. *The Covered Bridges of Pennsylvania: A Guide*. Harrisburg, PA: Pennsylvania Historical and Museum Commission, 1993.

Index

About the Authors

Over the past 18 years, these veterans of the outdoors, Rhonda (writer) and George (photographer), have collaborated on three eastern hiking guidebooks, half a dozen western guidebooks, and sold hundreds of articles on topics of nature, travel, and outdoor recreation. Retiring their hiking boots for a year, they decided to do their scouting from behind the wheel of a car and returned once again to the Keystone State—a familiar haunt, having recently explored the state on foot for *Hiking Pennsylvania* (Falcon Publishing, 1998). With *Scenic Driving Pennsylvania,* they invite you to come along for the ride and share a look out their windshield at the beauty and history of Penn's Woods.

Other titles by this team include *Hiking New York* (1996) and *Hiking Southern New England* (1997), both with Falcon Publishing, and *50 Hikes in Hells Canyon and Oregon's Wallowas* (1997), *California State Parks: A Complete Recreation Guide* (1995) and *100 Hikes in Oregon* (1992) with The Mountaineers in Seattle, Washington.